THE CLASSICAL CHRISTIAN GOD

THE CLASSICAL CHRISTIAN GOD

Douglas Kennard

Toronto Studies in Theology
Volume 86

The Edwin Mellen Press
Lewiston•Queenston•Lampeter

Library of Congress Cataloging-in-Publication Data

Kennard, Douglas Welker.
    The classical Christian God / Douglas Kennard.
        p. cm. -- (Toronto studies in theology ; v. 86)
    Includes bibliographical references and index.
    ISBN 0-7734-7223-1
    1. God. I. Title. II. Series.

BT103 .K46 2002
231--dc21
                                                    2001044585

This is volume 86 in the continuing series
Toronto Studies in Theology
Volume 86 ISBN 0-7734-7223-1
TST Series ISBN 0-88946-975-X

A CIP catalog record for this book is available from the British Library.

The Edwin Mellen Press   The Edwin Mellen Press
Box 450   Box 67
Lewiston, New York   Queenston, Ontario
USA 14092-0450   CANADA L0S 1L0

The Edwin Mellen Press, Ltd.
Lampeter, Ceredigion, Wales
UNITED KINGDOM SA48 8LT

Printed in the United States of America

Dedicated to my wife Janet Ike Kennard,
I went into teaching because I fell in love with
This classical Christian God
And I wished to share Him with all of my students
Of whom Jan is the most committed.

Table of Contents

Preface

By Millard Erickson

I am glad to write a brief endorsement. I think Doug Kennard has made a contribution in his book *The Classical Christian God* that needs to be heard. Doug has undertaken quite a project, of uniting both philosophical and biblical considerations, and has demonstrated the competence in both areas necessary to do this. My impression is that this is an attempt to show how the two areas of consideration fit well together when discussing the nature of God. Doug has obvious familiarity, not only with classical but also with contemporary authorities in philosophy, and has also developed well the biblical materials. The chapter on freedom and sovereignty seems to me to be especially strong. Such a combination of knowledge of the philosophical literature and biblical exegesis is not common these days.

Introduction

The twentieth century was full of creative developments in the doctrine of God. A brief mention of three shall illustrate my point: process, openness and postmodernity. These three approaches are fairly different but they show something of the range of theological options with which our current day is wrestling.

In 1925 Alfred North Whitehead delivered the Lowell Lectures at Harvard University, which were published in *Science and the Modern World*.[1] In this presentation a novel microscopic idealism emerged which tried to describe a relativistic universe in phenomenalistic language. In this volume and especially the idiosyncratic volume of the Gifford lectures, *Process and Reality*[2] to follow, the soft persuasive powers of the primordial nature of God were portrayed. This primordial nature is a transcendent omniscience of all possibilities (including the evil possibilities) which might take place. When such possibilities are seen as energized by the creative thrust a grand evolutionary universe progressively emerges. Each occasion and the societies of occasions, like humans, cooperate with this creative thrust to give their free will contribution to the next generation of occasions. The imminent consequent nature of God absorbs all the knowledge that can be known, namely knowledge of the past that has had sufficient time to be known by God, so that the primordial nature could suggest the next possibility for each occasion's consideration. In this model we can help God grow by

---

[1] Alfred North Whitehead, *Science and the Modern World* (N.Y.: The Free Press, 1925).
[2] Alfred North Whitehead, *Process and Reality* (N.Y.: The Free Press, 1929, 1978).

enabling the evolutionary process of the universe. Also in this model God's effect on the universe is portrayed as persuasion, which means that the evil of the universe is experienced because occasions have chosen awry, God is not to be blamed. In this model prediction is seen as an expression of the divine intention but there is no guarantee that this persuasive God will accomplish these prophecies or bring in the kingdom. In Tielhard de Chardin's version, the goal of history or omega point is Christ Who continues to evolve out in front of the evolving universe.[3] In a Whiteheadian model of process, everlasting life reduces down to being remembered by the consequent nature of God. Neither model portrays a final resolution of the evil experienced in this life for the universe continues to evolve and all the evil experiences are also remembered in the consequent nature of God.[4]

The openness of God model is a recent development of the theological landscape appreciating some of the points of process theology from within a context where an Arminian god concept had been previously. The book *The Openness of God*[5] presents a Christian God Who feels our hurt in suffering unlike the platonic simple god mystically beyond description or the Aristotelian god of pure actuality, which the patristic, medieval and scholastic church embraced. They view themselves as calling Christianity away from this Hellenistic god concept to a Biblical God, Who responds to humans in their prayer and faith. The Christian God is not seen as a-historically eternal with everything set in the decree, but the God Who is in history and reacts to the decisions we make as though our choices make a difference; they view man as having a libertarian free will.[6] Some of the philosophers, like William Hasker, see this libertarianism as a

---

[3] This is especially seen in Tielhard de Chardin, *The Divine Milieu* (N.Y.: Harper and Row, 1960), and *The Future of Man* (N.Y.: Harper and Row, 1964).

[4] These last points in the paragraph are illustrated in Marjorie Hewitt Suchocki, *The End of Evil* (Albany: State University of New York Press, 1988) and many other sources.

[5] Clark Pinnock, Richard Rice, John Sanders, William Hasker, and David Basinger, *The Openness of God* (Downers Grove: InterVarsity Press, 1994). The view is also even more simply developed in the volume by Greg Boyd, *God of the Possible* (Grand Rapids: Baker, 2000).

[6] David Basinger, *The Case for Freewill Theism* (Downers Grove: InterVarsity Press, 1996).

driving feature setting the framework for the openness model, whereas some of the theologians see that this libertarianism is merely an implication from a more basic idea that God is trinitarian with respect to attributes like love.[7] That is, for God to love and receive love God must be a free agent. Such freedom is seen as a facet of a person to give and receive love. Therefore, we humans have this libertarian free will in order to cultivate a love relationship meaningfully. Additionally, somewhat informed from process theology, God's omniscience is that God knows all that can be known, that is the present and the past, because the future is still largely open for us to decide how it will be. God is everlastingly in time and immutable in His character as He consistently initiates and responds to the circumstances, which occur in Biblical narrative and in our lives. There are a few things of the future, like the second coming of Christ, salvation for believer's in Christ, and God's ultimate victory in history that are established because God has guaranteed and predicted that they would happen.[8] Such a view sees evil and sin as the work of the human and angelic agents who choose awry from the revealed moral will of God, so God is not to be blamed for evil occurrences.[9] Additionally, since God guarantees the victory, God's salvation program is the answer for evil. They call people to faith in Christ, to be fervent in prayer and godly living because our choices really make a difference.

Postmodernity emerged progressively upon the landscape of the twentieth century. The first form emerging first in literary expression on the lips of Ivan Karamasov in Dostoevsky's novel *The Brothers Karamazov*.[10] However, with Ivan being redeemed in an orthodox way toward the end of the story by the generosity of his brother, a traditional orthodox God still amazes this form of

---

[7] The distinctive difference can be seen in the papers of the 47th Wheaton College Philosophy Conference, Oct. 26-28, 2000, namely: John Sanders, 'Mapping the Terrain of Divine Providence' and William Hasker, 'Antinomies of Divine Providence.' Also Clark Pinnock's works on trinity contribute here.

[8] Greg Boyd, *God at War: The Bible and Spiritual Conflict* (Downers Grove: InterVarsity, 1997).

[9] John Sanders, *The God Who Risks* (Downers Grove: InterVarsity, 1998).

[10] Fyodor Dostoevsky, *The Brothers Karamozov* (Chicago: Encyclopaedia Britannica, 1952).

postmodernity. A more blatant form of existential postmodernism can be seen in Friederich Nietzsche's *The Will to Power* in which he advocates the exercise of one's will to the extent that one's power will carry it.[11] Of course Nietzsche's postmodern tapestry as expressed by *Thus Spoke Zarathustra* shows his tendency toward autonomy within atheistic existentialism. It was in reaction to this existential postmodernity that Bernard Bell in 1926 coined the term 'postmodernism,' calling us back to modern rational thought.[12] However, much of what is known to be postmodernity today is more indebted to the communal form of conventional language or language games which Ludwig Wittgenstein developed mid-century in his *Philosophical Investigations*.[13] The effect of these existential and conventional postmodernities is extensive and I have elsewhere explored them at some length in my book *The Relationship between Epistemology, Hermeneutics, Biblical Theology and Contextualization.*[14] In the wake of postmodernity, pluralism is often embraced. Any individual may existentially choose a god of his own liking that will enable him to be a self fulfilled individual or any community may choose a god that fits their liking and tradition so that they might keep their faith. There is a danger here that evangelicals maintaining their traditional God will become just one more postmodern option in the theological smorgasbord, using the same postmodern techniques to keep their language game live for their audience. One way that some of these postmoderns view 'God' is that of a meaningful existential metaphor for individuals or communities to make sense of their lives. For example, Goddess as the Divine Feminine[15] need not be describing a

---

[11] I have found that the translations and notes by Walter Kaufmann to reliably capture Friedrich Nietzsche's works *The Will to Power* (New York, 1966) and *The Portable Nietzsche* (New York, 1954) in which *Thus Spoke Zarathustra* is found.

[12] Bernard Iddings Bell, *Postmodernism and Other Essays* (Milwaukee: Morehouse Publishing Co., 1926).

[13] Ludwig Wittgenstein, *Philosophical Investigations* (N.Y.: Macmillan, 1953, 1968).

[14] Douglas Kennard ed., *The Relationship between Epistemology, Hermeneutics, Biblical Theology and Contextualization* (Lewiston: Mellen Press, 1999).

[15] There are abundant examples, but these are two of them: Virginia Ramey Mollencott, *The Divine Feminine* (N.Y.: Crossroad, 1989) and Eleanor Rae and Bernice Marie-Daly, *Created*

metaphysical being of God as though she is gendered. Rather this at times is a subtle denial of metaphysical theology altogether and beings are not really in view at all. What is in view is a meaningful metaphor to make sense of the female Christian experience with metaphors to which some of our sisters can relate. This perspective would accuse the classical Christian God and an openness God as both being idols. They would claim that Goddess is not an idol because there is no actual being which is described even though referring to a goddess (as an equivocal metaphor) who is to be worshipped is a reportedly meaningful religious act.

I have previously developed a rationale for a critical realistic epistemology that takes the best of the tools that pre-modernism, modernism and postmodernism has to offer.[16] This critical realism model of epistemology has a place for modern philosophical precision as evidenced by my use of philosophy of religion in this work. Also the precision of the mostly modern discipline of Biblical theology presents a Biblical God that can be distinguished apart from the variety of traditions that try to proof-text the Bible. This precise Biblical theology mingles in a post critical move that returns to the pre-modern confidence of the Biblical text as our authority and merges with a post-modern passion for vividness of Biblical narrative compelling us to worship God more fully. That is, while all the chapters are trying to work the precision of truth about God (a modern idea) some of them are trying to do a very pre-modern thing like becoming devotional literature in the spirit of Anselm and also accomplish a post-modern goal as well, such as existentially compelling us to worship this God I love. It means that

---

in Her Image (N.Y.: Crossroad, 1990). Once at the American Theological Society I asked a goddess theologian if she wasn't in fact fostering idolatry and she responded that from her phenomenological perspective that she was not but that I was in danger of idolatry with a classical Christian God.

[16] Douglas Kennard, ed. *The Relationship Between Epistemology, Hermeneutics, Biblical Theology and Contextualization* (Lewiston: Mellen Press, 1999). I especially (from a postmodern or romantic perspective) developed this in the chapter of 'The Rise and Fall of Modern Philosophy as Illustrated in the Arts' (which is the transcript of an audio-visual presentation) but this was balanced by the more precise analysis of my positive epistemology in the chapter 'Faith and

unlike the criticism of some forms of classical Christianity, I am not platonic or Aristotelian.[17] I wish to distance myself from those Christian traditions that have read Platonism and Aristotelianism into their God concept. Wolfhart Pannenberg who makes these points about early Christianity embracing these philosophical templates also recognizes that some philosophical argumentation such as the causal inference in Romans 1:19 is a Biblical instance of cosmological argumentation, and thus such use of philosophy is Biblical and appropriate.[18] Philosophically, I desire to retain the precision of modern philosophy, without returning to the intuitional naiveté of classical philosophy. Nor am I guilty of the Christian charge of autonomy leveled at modernity, for I submit these philosophical disciplines to the services of theology and God ultimately with a devotion that wishes that the reader enter into these chapters to follow as devotional literature in the same way as Anselm proposed his works. I recognize that arguments for God's existence and Biblical narratives may be used in certain settings with apologetic value, but that is not my primary purpose here. So that I am not guilty here of a kind of liberalism, a human evangelical attempt to get to God by philosophy or to get behind the Biblical text to somehow bridge Lessing's ugly ditch. Rather, following thinkers like Alvin Plantinga, my methodology merges the concerns of faith and knowledge together in a manner that refuses to separate them.[19] Furthermore, when I explore the Biblical text and the Biblical theology that comes from texts, it is to unpack the meaning in the text within its

---

Knowledge.' Each of these sides of my model of critical realism come together in my hermeneutical model, which is expressed in the chapter 'A Thiselton-Ricoeur Hermeneutic.'

[17] John Sanders in *The Openness of God,* pp. 59-76 develops the platonic development of the patristic God concept. Likewise, Wolfhart Pannenberg in *Basic Questions in Theology* (Philadelphia: Fortress Press, 1971) volume 2, pp. 119-183 develops how the patristic embracing of philosophy embraced a platonic God concept as well. I agree with these authors that it is unfortunate that the early church became so platonic in its tradition. The classical Christian God that I am exploring is not platonic but is still accessible in part through philosophical argument.

[18] Wolfhart Pannenberg, *Basic Questions in Theology, Vol.* 2, p.158.

[19] I have defended this view in my book: Douglas Kennard ed., *The Relationship Between Epistemology, Hermeneutics, Biblical Theology and Contextualization* (Lewiston: Mellen Press, 1999), especially chapter 3, "Faith and Knowledge," pp. 35-70.

ancient Near Eastern context.[20] What I am trying to do in this book is to portray
God in such an accurate and lofty and compelling way as to prompt faith in my
readers for the God I love and to woo them to inform their theology and worship
my Beloved God. I recognize that Augustine, Anselm, Aquinas, Melanthon,
Calvin, Edwards each combined the precision of their philosophical thought with
Biblical exposition in a manner that tried to be true to both and their subject, God,
as well. I am trying to follow in their big footsteps here as we enter into the
twenty-first century. I realize that one approach would be to provide chapters that
critique each of these models, however I find more of what I have said I am trying
to do able to be accomplished through a positive statement, rather than critique.
So as I spin the positive web of belief about our beloved God there will be
occasional moments of critique to clarify how I understand God to in fact, be. In
this work I find that I resonate with Millard Erickson's excellent work, *God the
Father Almighty*,[21] which is trying to accomplish something of the same task as
my volume here. I enjoy his command of history and irenic style and tried to
emulate it here. I am not trying to duplicate this work by Erickson but trying to
be complementary in exploring a purer look at my disciplines of Biblical theology
and philosophy of religion to find the intersection between them to inform a
systematic theology with devotion to God and practicality in life. Part of my
motive in exploring these disciplines in the purer and more blatant way was that it
seemed to me that each side of these creative options and of their critics was
being very selective in noticing only the evidence that supported their own view
thus selectively slanting texts without acknowledging that they were eisegeting
Scripture. That is, instead of an ideological hermeneutic I follow Gabler in a
descriptive Biblical theology methodology. So my model ends up more varied

---

[20] My hermeneutic and Biblical theology method is explained in Douglas Kennard ed.,
The Relationship between Epistemology, Hermeneutics, Biblical Theology and Contextualization
(Lewiston: Mellen Press, 1999), pp.117-151, 181-185. Additional explanation and rationale is
also provided in two papers: "The Reef of Biblical Theology" (ETS paper presented Spring, 2000)
and "Biblical Authority in the Contemporary Hermeneutical Scene" (Wheaton Theology
Conference, April 2001).

[21] Millard Erickson, *God the Father Almighty* (Grand Rapids: Baker Books, 1998).

and complex wherever the texts and arguments take me, sometimes *for* tradition and sometimes *against* tradition. Provided that I see a way of making sense of these complex composite views that is free from contradiction, I consider that this view which I present in this book is a more complete or corresponding critical realist view of the way God, in fact is, in reality. One of the advantages of this approach is that many of the reasons and points to which these opposing views call us will be realized within my view in a complex hybrid. That is, the evidence often for each side supports my hybrid view. The accompanying difficulty is that some may find difficulty holding in tension the extent of hybridization, which my view maintains. However, often the complexity reflects the complexity of the Biblical text. Ultimately, it is not a detriment to be as complex as God has revealed things to be.

Because this book about God is an attempt to present a positive model in systematic theology, it would be helpful to briefly state what I am trying to do in this theological work. Systematic Theology, in my tradition, can be defined by Lewis Sperry Chafer as: "The collecting, scientific arranging, comparing, exhibiting, and defending of all facts from any and every source concerning God and His works."[22] To accomplish this task, systematic theology would have the following goals: 1) Systematic theology under this definition should evidence the development of a method (indicating "the collecting, scientific arranging, comparing, exhibiting, and defending" process), so I intend to show method as well as a product. This is why at times some of my chapters emphasize the philosophical method or Biblical theology method or historical traditions. Following the classical pattern, as in Aquinas, I first explore the philosophical

---

[22] Lewis Sperry Chafer, *Systematic Theology* (Dallas: Dallas Seminary Press, 1947) vol. 1, p. 6. This definition is merely a starting point out of which I wish to develop my theological method as explained here and in Douglas Kennard ed., *The Relationship between Epistemology, Hermeneutics, Biblical Theology and Contextualization* (Lewiston: Mellen Press, 1999), pp. 181-185. Additional explanation and rationale is also provided in two papers: "The Reef of Biblical Theology" (ETS paper presented Spring, 2000) and "Biblical Authority in the Contemporary Hermeneutical Scene" (Wheaton Theology Conference, April 2001).

concept of God as illustrated in the Biblical text and then the Biblical concept of God, which is philosophically consistent. Unlike some evangelicals, I see the philosophical and the Biblical concept of God to be essentially describing the same God. 2) The method for doing systematic theology would be especially dependent upon Biblical authority and the Biblical theology appropriate to the texts of Scripture. Some of the chapters are Biblical theology expositions of texts that focus upon God. 3) Such a Biblical interpretation requires the Biblical text to be understood in the ancient Near East context, rather than proof-texted to fit into a logical point. 4) Such a systematic theology would interact with the primary historical options of church history and incorporate the ones to which our orthodox Christian and evangelical traditions have tended to be defined. 5) A fully funded systematic theology would also think through the spoils of philosophy of religion and incorporate the proper level of engagement of this discipline. A few chapters approach the concept of God primarily from this philosophical side. 6) A theological method that is thought through for its epistemic concerns should be utilized so that the readers see why each feature is inclined to be included. 7) Systematic theology should engage the student where they are in their stage of life development. Some of my chapters and parts of the others chapters try to practically apply the theology in ways that connect with the reader, as in prayer. 8) Systematic theology should also engage the contemporary arena of theological options, while calling the student to truths that transcend the contemporary arena. 9) Systematic theology should provide an apologetic for the points being made so that they are not merely presented dogmatically but have a compelling rationale. This is the challenge I have in this volume but our God is well worth this effort so that He might be known, loved and worshipped.

The Nature of Necessity: A Case for Classical Theism in Opposition to the Openness of God Model

Necessity as a concept is used in several ways but these ways can be primarily organized into either logical necessity or actual necessity. Logical necessity normally requires an argument with assumed premises to establish the logically necessary relationship of cogency. In such an instance "cogent" simply means that the argument is logically tight or logically necessary. Of course, this does not require that a cogent argument is compelling and thereby accepted by the reader, for the assumed premises of the argument may not be granted by the reader. With the granting of the premises such logical necessity has implications governing reality.[1] At times, something in the experience of reality logically necessarily requires there to be a particular being in reality. For example, Descartes' maxim of "I think therefore I am" guarantees that for any experience of thinking or doubting that at least this thinker exists in reality as a thinking being. However, sometimes logical necessity governs reality without an experiential ground merely because the concept under consideration logically necessarily requires it to be so. For example, a square circle can never exist in reality for the concept is logically necessarily contradictory. The concept of square mutually excludes the concept of circle from describing the same object simultaneously.

The concept of actual necessy or modal necessity describes a being whose immutable existence is logically necessary and eternal. That is, such a necessary being must exist in reality if it exists at all. The four Aristotelian categories of modality include: impossibility (like square circles will never exist in any reality), possibility (might existence or a potentially dependent being), actuality (happen to be in reality, can actually dependent being, or a contingent or changing being), and actual necessity (must be immutable eternal existence). Each human has occupied both the category of possibility (as their parents contemplated their conception, birth and the changes that would make to their family) and actuality (as they exist aa dependent happen-to-be-growing being now). That is, we are dependent upon our parents for our existence and such things as food and circumstances for continued growth in existence.   Such categories as possible and actual would most likely have temporal sequence of: having possibilities change as events happen, being a particular way then being a different way. If such an actual being continued forever, as in everlasting life, then everlasting (continued temporal existence in which change would continue to occur) would be the appropriate description rather than eternal (existence outside time and sequence, with no essential change). An actually necessary being, if there is such a being, could not merely be a possible or an actual being, for it would not be in the same dependent kind of relationship or happen-to-be kind of existence or merely everlasting existence as thee two categories imply. So, if an actually necessary being exists at all then it must necessarily exist in reality, and if not then, it could never exist for it would then be impossible. However, we can not merely assume or illustrate such a necessary being into existence, as though through some sort of a Platonism[2] we were guaranteeing an eternal form from our

---

[1] For a defense that the logically necessary is the real, cf. Douglas Kennard, *The Relationship of Epistemology, Hermeneutics, Biblical Theology, and Contextualization* (Lewiston: Mellen Press, 1999), pp. 42-43.

[2] The author acknowledges that the classical model of God as a necessary being emerged as a Platonic and Aristotelian concept among the fathers and scholastics of Christianity however this paper is an attempt to show that the concept should be maintained without dependence upon them. Actually, this author is far more indebted to Locke, Leibniz, Kant, Pierce, Wittgenstein,

belief or discursive reasoning. Furthermore, if we maintained such a belief about the existence of God by merely tradition, then such a basic belief could probably be strengthened by examining its rationale. This paper will explore this rationale by examining: 1) an ontological argument, 2) the nature of a maximally great being defended by this ontological argument, 3) a cosmological argument, 4) the nature of an actual necessary being defended by these arguments, and 5) a Biblical assessment of whether the God of the Bible is described by these philosophical concepts and arguments.

An Ontological Argument

An ontological argument is informed by a powerful concept like that of a maximally great being. For our purposes, a maximally great being will be defined as *that being which has the maximally great set of metaphysical attributes.* One implication from this definition is that such a being is not contradictory, and thus normally considered to be not impossible, for the concept underscores that each of the attributes in the set will mutually limit the other attributes of the set so that no grotesque (a being with one attribute in the extreme) or contradictory being will ensue. For example, omnipotence in such a maximally great being could not mean "all powerful" because omnipotence limits omnipotence in that he could not make a stone so large that he could not move it. Omnipotence for this maximally great being would mean that this being, if it existed, would have the maximal degree of power it is possible to exemplify including:

1) There are no independent externally determined constraints on divine power; there are no rival beings that could thwart a maximally great being.
2) All God's internal attributes are fully empowered to perform all that is intrinsically better to have than to lack.

Hackett, Plantinga, Thiselton, and Ricoeur than these classical influences. The author is also

3) God is the sole source and continuous support of all the power there is or could be; all the power of every entity is contained within and derives from God.

Each of these premises is required from the nature of a maximally great being, if it is a being at all.   Because we conceive of a matrix of attributes in the set of divine attributes, if there is such a maximally great being then these attributes will be fully empowered (2).   Other beings, like ourselves, would be empowered fully from this maximally great being in such a manner that there would be no power which another being has that the maximally great being didn't source without diminishment to His own power (3).   Therefore there can be no rival because all other beings are empowered by the power which they have ultimately from this maximally great being, if there is such a being (1).   With attributes like this, a maximally great being would be incomparable, in that no other being could be favorably compared to this being.   A maximally great being would always be superior.   Thus there would only be one maximally great being as a monotheism. Furthermore, such a maximally great being would be a necessary being if he existed.   For example, a maximally great being would not change, come into being, go out of being or depend on another being for it's existence.   If such a necessary being exists, he could not merely happen to exist or be potentially existent or be a dependent being.   Therefore, a maximally great being is either necessary or impossible.   With attributes like these, an ontological argument may be constructed following Al Plantinga[3] as follows:

4) If a maximally great being exists, his existence is actually necessary.

5) If a maximally great being does not exist, his existence is impossible.

6) Either a maximally great being exists or he does not exist.

7) A maximally great being is either actually necessary or impossible.

---

committed to Biblical theology, which takes us in a very different direction.
[3] Alvin Plantinga, *The Nature of Necessity* (Oxford: Clarendon Press, 1974), pp. 196-221.

8) A maximally great being is not impossible.

9) Therefore, a maximally great being exists as an actually necessary being.

Premises 4 and 5 reflect the modal options from the previous discussion of necessity. Premise 6 identifies that there are only two mutually exclusive options available: existence or nonexistence. Premise 7 replaces premise 6 terminology by the implications from premises 4 and 5. Plantinga affirms premise 8 as a basic belief, which is quite natural when we recognize that we do not normally consider a concept to be impossible unless it is shown to be impossible, and a maximally great being has already been shown to be not a contradictory concept. Provided the reader does not approach this issue with the bias of skepticism it is reasonable to assume that a maximally great being is not impossible as a being and not just a concept. Additionally, if any argument for God's existence is compelling for the reader (like the cosmological argument to follow) then such an argument could confirm premise 8. However, premise 8 does not need nearly so strong an argument as this, so I will explore two other arguments for premise 8 to help compel the reader to grant it within this framework.

Within the heritage of William James' *Varieties of Religious Experience*, an inductive argument for the nonimpossibility of a maximally great being following Clement Dore[4] could be constructed as follows:

10) It is reasonable to consider that any concept that is internally consistent which is claimed to have been experienced is not impossible.

For example, if you walked into the local police station this Friday night and consistently claimed to have just had the experience of robbing the local convenience store, the police would assume that it is not impossible that you might in fact have robbed this store so they would usher you into the back room for further questioning and probably call that convenience store to check out your story. Depending on how your story checked out with their investigation you would either be prosecuted or sent to a hospital to deal with mental issues. The police began to check out the story because they assumed that an internally consistent concept claimed to have been experienced is not impossible. However, to float this premise all that is needed is the first assumption that anything internally consistent that is claimed to have been experienced is not impossible. With this framework the inductive argument for premise 8 would be as follows:

11) A maximally great being is by definition internally consistent.

12) Isaiah 40-48 claims to have experienced a maximally great being under the rubric of incomparability.

8') Therefore, it is reasonable to consider that a maximally great being is not impossible.

This argument does not require Isaiah to be authoritative Scripture but merely a testimony of a claimed experience of an incomparable being. Labuschagne develops the ancient Near East concept of incomparability as essentially the philosophical concept of incomparability in his work *The Incomparability of Yahweh in the Old Testament*[5]. That is, the philosophical concept involved in the ontological argument is also a Biblical concept. No actual or potential rival can be favorably compared to Yahweh, Who as sovereign is greater than all comers individually and combined (Isaiah 40:18-28; 41:4, 23-24; 42:5; 43:10-13; 44:6-8; 45:5, 21-22; 46:9-10; 48:12-14). It is Yahweh who, when talking with Isaiah, is reported to be always present to: be able to create, know history from its beginning, and predictively reveal the future because He continues to create history by bringing about His will. He has no rival. This incomparable Yahweh

---

[4] Clement Dore, "The Possibility of God," *Faith and Philosophy*, 1 (1984), pp. 303-15, and "God, Suffering and Solipism" (Unpublished manuscript, 1986), pp. 3-42, 108-119.

is testified to by Isaiah as having talked with him and challenged him and others to take the incomparability of Yahweh seriously, putting away idols and holding to Yahweh alone as their sovereign. Isaiah's experience of such an incomparable being renders such a noncontradictory concept to be not impossible to be experienced. Therefore, an incomparable being is not impossible. Furthermore, the impossibility of such an incomparable being cannot be experienced, for with the concept of an incomparable being having freedom from contradiction such a claim would mean that a person is claiming to have experienced the full range of available experiences in the universe and concluded that such a being is not available to be experienced. However, such a claim to have experienced the full range of available experiences is essentially an omniscience claim, which itself is impossible for a finite human person to experience. Because the concept of incomparability is championing Yahweh as over all options, real as well as hypothetical ones, the concept of incomparability is essentially identical to a maximally great being. Therefore, premise 8 is affirmed; it is reasonable to consider that a maximally great being is not impossible.

A deductive argument for the nonimpossibility of a maximally great being is available within Plantinga's construction of possible worlds.[6] A possible world is a logically possible state of affairs as indicated by freedom of contradiction both as a concept and with other constituents within that possible world. Nonimpossibility is normally defined as that which is logically conceivable without contradiction. However, since it has already been shown that a maximally great being is free of internal contradiction, the issue here is with regard to compossibility (whether this consistent concept of a maximally great being can be instantiated without contradiction with the truths which are conjunctively the case in all possible worlds). Plantinga defined a maximally great being as within each possible world but this is an arbitrarily weaker

---

[5] Labuschagne, *The Incomparability of Yahweh in the Old Testament* (Leiden: Brill, 1966).

[6] Plantinga, p.218-19.

definition because like a necessary being a maximally great being will be a transworld entity if he exists at all. For example, a necessary being in possible worlds is defined as *that being, when considered from the standpoint of any possible world, is understood to immutably exist in any and all possible worlds.* Likewise, a maximally great being is defined as *the being, when considered from the standpoint of any possible world, is understood to have maximum metaphysical greatness in any and all possible worlds.* Therefore, if a maximally great being exists, then any proposed world which contradicts such a maximally great being is not even a possible world. However, Plantinga claimed that a maximally great being in possible worlds terminology does not require one to assume that a maximally great being must exist. He proposed that there are two options besides a maximally great being. However to make those two options in fact mutually exclusive options the definitions of maximally great being must be the same in all these options or they will not in fact exclude a maximally great being from nonimpossibility and actual necessary existence. The first alternative is no-maximality, defined as the claim that a maximally great being does not exist in any possible world. The second alternative is near-maximality, which is defined as a maximally great being exists in some possible worlds but does not exist in other possible worlds including the actual world. Plantinga correctly concludes that all conceptual options are included within these three mutually exclusive options: maximally great being, no-maximality, and near-maximality. This framework permits the following argument: The only available nonimpossible option is the one conceptually consistent and compossible option from the following fully inclusive and mutually exclusive options: a maximally great being exists, no-maximality exists, or near-maximality exists.

13) A maximally great being is by definition internally consistent.

14) No-maximality is internally contradictory when the meaning of maximally great being is clarified in the definition as follows: *the being when*

considered from the standpoint of any possible world, is understood to have maximum metaphysical greatness in any and all possible worlds does not exist in any possible world.

15) Near-maximality is internally contradictory when the meaning of maximally great being is clarified in the definition as follows: *the being when considered from the standpoint of any possible world, is understood to have maximum metaphysical greatness in any and all possible worlds* exists in some possible worlds but does not exist in other possible worlds including the actual world.

16) Because no-maximality and near-maximality are contradictory concepts they cannot meaningfully exist as states of affairs.

8'') With two of the fully inclusive and mutually exclusive options as contradictory, the only available option must be that a maximally great being is not impossible.

Therefore, a Maximally Great Being necessarily exists in reality. Premise 8 brought us to that conclusion, whether by basic belief, an argument from testimony or an argument from possible worlds. Additionally, if one grants the modality of possible worlds, then God knows all possibilities or counterfactuals as counterfactuals since this Maximally Great Being is a transworld Being.

The Nature of a Maximally Great Being

There necessarily exists a Maximally Great Being Who is defined by the maximally great set of attributes it is possible to have. Since the kinds of possibility include not just logical possibility but also actual or compossibility as well, then no proposal is credible in which this being entails a contradiction through internal (e.g. claims of contradiction within attributes) or external (e.g. claims of contradiction with the problem of evil) means. All such claims for contradiction with the Maximally Great Being are not even possible because the transworld quality of the Maximally Great Being excludes them from all possible worlds. This means that the Maximally Great Being's attributes are those which when combined in a set are the maximum possible to exemplify as illustrated by omnipotence above (e.g. premises 1-3). The attribute of infinity, which would include transcendence, can describe these attributes by indicating that the Maximally Great Being is not limited by anything other than the necessary relationships among its own maximally great qualities.[7]

Such a Maximally Great Being would be imminently omnipresent and thus immaterial or spiritual as well. That is, the availability and accessibility of objects in the spatial-temporal world is a good trait making them useable to us. Likewise, the availability and accessibility of an imminent, omnipresent and everlasting being would be very fitting for the Maximally Great Being as well. However, the Maximally Great Being's omnipresence would be necessarily everywhere without variation or sequence. So such omnipresence would be nonbodily (i.e. spiritual) and immutably (i.e. eternal even though such a being might be glimpsed within creation as everlasting). So the spiritual and eternal omnipresence which the Maximally Great Being would instantiate would be exhibited in a non-spatial and nontemporal manner similar to another dimension beyond space and time. Perhaps Tillich's dimensional model for spirit as an imminent causal ground which creates and sustains the whole of creation serves as a paradigm for making sense of omnipresence of this eternal spiritual Being. That is, a person would not expect each location of the universe to contain an instance of the fullness of God but that God's fullness is present to each location in a continuous causal manner creating, determining, sustaining, protecting, relating, knowing from that perspective and recreating the whole of the universe into His kingdom.

---

[7] Such a view would not entail infinite options, for possibilities are limited to that which is not contradictory to the Maximally Great Being, thus excluding the renaissance maximal possibilities which Leroy Howe suggests in "Existence as a Perfection: A Reconsideration of the Ontological Argument," *Religious Studies* 4 (1968):92-94. Additionally the concept of a process

Such a Maximally Great Being would be actually necessary, immutable, and eternal. This being could not come into being or go out of being for He would always possess the maximally great set of attributes. Likewise, this being would not grow or degenerate for He would always possess the maximally great set of attributes. Without change in these attributes He is immutable, without chronological sequence He is thus eternal. More on this later when a necessary being is unpacked after a cosmological argument is presented within this chapter.

Since such a Maximally Great Being is defined by His nature, in which the maximally great set of attributes is embraces meaningfully distinct attributes held together in a set, the concept of simplicity embraced within Platonic and Aristotelian Christianity is excluded as contradictory. That is, the following features of the Aquinas/Stump definition of simplicity[8] would be excluded by the divine nature: "there cannot be any real distinction between one essential property and another in God's nature" and "there cannot be a real distinction between essence and existence in God." The meaningfully distinct attributes (such as God's goodness and wrath, or transcendence and immanence) show the impossibility of the Maximally Great Being as this kind of a simple Platonized Christian god because such a simplicity view is contradictory.[9]

The Maximally Great Being is incomparable and thus monotheistic, with no individual or corporate rival. So dualism and polytheism is excluded. No Satan or group of humans could thwart the plan of this Maximally Great Being. That is, a Maximally Great Being could not be a part of a whole which is greater than the former Being alone, so He becomes the sole source and continuous support of all power and all beings who exercise power.

---

primordial nature would be excluded or severely limited to only those compossible possibilities to a Maximally Great Being.

[8]Thomas Aquinas, *Summa Theologica*, vol. I, Pt. 1, Q3, A7, and Eleonore Stump, "Simplicity" in Quinn and Taliaferro, *A Companion to Philosophy of Religion* (Cambridge: Blackwell, 1997), p. 250, and Stump and Kretzmann "Absolute Simplicity," *Faith and Philosophy* 2(1985), pp. 353-81.

[9] The author has argued this in the chapter "A Few Philosophical and Biblical Theology Problems with Statements of the Trinity," within this book, which is indebted to Alvin Plantinga, *Does God Have a Nature?* (Milwaukee: Marquette University Press, 1980).

Another way to approach maximal greatness is to recognize good traits among humans, and then maximally surpass these good traits to determine maximal greatness. In this process, humans make a good model since they are near the top of any list of naturally known beings that can vie for metaphysical greatness. So the beneficial or great traits that humans have (such as being personal in interacting with those around, knowing what is happening around them, empathizing with others, having a will to act, and doing good) can also be found in the Maximally Great Being. Furthermore, these human traits are surpassed by His maximal greatness, so that God would excel humans in manifesting such personal and good traits. This approach excludes noninteractive god concepts such as deism and a fully actualized Aristotelian god who does not feel and interact with those around him. Notice that this technique does not reduce to Feuerbach's anthropomorphized God concept because there is an argument to support the necessary existence of this Maximally Great Being; He is not merely a wish fulfillment. Such a maximally Great Being would be personal, communicating to others and receiving prayers as a meaningful communication from them. Since it is advantageous in communication to tell the truth, such a Maximally Great Being would be known for only telling the truth without any lie (e.g. Titus 1:2). Additionally, such a Maximally Great Being would be an empathetic, compassionate, merciful God Who purposes to protect and cultivate those He has chosen (e.g. Jer. 31:20; Hos. 11:8). As a result of protecting His own, there would probably be a place for a Maximally Great Being to express righteous anger against those who attempt to destroy those who are His (e.g. Nah. 1:2). Since this being is omnipresent, He would know everything that happens, feel empathy for all, and sovereignly act for the good of the whole creation. Such an interactive Maximally Great Being would be multiple persons, for in eternity before the creation the interactive communication, empathy, and love occurring would happen necessarily within Themselves. However, there is not enough here to require that this configuration must be a trinity,[10] though it may need to be more than two persons for the communal value of these attributes to be engaged. This would mean that creating would not be a necessary requirement for the Maximally Great Being but it would be a very natural choice on His part. With the act of creation would come continued involvement, so that the creation would reflect His qualities as it also shows forth the qualities of beings of creation as well.

A Cosmological Argument

Another way to argue for a necessary being involves the inductive, and thus not logically tight, means of the cosmological argument. However, this argument is often easier to follow because it starts with the experience of existence and floats its argument within empirical experience of creation. Additionally, unlike the ontological argument the cosmological argument has some evidence of its use within the Bible for purposes of fostering worship, gospel, and judgment. For example, Psalm 19:1 testifies to God's grandeur as known from the creation: "The heavens are telling of the glory of God; and their expanse is declaring the work of His hands." Additionally, in a context of gospel proclamation, Paul develops a common ground with the Athenians between the rival Epicurean and stoic philosophies by appealing to the remembered experience of a plague being averted as pointing to a creator sovereign God Who is acknowledged by them but remains largely unknown to them as He is the One Who has resurrected Christ (Acts 17:18-31). This gospel was effective enough for some to come to a saving knowledge of Christ even though most seemed to reject it at the point of Christ's resurrection. For those who reject the gospel or who have never heard the gospel, God is still righteous in judging them with wrath "because that which is known about God is evident within them; for God made it evident to them. For since the creation of the world His invisible

---

[10] Contra Augustine, Anselm, Swinburne, et al.

attributes, His everlasting power and divine nature, have been clearly seen being understood through what has been made, so that they are without excuse" (Rom. 1:19-20). In Paul's perspective, there is enough evidence in creation to point to God as an everlasting powerful and immortal being. The cosmological argument is one form in which this voice from creation is precisely heard.

The particular cosmological argument that is presented here is framed by three mutually exclusive options that cover the whole array of origins contemplated. First, 'Uncaused' beings are those, which are eternal and through this argument are seen to be actually necessary. Second, beings which are "caused by another" in this framework are contingent, with all the changeability and dependence of "happen to be" beings. Third, the option of being self-caused has in view a range of options like: Stephen Hawking's view that within an everlasting universe with imaginary time, the big bang brought about the expanding universe and positive time without outside cause, or microscopically Donald Sherburne's naturalistic process, or Fred Hoyle's continuous creation of Hydrogen molecules, or extreme forms of existentialism which see choice involved in creating one's own existence in the first place. From this framework the cosmological argument may be run as follows:

17) If any being exists, then it is either: uncaused, caused by another, or self caused.

18) Some contingent beings exist (e.g. I exist).

19) Contingent beings are not uncaused because they are dependent in their "happen to be existence" (e.g. I had a beginning and need food for growth).

20) Human experience indicates that non-existent contingent beings do not cause themselves to exist (i.e. you cannot be prior to yourself).

21) Therefore, contingent beings are caused by another (e.g. I have parents).

22) The cause for these contingent beings existing is either an infinite regress of contingent beings or ultimately a necessary being.

23) An infinite regress of contingent beings is unreasonable because the universe evidences a finite age from observations of its expanding nature.

24) Therefore, it is reasonable to conclude that a necessary being exists, which we call God.

The weakest premise is probably premise 21 because the views of Hawking, Sherburne, Hoyle and extreme existentialists are not stopped by this popular human appeal. However this is not very significant because each option could be diminished. For example, most astronomers do not embrace Hoyle's view of continuous creation because they accept the law of the conservation of energy and explain hydrogen gas clouds in relation to the forming or exploding of a star. Carl Sagan popularized this view. Alan Gluth of MIT extends this view in his conjecture which he calls inflation, namely that a propelled expansion of space smaller than an atom caused the creation of matter. Most existentialists do not develop these details but recognize that one needs existence in the first place for there to be meaningful choice to frame one's essence, and this argument is about explaining where this initial existence comes from. Hawking's basic belief entails an everlasting universe before the big bang which we know nearly nothing about. However, he has the assumption that the rules for our universe are so compelling that they or some aspect from the unknown universe could instigate the big bang without any further cause. The expanding universe known to human experience has no observed mechanism to explain the instigation of the big bang. Hawking's basic belief is for a claim of which he has no explanation of the process. Others, like Richard Gott and Li-Xin Li of Princeton, join him by mapping a model that permits the universe to become its own mother. Sherburne's naturalistic process denies the God of most process advocates and adds the personal quality of occasions, which is extremely foreign to most scientific microscopic analyses. These unusual modifications leave the group of adherents rather small. So perhaps a popular appeal is not hindered by the few who would still slide through. For most, the verse sung in the "Sound of Music" still makes sense, "Nothing came from nothing, nothing ever could." Thus, premise 21 will hold for most; human experience indicates that non-existent contingent beings do not cause themselves to exist.

Premise 23 has within it the possibility of the cause for contingent being to be a set or nexus of contingent beings, but each set or nexus would then be dependent upon some contingent beings or set of contingent beings. Ultimately this sequence of causes for contingent beings or sets of beings is either an infinite regress of contingency or ultimately begun by a necessary being.

Premise 24 used to be a difficult chasm to close before the current big bang theory which has made this significantly easier for those who are scientifically inclined. At the turn of the century, Henriet Levit recognized that the length of time it took to fix the image of a sephiad star on a photographic plate indicated the distance this star was from the earth. Edwin Hubble used this understanding to recognize that the more distant stars had a spectrographically redder Doppler shift of light, and thus an expanding universe. From this awareness, he proposed Hubble's law, which states that distance to stellar objects is proportional to velocity (i.e. twice as far away means twice as great a velocity). From these experimental facts the theory of the big bang is constructed. At least the expanding universe is scientifically observable, whether this means that the big bang occurred where this expanding universe originated or whether creation merely emerged as an earlier stage of this expanding universe is largely dependent upon one's presupposition for an old or young universe. In the early 1970's the theory of the oscillating universe was floated but it has few adherents today because there is rather broad agreement that the observed masses in the universe are rather small when compared to their high velocities and great distances. The oscillating universe also multiplies inexplicables such as: a mechanism for the repeated big bangs, how to turn a black hole of the big crunch into the big bang, how to overwhelm entropy that would then decay the oscillations so that everlasting oscillations would be impossible, and the cause for the infused energy/matter which would then overwhelm entropy. A further nail in the coffin for the oscillating model is the recent study, by both the University of Berkeley and Harvard University comparing supernovae from one to ten billion light years away from earth, which seems to indicate that the universe is expanding at an increasing rate.[11]

With an infinite regress of contingent beings as unlikely, then the best explanation for the existence of the expanding universe is an actually necessary being which we call God (premise 25).

The Nature of a Necessary Being

Both the ontological argument and the cosmological argument propose that an actually necessary being exists which we will call God. This necessary being is always existent immutably and eternally. This level of immutability and eternity means that there is no sequence within God. There is no chronological experience in order for God to not change from non-being to being in a certain way.[12] Furthermore, the knowledge He knows He has always known without variance. God would know all there is to be known for the whole of time as an eternally present experience, without change. However, this does not cause God to be opposed to the knowledge of His creation, for He would always know what every feature of the creation knows from the creation's perspective in space and time while also knowing simultaneously from His unique vantage point. For example, He would eternally know my knowing of the past and my fears of the future from my vantage point and the perspective of every created thing in

---

[11] As reported by Douglas Duncan, associate professor of astronomy at the University of Chicago, during "Odyssey" program interview on Chicago public radio station WBEZ Jan. 16, 1999 about 11 a. m.

[12] This means that the kenotic view of the divinity of Christ emptying Himself of His divine attributes so that He could become incarnate that Satori proposed in 1831 is excluded as well as the evangelical softened version of a willing nonuse of divine attributes which He continued to possess for both options describe essential change which is impossible for an immutable being. For a further discussion of this see Douglas Kennard, "A Few Philosophical and Biblical Theology Problems with Statements of the Trinity" in this book.

addition to His unique additional perspectives. So that in our Einsteinian relativistic universe we may have problems defending simultaneity of events but God would know simultaneity because He is not limited by our finite empirical ways of knowing. However, this does not render eternity to be static, for Boethius defines eternity in a more determining manner as the complete possession all at once of illimitable life.[13] The complete possession is an atemporal sourcing that does not change and is not limited but brings about all that has changed in its expressions of finiteness. This means that eternity is the source for all power and life, as previously described under the section on omnipotence above. So eternity is not primarily to be known for it's static comprehensive determining knowledge but for the life revealed to have come from God in His revelational creation. Because God initiates the whole of the creation including all of its details His knowledge essentially also determines choice. God's choices are eternal and essential to His nature without variance. To have God as an actually necessary being means His sovereign choice is set. This means that the level of necessity for God includes all of God's thoughts and sovereign choices eternally and immutably. God is not open in growing and gaining more knowledge and choosing in response to this knowledge. God's knowledge and choice would in fact be set within God's essential nature as determinative for the existence, essence, and choices the whole of creation makes.[14] With God's knowledge and choice as essential to His nature, then there is no logical order in God either. This means that all the reformation options expressing the order of the decree would in fact be contradictory to God's essential nature. Additionally, conjectures about Molinist counterfactual possibilities informing God's foreknowledge before His choice would also be

---

[13] Boethius, *The Consolation of Philosophy*, Book V, Prose 6; and *De trinitate*, chapter 4 in E. K. Rand, ed., *Boethius: The Theological Tractates and The Consolation of Philosophy* (Cambridge: Harvard, 1973).

[14] For a further discussion of how the determining sovereignty of God and freedom of man fit in a non contradictory manner that consistently reflect the Biblical text see the paper by Douglas Kennard, "God's Sovereignty and Human Free Will," in this book. In that paper a compatiblism of Anselmic/Thomistic determinism with Edwardsian free will is defended.

contradictory to God's essential nature. There would not be a logical sequence within God Who simultaneously knows and chooses without sequence (i.e. eternally). This should not surprise us, for there are no Biblical texts that talk about any logical or chronological sequence within God of an order of salvation either; all these claimed texts at best indicate that when it comes to the application of God's choice out into the chronologically changing creation that such choice has a sequence of application for the recipient. For example, no texts that develop hypothetical counterfactuals (e.g. 1 Cor. 2:8) identify that God is somehow informed of these possibilities in order to choose. Such Molinism would imply a clear logical sequence if not chronological sequence in a Molinist God in which foreknowledge of all possibilities is the first step and God's choice (of the possible world, which will be the actual world) is the second step. Likewise, the order of the decree would have clear logical sequence if not chronological sequence. These sequential views of God's essence would be excluded by the affirmation of necessity. However, there is no problem in maintaining an essentially necessary God Who applies His decisions to the creation in a chronological or logical order. For example, there is a clear logical and chronological sequence in applying the divine election (*ekletois*) as foreknown, preparative sanctifying the person so that the outcome (*eis*) of this sanctification ushers in obedience and atonement (1 Pet. 1:1-2). At other instances of sequence of the application of salvation there is encouragement for the Christian who has experienced some of the salvation benefits, such as justification, who can be reassured that the other benefits, such as glorification, will also be his in time (e.g. Rom. 8:29-30). So the whole post-reformation discussion of the order of the decree and the order of salvation within God's essence was an unfortunate exploration that does not apply to this necessary, immutable, and eternal God. Any linkage of logical order or chronological sequence in such works of God is an expression of application order or revelation purpose. Any attempt to communicate eternal truths into a constantly changing environment such as the creation will reflect them in sequential ways partly because of the sequential nature of the environment and partly to accommodate to our human understanding. For example, the textual sequences above convey that God graciously applies and guarantees the fullness of salvation to each Christian personally, which is a revelation purpose consistent with God's immutable nature. Any apparent change in God is actually the refraction of a changeless God through the lens of the changing environment for purposes of applying some benefit to the creation, such as salvation or the communication of certain select truths to a certain group in time. The fact that the truths of God are accommodated to the means of communication does not limit the truths of God, but the context indicates the primary hermeneutical purpose and how the descriptions of God are merely supportive of this purpose.

Biblical Assessment

In this section the philosophical model for God that has been explored will be compared to the Biblical presentation of God. To do this assessment the Biblical model will be unpacked and then compared to that of the previously explored philosophical model. Other issues could be explored in other papers but this section is limited to a Biblical assessment of this particular model.

The attribute of necessity is never referred to in the Bible however God is described as an immutable being, which is a major aspect of necessity. For example, James points out that in the context of temptation that the divine Father is the generous provider of every good gift and that He continues to give these good gifts without mixing any temptation or sin among these gifts (Jas. 1:17). So the Christian can reassure himself that God will continue to give good without any evil. Likewise, Jesus is the same yesterday, today, and forever as the everlasting king and focus for our faith (Heb. 1:12; 13:8).[15] Additionally, God is

---

[15] This means that the kenotic view of the divinity of Christ emptying Himself of His divine attributes so that He could become incarnate which Satori proposed in 1831 is excluded as well as the evangelical softened version of a willing nonuse of divine attributes which He

consistently described as the first and the last, identifying that God will continue from creation to the climax of history as the one Who engages in history to accomplish His purposes, especially blessing those who remain faithful (Isa. 41:4; Rev. 1:8; 21:6; 22:13).

The attribute of eternality is never referred to in the Bible but God is described as an everlasting being, which identifies that God in the Bible is being described phenomenolistically from the vantage point of how He is viewed from within the creation. So the same level of philosophical description need not be expected, provided the creation-based description approximates that of the necessary being. The words for "everlasting" in Hebrew (*'olam)* and the Greek *(aionios)* both have a temporal meaning such as "from age to age" or "perpetual within time." For example, the kingdom of God is an everlasting reign from age to age (Dan. 4:3, 34; 7:14, 18, 27; 1 Tim. 6:16). Furthermore, the Noahic covenant is an everlasting covenant as long as there are humans, animals, and rainbows (Gen. 9:8-17). Likewise the Davidic covenant is as everlasting as the sun and moon continue to shine (Ps. 89:2, 36-37). None of these texts address an eternal nonsequentiality beyond time but rather they support a continuous everlasting character. Within this creation-based framework God is viewed as everlasting (Rom. 16:26). Additionally, Christ calls his followers to everlasting life as opposed to everlasting judgment; neither option has an end (Mt. 25:41,46).

God's omnipresence is claimed by a myriad of examples in the Bible rather than a universal statement. One of the most concentrated examples of these claims can be found within the hymnic part of Psalm 139:7-12. David asks where can he go from God's controlling presence or Spirit that encircles him with His knowledge. In this omnipresence God is expressed as a spiritual Being. When David considers a range of hypothetical circumstances he reassures himself that he cannot escape God's presence. David first considers a merism with the height

---

continued to possess. Both options describe essential change which is impossible for an immutable being. For a further discussion of this see Douglas Kennard, "A Few Philosophical and Biblical Theology Problems with Statements of the Trinity," in this book.

and close proximity to God's throne room in heaven as compared to the deepest pit and furthest from this throne room. God is in both places and thus to be thought of as everywhere in between and thus throughout the creation. Poetically emphasizing this again, David considers travelling as fast as the dawn, which as a tool of God brings light to the creation isolating chaos to the dark of night. Then like *sheol,* the remotest part of the sea is deeply associated with chaos. However, God is not only present to these opposites of chaos conquest and chaos immersion but controlling throughout the whole of the creation by His presence as well. "Even there Thy hand will lead me and Thy right hand will lay hold of me." David contemplates that in the contexts of darkness and chaos that he will be overwhelmed by the forces of chaos and concludes that since God's presence is with him, even the darkest most chaotic environment is penetrated and brightened by the light of God. God's omnipresence, to be wherever David could think of escaping from God and of course to be wherever David in fact *is,* is profoundly reassuring of God's control and protection in his life. Such a view of omnipresence for God in a relativistic universe has implications on God's everlastingness, namely because space and time are dimensionally related, God Who is everywhere is also everywhen. This will be developed further in the chapter, "Eternity and Everlasting."

God is described at times with special local presence to portray some divine purpose with and in His creation. For example, the burning bush presents Yahweh as the God who always will be there to help in time of need and in fact was helping then by sending Moses back to lead Israel out of Egypt (Ex. 3:1-22).[16] When the tabernacle is constructed according to the pattern, God indwells it showing His pleasure and glory to authenticate and lead Israel to the promised land (Ex. 40:34-38). Additionally, when God called prophets He sometimes

---

[16] In Exodus 3:14 the verbal ideal of the name of Yahweh is either Qal imperfect, "I am Who I am" or existential presence to help or Hiphil imperfect, "I will be Who I will be" or promised presence to help; this is not a good passage to teach the eternal existence of God or aseity.

presented Himself to them in a vision (e.g. Isa. 6). Climactically, when the divine
logos added humanity and walked among His creation, He was a concentrated
expression of God through His humanity (Jn.1:1-18). These expressions are not
excluded by God's necessity, immutability, and omnipresence, for God would
have remained with these attributes without any kenotic diminishment or nonuse,
but phenomenologically from the vantage point of the creation, the visual
presence of God in these ways functions as a powerful accommodation of Himself
to man to communicate truths about God that would probably not otherwise be
grasped. However, these expressions of God within creation, and thus seen as
locally and temporally present, go beyond merely that of communication, for God
is also One Who engages in: creation, transformation of history, and
reconciliation; the divine presence communicates and accomplishes His purposes
within the creation. These dramatic engagements do not take away from the
essential necessity, immutability or omnipresence but rather show God to be the
gracious glorious God He is. Such engagement and compassion for creation
would only be seen from the vantage point of creation as temporal locally present
phenomena. While the shekinah glory was present in the tabernacle He was also
present everywhere as David praised Him to be (Ps. 139:7-12). Likewise, while
the grace and truth of God was expressed through the local presence of the divine
Son Who fleshes out and explains God, the divinity of the Son is also
omnipresent, for He does not change yesterday, today or forever (Heb.13:8;
Rev.1:17).

God's omniscience is claimed in the Bible by a myriad of examples rather
than a universal statement. For example, the divine speeches in Job barrage Job
with an array of questions he cannot answer but presumably God can. However,
probably the most concentrated section to examine the omniscience of God is in
the hymnic section of Psalm 139:1-6, 13-18. David declares that God has carried
out a complete investigation as in spying out the land or in a legal brief. This
results in God's complete truthful knowledge as expressed through the merism of

God knowing his sittings and risings. As a merism God also knows all the other events, too. However, this knowledge reaches to David's internal thoughts as well, for perceived distance to God does not hamper God from knowing them all. Another merism shows that God knows David's path or way or plans of life and when David is resting from these plans. "God is intimately acquainted with all my ways." That is, all of David's action and behavior is truthfully known by God. God is not limited by knowing things only after the fact for He knows what David will speak before he himself does as an indication that God knows everything. In fact, God's knowledge is controlling because it so extensively surrounds David like a fortress (so high that David can't assail it or overpower it or, as we saw previously under the discussion of God 's omnipresence, David can't escape it either). Beneath the omniscience and omnipresence is the realization that God is the initiator, for God knows so well because He made David. God's creation of David involves weaving out the tapestry of his life while David was still in the womb. Because God's creating of David frames and fills out who David will become even while he is hidden from all others view, shows the extensive knowledge of the craftsman. God has blueprinted David's embryo and history before David had even begun any of them. God's knowledge is the initiating, creating, determining, and controlling thing in David's life and David lives out his life reflecting this condition of being so extensively known by God. These thoughts are too many to count about any one individual that David is overwhelmed by God's omniscience.

Job and Revelation especially portray God to be an omnipotent being Who has no individual or corporate equal and will thus accomplish His will in spite of all opposition. Biblically the concept of omnipotence is seen through the Latin *omnipoens* which reflects the Hebrew *shadday* and the Greek *pantokrator*. The rabbinic analysis of the word *shadday* is that it is composed of the relative *she* "who" and the word *day* "enough" or *shadday* "self-sufficient."[17] More recently

---

[17] Babylonian Talmud Hagigah 12a.

shadday has been connected with *shadod* "to destroy," hence the powerful destroyer. These meanings could fit in the context of Job (e.g. Job 5:17; 6:4; 8:3; 11:7; 32:8; 40:2) but not in the few texts of Genesis 17:1; 28:3; 35:11; 43:14; 48:3 and Exodus 6:3 where the contexts for *shadday* are more of blessing and covenant. A widely held suggestion today is to connect *shadday* with the Akkadian word *zadu* "mountain," as God's abode. The *-ay* suffix would be understood as "of the" which has been demonstrated by Ugaritic. While this is possible, few *shadday* references have a mountain context and Job's *shadday* is the creator and enabler of all; if mountains are thought to be *shadday's* home then He is no localized deity but the One powerful sovereign to whom Job must submit. When the imagery transposes into the N.T. the *pantokrator* is the Almighty Who confronts John in vision destroys His opponents and brings in the kingdom (Rev.1:8; 4:8; 11:17; 15:3; 16:7, 14; 19:6, 15; 21:22). So the Biblical emphasis for omnipotence is that God is the creator, provider, covenant or conqueror, and establisher of His kingdom. Programs for evil will fail because the almighty God will establish His kingdom. There is no group of beings who can thwart Almighty God's plan.

Foreknowledge of God is a determined intimate knowledge of a person or event experientially prior to it appearing in creation, from the perspective of those in creation. For example, Peter uses foreknowledge as a parallel word to communicate a predetermined plan (Acts 2:23). Thus, foreknowledge is not God responding to human activity but rather God having determined an event, which, when seen from the perspective of the creation, appears to be known before it happens. This is how eternal omniscience would be perceived from the creation; technically God does not know in advance, He knows *outside* of time and sequence. So, foreknowledge is a metaphor that communicates features of God's eternal omniscience into a temporal creation so the creation might be encouraged by the sovereign intimacy of God. Peter elsewhere points to God's foreknowing Christ before the foundation of the world from the vantage point of the creation so that in more recent times Christ appeared in the world for our sake so we would believe in Him and His redemption (1 Pet. 1:20). In this case the knowledge within foreknowledge is not an event but intimate personal and relational. Foreknowledge in these contexts simply would not make sense in a classical Greek, or Arminian, or Molinist way for here the person is known and the redemption is determined by God; God is not held captive by human initiation to bring about His plan for He is the initiator of redemption. The Father knows Christ essentially and eternally within the trinity. This trinity is emphasized within these contexts as seen in the description of the recipients and longer blessing in 1 Peter 1:2, 3-12 or in the foreordaining God who exalts Christ to be Lord enabling Him to pour forth the divine Spirit (Acts 2). This same trinity is intimately involved in the salvation of the Christian. For example, the election of those who become Christians is foreknown by the Father in eternity because the same contrast is made in 1 Peter 1:1-2 as is made in 1:20; the foreknowledge is an intimate determining aspect of divine omniscience recognized to be known from the viewpoint of the creation as prior but it is applied in the creation in time. In this case the election is divinely applied through the preparatory sanctifying of the Spirit which brings about the outcome (*eis*) of obedience and atonement. Notice that God is the initiator for the first act of obedience that identifies this person as within the atonement and which is brought about as a result of the divine election being applied by the Spirit.

God's sovereignty is Biblically claimed in countless ways. Yahweh is the king Who continues to reign overall while the earthly kings reign over miniature plots for a moment (Isa. 6). Yahweh presents Himself as a suzerain or great king though the form of documents of revelation (namely: Exodus-Leviticus, Deuteronomy, and Joshua 24). When suzerain Yahweh challenged Egypt, the most powerful nation of that time, Yahweh destroyed Egypt and their pantheon of gods in order to lead Israel out to the promised land. Yahweh is the incomparable One Who is superior to all and thus accomplishes His will of judging sinners and rescuing those He has chosen (Isa. 40-48). As sovereign, Yahweh predicts and guarantees that the predictions will come to pass for there is no rival to God (Isa. 44:6-8). When the history of the world runs its course God's kingdom will again conquer, indicating that He continues to reign (e.g. Dan. 2:45).

God's sovereign choice includes everything within the decree as divine initiation determining what would come to pass.[18] Paul in Romans 9 explains the process of God's determinism as dependent and initiated by Him so that the Christians do not have to fear being overwhelmed by evil. God overwhelmingly conquers for the Christian even as some are dying a martyr's death so their inheritance with Christ is guaranteed. God's purpose is initiated by Him in promise before any choice could be made by the participants "in order that God's purpose according to His choice might stand, not because of works, but because of Him who calls" (Rom. 9:6-13). Since it is God's sovereign initiation which determines whether an individual or nation is saved and blessed or actively rejected for curse, the determinism of their fate is set without their works even though their works are involved in playing out the dramatic narrative. Quoting Malachi, 1:2 God declares "Jacob I actively loved, but Esau I actively hated" to indicate that the choice stands determined by God Who has set their fate. This is a harsh statement but is the only meaningful one to make sense of the question in the next verse, "There is no injustice with God is there?" (Rom. 9:14). God initiates and determines the action for such a question to be raised. God is the One Who has mercy or compassion to include in blessing so the choice does not depend on the will of man or the activity of man but on God as the initiator (Rom. 9:15-16). Options like Molinism or Arminianism do not reflect that God is the initiating determiner as this passage portrays. However, the determinism is not merely of the good of mercy but also the active curse as illustrated by the hardening of Pharaoh. The verse quoted in Romans 9:17 is the one in Exodus

---

[18] For a further discussion of how the determining sovereignty of God and freedom of man fit in a non contradictory manner that consistently reflect the Biblical text see the chapter "God's Sovereignty and Human Free Will," in this book.

4:21 where God predicts and informs Moses that He has raised Pharaoh for this destruction in order to demonstrate His sovereign determining in the salvation of His people. This sovereign determining is the emphasis in the Exodus context as illustrated by the majority of instances in which God is declared to harden Pharaoh's heart (Ex.4: 21; 7:3; 9:12; 10:1, 20, 27; 11:10; 14:4, 17). There are other verses in the context that could be taken as divine determinism but these listed unquestionably emphasize that God is the initiator and determiner of Pharaoh's fate. However, this determinism works compatibly with human choice, for Pharaoh is recorded as having taken an active hand in hardening his heart in a few instances as well (Ex. 8:15, 32; 9:34). In Paul's context the sovereign determinism is the feature being emphasized as well; "So He has mercy on whom He desires, and He hardens whom He desires" (Rom. 9:18). Unless one recognizes this strong sovereign determinism as what is happening in this context, the next verse's questions do not make sense: "For why does He still find fault?" for "Who resists His will?" (Rom. 9:19). The answer keeps the determining initiative with God, "Who are you, O man who answers back to God? The thing molded will not say to the molder, 'Why did you make me like this,' will it? Or does not the potter have a right over the clay, to make from the same lump one vessel for honorable use, and another for common use?" (Rom. 9:20-21). In a similar context exploring the features of salvation, such as predestination accomplished within the heavenly benefits, Paul reminds his readers that God works all things after the counsel of His will (Eph. 1:11). This determinism is exhaustive and includes everything, for in this context the salvifically determined events are seen as within a greater context of the "all things" of God's sovereignty.

God can be viewed in this model as the continuous final causal ground for all existence and events. So God both determines and omnisciently knows (another divine initiating and determining motif) all the creation. God continues to sustain all the creation as well. In His active sustaining role God is better understood as an efficient cause as well. More explanation will be provided on divine efficient causality in the chapter on "Sovereignty and Free Will."[19] God will bring the whole of the creation within His goal, for as omnipotent and incomparable He is fully able, and as sovereign determiner He is fully willing to do so. God has no challenger who can thwart His plan.

This model handles the passages with which the openness model challenge us. Many of them have already been folded into the discussion however two texts in Genesis stand out as examples of openness challenge.[20] Genesis 6:5-7 presents an evaluation of humans prior to the Noahic flood that recounts Yahweh seeing man's wickedness to such an extent that He is grieved in heart and repents from His blessing to now destroy the world in judgment. Certainly, Yahweh is consistent with His nature in His blessing His creation until in their disobedience they transgresses His standard (e.g. Gen. 2:17; 3:14-20; 4:7-12). The text does not comment on this being a plan of Yahweh, for it leaves it as a description from the vantage point of the changing historical narrative and such phenomenological language is to be expected in a narrative account. Now that man's thoughts were only evil continually, God's destroying judgment is to be expected. The other account is in Genesis 18 where Yahweh appears before Abraham and takes him into confidence concerning Sodom and Gomorrah's judgment. In this context Yahweh engages in conversation with Abraham predicting that Sarah would bear a child within a year's time (Gen.18:10). When Sarah overheard this prophecy she laughed in disbelief and tried to cover it up but Yahweh knew and corrected her so that she did laugh, for nothing is too difficult for Yahweh (Gen. 18:13-15). Then Yahweh took Abraham into confidence about the judgment that He was about to accomplish (Gen.18:17). The interactive interchange that follows demonstrates that Abraham and Yahweh are both righteous. God is so committed

---

[19] Cf. Chapter "God's Sovereignty and Human Free Will," in this book.

[20] Other examples could be given, such as 1 Samuel 15:11 which John Sanders develops in *The God Who Risks: A Theology of Providence* (Downers Grove: Inter Varsity Press, 1998), but they can be answered in the same method as illustrated in the above examples by appealing to near contextual statements, such as 1 Samuel 15:29.

to the righteous that if there were ten righteous in the city then the whole city would be delivered (Gen. 18:23-32). By going down to Sodom to see if the conditions of Sodom were as bad as the outcry and then he would know shows Abraham and the readers that God is completely righteous so as not to destroy any righteous (Gen. 18: 21, 25; 19:13). God's accommodation of communication of Himself to metaphors of experiential knowledge serve a higher purpose in the passage of emphasizing God's righteousness. God's righteousness is further demonstrated by having not found ten righteous. The few righteous found were still saved while the wicked perished in the judgment God had purposed to bring about in the first place. The previous plan of God was accomplished and God showed Himself to be consistently righteous and compassionate at the same time.

The Biblical presentation of God is greatly analogous both to the philosophical description of the Maximally Great Being and an actually Necessary Being. Biblically and philosophically God is described as a monotheistic sovereign creating and determining Being Who is immutable, omniscient, spiritually omnipresent, omnipotent and incomparable. Apart from the philosophical view of an essential being (e.g. eternal) as compared to the phenomenological view of a Biblical sovereign (e.g. everlasting), the presentations are basically in agreement. There is also broad agreement with the personal attributes of the Maximally Great Being and that of the Biblical presentation of God as interactive, true, affirming, empathetic, compassionate and merciful in practical ways. Furthermore, each model compliments the other by providing a degree of precision that the other model lacks, while being amenable to it. For example, precision is provided by the philosophical model's universal statements as in the discussion of omnipotence above. Additionally, the philosophical analysis provides a tightness of analysis that can provide warrant to alternate worldviews. Likewise, the Biblical text is clearer than the philosophical with regard to issues like the trinity. The narrative and personal lives recounted within the Biblical text as yoked with God makes the presentation often more vivid and personally compelling.

Eternity and Everlasting

"Eternity is the complete possession all at once of illimitable life."
Boethius.[1]

"Lord, Thou hast been our dwelling place in all generations. Before the mountains were born, or Thou didst give birth to the earth and the world, even from everlasting to everlasting, Thou art God." (Ps. 90:1-2).

God (ontologically or in Himself) is eternal (outside of time) and yet once He began to create He is everlasting in time in relationship to this creation. God's eternality is defended philosophically and hinted at Biblically. While the main Biblical pattern develops a God, Who at least in relationship to creation interacts and reacts with this creation in time forever and always will. This is not a contradiction, since eternity describes God ontologically; everlasting in time describes God's relationship to the creation. In this paper I will define time, everlasting, and eternity. Then I will explore how these work out for God ontologically and relationally.

Time is the relationship of sequence for any one thing. Time is not merely an absolute Newtonian framework (in which everything experiences the same sequence simultaneously) or a Kantian phenomenological grid for perception (in which sequence merely becomes a mental category not descriptive of reality) but an Einsteinian metaphysical relationship of anything's experience in relationship to another experience.   As such, time is not merely an experience[2] but a metaphysical reality in relationship.   For example, Einstein's time dilation is relative to the velocity at which any object moves in relationship to another as expressed though the equation: an object's relativistic time equals observed time divided by the square root of [1-(velocity squared divided by speed of light squared)].   This makes time a fourth dimension along with the three spatial dimensions and all four of these are effected by the velocity of the object in relationship to another to which they are referenced, as expressed by the dilation equations.   This theoretical time dilation was experimentally verified by the MIT physicists Frisch and Smith in 1961 who showed that for the mu-mesons (small particles found in both the atmosphere and outer space) that were being stopped at sea level, their time had been slowed down by their longer experience at a velocity near the speed of light as compared to the time of the earth observers or the time of the mu-mesons which were stopped and held relatively stationary in the cloud chamber on the top of Mt. Washington.   The mu-mesons which traveled faster for longer then lived longer verifying the Einsteinian expectation that time is in fact a metaphysical reality for anything in relationship to another.   In this way, time can be thought of as a metaphysical sequence.   Anything that has the experience of sequence is then in its own time.   Likewise, anything that is related to the experience of sequence is then also in its own time as well.   It is in reference to God's creation of the universe and the experience of the sequence of this creation that God is drawn into time as an everlasting being.   For example, one implication of our previous defense of God being everywhere (from the nature of necessity or Psalm 139 chapters)[3] is that God would be everywhen as well.   This means that the fact of creation draws the everywhere and everywhen God into everlasting experience of all things and all times.   God in relation to creation experiences the creation's sequence.   These metaphysical expressions of

---

[1] Boethius, *Consolation of Philosophy* 9-11.
[2] In contrast to Hume's ocassionalism.
[3] Cf. This book pp. 11-39, 113-18.

time continue to unfold in one direction; what is the future of any one thing eventually becomes the present of that thing and then becomes the past of that thing. Or more simply the rock group Seal reminds us in its pop song "Fly Like an Eagle," that "Time keeps on slipping, slipping, slipping into the future."

Everlasting means persistence through time. Everlasting would be any temporal experience that does not end, or a being which is perpetually in relationship to time. For example, *aionion* is used in the Bible in this sense of perpetual temporal experience. An instance of this is the everlasting life that the believer in Christ experiences already in contrast to the judgment that the nonbeliever is already under (Jn. 3:15-16). The fact that everlasting life is already being experienced as a temporal experience shows that everlasting life will always be experienced within time but that this time just does not come to an end.

Eternal would mean atemporality, or outside of time and sequence. This concept of eternity is understood by Boethius as an eternal duration of providentially sourcing life.[4]

> Eternity ... is the complete possession all at once of illimitable life. This becomes clearer by comparison with temporal things. For whatever lives in time proceeds as something present from the past into the future, and there is nothing placed in time that can embrace the whole extent of its life equally. Indeed, on the contrary, it does not yet grasp tomorrow but yesterday it has already lost, and even in the life of today you live no more fully than in a mobile, transitory moment ... [A temporal thing's] life may be infinitely long, but it does not embrace its whole extent simultaneously ... Therefore, whatever includes and possesses the whole fullness of illimitable life at once and is such that nothing future is absent from it and nothing past has flowed away, this is rightly judged to be eternal, and of this it is necessary both that being in full possession of it self it be always present to itself and that it have the infinity of mobile time present to it.[4]

Such a duration view of eternity may be helpful in showing the oddity of eternity but technically such expressions as "present to itself" and "simultaneous" are not appropriate of eternity for there would be no expression of sequence of any kind

---

[4] Boethius, *Consolation of Philosophy*, Book V, ii, 9-18, 22-31.

within an eternal God.   Eleonore Stump and Norman Kretzmann explain this

concept of eternity as follows:

> Because an eternal entity is atemporal, there is no past or future, no
> earlier or later, *within* its life; that is, the events constituting its life
> cannot be ordered sequentially from the standpoint of eternity.
> But, in addition, no temporal entity or event can be earlier or later
> than or past or future with respect to the whole life of an eternal
> entity, because otherwise such an eternal life or entity would itself
> be part of a temporal series.   Here it should be evident that,
> although the stipulation that an eternal entity completely possesses
> its life all at once entails that it is not part of any sequence, it does
> not rule out the attribution of presentness or simultaneity to the life
> and relationships of such an entity, nor should it.   In so far as an
> entity *is,* or *has* life, completely or otherwise, it is appropriate to
> say that it has present existence in some sense of "present;" and
> unless its life consists in only one event or it is impossible to relate
> an event in its life to any temporal entity or event, we need to be
> able to consider an eternal entity or event as one of the *relata* in a
> simultaneity relationship.[5]

Both the ontological argument and the cosmological argument propose

that an actually necessary being exists eternally, which we will call God.   This

necessary being always exists immutably and eternally.   This level of

immutability and eternity means that there is no sequence within God.   There is

no chronological experience in order for God to change from non-being to being

in a certain way.[6]   Augustine develops this ultimate Being's existence as

immutable eternal existence.

> That which is changed does not retain its own being, and that
> which can be changed, even it is not actually changed, is able not

---

[5] Eleonore Stump and Norman Kretzmann, "Eternity" in *Philosophy of Religion: The Big Questions* (ed. Eleonore Stump and Michael Murray, Maiden: Blackwell Publishers, 1999), pp.44-45.

[6] This means that the kenotic view of the divinity of Christ emptying Himself of His divine attributes so that He could become incarnate that Satori proposed in 1831 is excluded as well as the evangelical softened version of a willing non-use of divine attributes which He continued to possess, for both options describe essential change which is impossible for an immutable being. For a further discussion of this see the chapter "A Few Philosophical and Biblical Theology Problems with Statements of the Trinity," in this book.

to be that which it had been. For this reason, only that which not
only is not changed, but also is unable to be changed in any way, is
most truly said to be.[7]

In such a model Aquinas defends that God's eternity is like an event through
which God sees all events as present.

> Were someone to see many travelers along a road successively,
> over a certain period of time, in each part of that time he would see
> some passersby as present, so that over the whole time of his
> vision he would see every traveler as present. He would not see all
> as present at once because the time of his seeing is not all-at-once.
> If his seeing were able to exist all at once, he would see at once all
> as present, although they do not all pass by as present at once.
> Whence because the vision of God's knowledge is measured by
> eternity, which is all at once and yet includes all of time ... God
> sees what happens in time not as future but as present.[8]

While this view has influenced eternity development significantly, it still
maintains analogies of time, such as "all at once," to communicate what is
essentially beyond time and sequence. So as a model, the temporal analogies still
fall short of God's eternal essence.

The classical Christian theologian who most captures the essence of
eternity is Anselm, with his view that eternity is like a super-temporal dimension

> Everything that is in any way bounded by place and time is less
> than that which no law of place or time limits. Since, then, nothing
> is greater than thou, no place or time contains thee; but thou art
> everywhere and always. And since this can be said of thee alone,
> thou alone art uncircumscribed and eternal.[9]

Such a Maximally Great Being would be imminently omnipresent and thus
immaterial or spiritual as well. That is, there could be no sequence or variation
temporally or spatially for this God. Likewise, this God would be available and

---

[7] Augustine, *The Trinity*, Book V, ii, 3.

[8] Aquinas, *Of the Truth*, 2.12.

[9] Anselm, *Proslogium,* chapter 13.

accessible as an imminent omnipresent and everlasting Being under the rubric of a Maximally Great Being. This Maximally Great Being's omnipresence would be necessarily everywhere without variation or sequence. So such omnipresence would have no body (i.e. spiritual) and be immutable (i.e. eternal even though such a being might be glimpsed within creation as everlasting). So the spiritual and eternal omnipresence which the Maximally Great Being would instantiate would be exhibited in a non-spatial and non-temporal manner similar to another dimension beyond space and time. Perhaps Tillich's dimensional model for spirit as an imminent causal ground which creates and sustains the whole of creation serves as a paradigm for making sense of the omnipresence of this eternal spiritual Being. That is, a person would not expect each location of the universe to contain an instance of the fullness of God but that God's fullness is present to each location in a continuous causal manner creating, determining, sustaining, protecting, relating, knowing from that perspective, and recreating the whole of the universe into His kingdom.

Brian Leftow describes the level of absolute immutability that ensues with such an eternal necessary Being as ontologically unreactive.[10]

> A timeless God does not remember, forget, regret, feel relief, or cease to do anything. For a timeless God has no past, and one can remember, forget, etc., only what is past. A timeless God does not wait, anticipate, hope, foreknow, predict, or deliberate. For a timeless God has no future, and one can anticipate, etc., only what is in one's future. A timeless God does not begin to do anything; if one can begin to do only what one then continues to do. If timeless, God does not change: what changes first has, then lacks, some property, and so must exist at least two times. Thus a timeless God never learns or changes His attitudes or plans. All His knowledge and intentions are occurrent, not dispositional. Further, if God is timeless, there is no temporal gap between His forming a plan and executing it, or executing it and seeing all its consequences. If timeless, God's life lasts forever in the sense that at every time, it is true to say that, timelessly, God exists. Yet in

---

[10] This concept can be seen to be essentially the Aristotelian concept of full actualization in God's ontological nature.

> itself, God's life is neither long nor short. We may say that a
> timeless God is forever unchanging. But from His own
> perspective, He knows and does what He does in the flash of a
> single now. A timeless God lives His whole life in a single present
> of unimaginable intensity.[11]

Anselm's solution to this unreactive eternity has God, Who does not exist in time

or place having all things existing in Him.[12]   "This thought is a kind of

expression of the objects created, like the expression which an artisan forms in his

mind for what he intends to make."[13]   Brian Leftlow follows him in this idea.

God's knowledge would then be the storehouse of all actualities of all time.[14]

Furthermore, the knowledge He knows He has always known without variance.

God would know all there is to be known for the whole of time without sequence

and without change. However, this does not cause God to be opposed to the

knowledge of His creation, for He would always know what every feature of the

creation knows from that creature's perspective in space and time while also

knowing simultaneously from His unique vantage point. That is, spatially or

temporally referenced knowledge claims will be referenced from the vantage of a

knower or as an avenue through God's everlasting omnipresence which would

know what would be known from that time and space if any other knower would

have been there. For example, He would eternally know my knowing of the past

and my fears of the future from my vantage point and the perspective of every

created thing in addition to His unique additional perspectives. So that in our

Einsteinian relativistic universe we may have problems defending simultaneity of

---

[11] Brian Leftow, 'Eternity,' in *A Companion to Philosophy of Religion* [ed. Philip Quinn and Charles Taliaferro, (Cambridge: Blackwell Publishers, 1997)], p. 257.

[12] Anselm, *Proslogium* 19, *Monologium* 9-14.

[13] Anselm, *Monologium* 10.

[14] This would be a Grand Mind idealism, which by His commitment to creation perpetually supplies the creation with its reality. We humans will know of this creation through critical realism [Cf. Douglas Kennard, *The Relationship between Epistemology, Hermeneutics, Biblical Theology and Contextualization.* (Lewiston, The Mellon Press, 1999), chapters 2 and 3]. This omniscient Sovereign superintends the actualities of the creation. This would contrast with the process primordial nature of God in that far more than possibilities would reside in God's mind and these thoughts of God would then be determinate for whatever happens. For more on this see the chapter, "God's Sovereignty and Human Free Will," in this book.

events but God would know simultaneity because He is not limited by our finite empirical ways of knowing. However, this does not render eternity to be static, for Boethius defines eternity in a more determining manner as the complete possession all at once of illimitable life.[15] The complete possession is an atemporal sourcing that does not change and is not limited but brings about all that has changed in its expressions of finiteness. This means that eternity is the source for all power and life, as previously described under omnipotence above.[16] So eternity is not primarily to be known for its static comprehensive determining knowledge but for the life revealed to have come from God in His revelational creation. Anything that knows and enlivens others should be thought to be alive. Because God initiates the whole of the creation including all of its details His knowledge is essentially also determining choice. God's choices are eternal and essential to His nature without variance. To have God as an actually necessary being means His sovereign choice is set. This means that the level of necessity for God includes all of God's thoughts and sovereign choices eternally and immutably. This means that God is not open in growing and gaining more knowledge and choosing in response to this knowledge. God's knowledge and choice would in fact be set within God's essential nature as determinative for the existence, essence, and choices the whole of creation makes.[17] With God's knowledge and choice as essential to His nature, then there is no logical order in God either. This means that all the reformation options expressing the order of the decree would in fact be contradictory to God's essential nature. There would not be a logical sequence within God Who simultaneously knows and chooses without sequence (i.e. eternally). This should not surprise us, for there are no Biblical texts that talk about any logical or chronological sequence within God of

---

[15] Boethius, *The Consolation of Philosophy*, Book V, Prose 6; and *De trinitate*, chapter 4 (in E. K. Harvard, 1973).

[16] Cf. pp. 13-14.

[17] For a further discussion of how the determining sovereignty of God and freedom of man fit in a non contradictory manner that consistently reflect the Biblical text see the chapter " God's Sovereignty and Human Free Will," in this book. In that paper a compatiblism of Anselmic/ Thomistic determinism with Edwardsian free will is defended.

an order of salvation either; all these claimed texts at best indicate that when it comes to the application of God's choice out into the chronologically changing creation that such choice has a sequence of application for the recipient. For example, there is a clear logical and chronological sequence in applying the divine election (*ekletois*) as foreknown, preparatively sanctifying the person so that the outcome (*eis*) of this sanctification ushers in obedience and atonement (1 Pet. 1:1-2). At other instances of sequence of the application of salvation there is encouragement for the Christian who has experienced some of the salvation benefits, such as justification, who can be reassured that the other benefits, like glorification, will also be his in time (e.g. Rom. 8:29-30). So the whole post-reformation discussion of the order of the decree and the order of salvation within God was an unfortunate exploration that does not apply to this necessary, immutable, and eternal God. Any linkage of logical order or chronological sequence in such works of God is an expression of application order or revelation purpose. Any attempt to communicate eternal truths into a constantly changing environment like the creation will reflect them in sequential ways partly because of the sequential nature of the environment and partly to accommodate to our human understanding, which is sequential in its learning and contemplation process. For example, the textual sequences above convey that God graciously applies and guarantees the fullness of salvation to each Christian personally, which is a revelation purpose consistent with God's immutable nature. So that any apparent change in God is actually the refraction of a changeless God through the lens of the changing environment for purposes of applying some benefit to the creation, such as salvation or the communication of certain select truths to a certain group in time. The fact that the truths of God are accommodated to the means of communication does not limit the truths of God, but the context indicates the primary hermeneutic purpose and how the descriptions of God are merely supportive of this purpose.

However, these classical presentations of an eternal God still permit many authors to say things of God in relationship to the world which we have seen would be inappropriate of God's eternity ontologically. For example, after Anselm defends the eternity of God he also defends that God creates everything,[18] permeates all and sustains all that exists,[19] and expresses compassion.[20] Since God in relationship to the world is the way God reveals Himself in the Bible, it is also true that we should say these revealed statements of God as well. However, Anselm is not contradicting himself in these claims for he acknowledges and expresses the lack of pathos ontologically within God and the clear compassionate results of the salvation, which God provides for us.[21] God is relationally temporal even though He is ontologically eternal. In fact, since time is the relationship to sequence, the very fact that God is related to the creation as source draws God automatically into relationship to this very sequence of the creation, and thus relationally into time. This temporal relationship is best understood for God as everlasting.

The Biblical authors express that God's life is without beginning and end in ways described as everlasting in time. William Craig suggested that God was eternal until creation in which God became temporal as everlasting.[22] However, God cannot first be timeless and then later be temporal, for then God's timeless phase is earlier than His temporal phase, and whatever is earlier than something else is in time.[23] Additionally, such a change from timeless eternity to temporal everlastingness calls into question whether God was in fact eternal at all for this very language contradicts the level of immutability that an eternal God would be. The solution I propose does not have this problem for God remains timeless in eternity, and with regard to creation, God reveals Himself relationally to be in

---

[18] Anselm, *Proslogium* 5, *Monologium* 8.

[19] Anselm, *Proslogium* 20, *Monologium* 9.

[20] Anselm, *Proslogium* 8.

[21] Anselm, *Proslogium* 8.

[22] William Craig, meeting of the Evangelical Philosophical Society, Nov. 20, 1999.

[23] Brian Leftow, "Eternity," in *A Companion to Philosophy of Religion*, ed. Philip Quinn and Charles Taliaferro (Cambridge: Blackwell, 1997), p.259.

time. Technically God is not in time but any expression of any relationship between an eternal being and the temporal will portray the eternal in temporal ways. This does not make God to be a deceiver for God accurately describes God's relationship to the creation in temporal ways that have a beginning in the creation act. In fact, the alliteration of the BRA sound of the first two words of the Hebrew Bible draw the concept of creation together with the beginning of time; time begins with God's creation (Gen. 1:1). So that God is ontologically eternal as a being but relationally everlasting once creation has occurred, as time begins. The Biblical text emphasizes the relational connection of God to the creation because of course the Bible is not trying to tell us everything about God, instead it focuses on God's relationship with His creation. The main point of the creation stories of Genesis 1-2 is to develop the privileged place humankind has within the creation in relation to God as the image of God, God's son and daughter, blessed and obligated for God's purposes.

Isaiah gives a helpful window into how God relates to time. Men, idols and false gods are in time and bound by it, while Yahweh is far superior, being beyond time and everlasting with time. Yahweh is the First and the Last, before Whom no being was formed and after Whom nothing will exist (Isa. 40:28; 41:4 43:10ff.; 44:6; 48:12). God is here contrasted with history in its totality ("and with the last I am still He").[24] This contrast includes a strong polemic against all other gods who are temporal. These declarations of Yahweh's transcendence over the world and time provided a basis for comfort within Judah's captivity as well as revealing Yahweh to be the God Who extends beyond the bounds of time. Isaiah uses verb tenses, which may even imply that the past, present and future of time is present to Yahweh. Christopher North explores this concept with passages such as Isaiah 48:4-5, which say, "I *knew* how stubborn you *are*" and "therefore I told you long ago," before the nation existed.[25] In these texts there is no clear development of God's eternality but Yahweh may be hinted at as being

---

[24] Westermann, *Isaiah 40-66,* p. 65.

contemporary with all history. "Ever since anything came to pass, there am I"
(Isa. 41:4; 48:16).

The Biblical case from word studies defends God in His relationship to
creation as everlasting in time. There are no Biblical texts that clearly develop
God's eternity beyond time. The primary word in the O.T. is *olam*, which means
everlasting in time. It can mean everlasting in the past or ancient (e.g. Gen. 6:4;
Dtr. 32:7; Pr. 22:28; Isa. 44:7). *ʿŌlām* can mean continuing as in a continuing
covenant relationship between God and creation through time (e.g. Gen. 9:12, 16;
13:15; 17:7-19; 2 Sam. 7:13-29; 1 Chr. 16:17-41; Ps. 105:10; Isa. 61:8). From
this temporal continuing everlastingness, God is said to be everlasting (Gen.
21:33; Pss. 41:13; 90:2; 93:2; 103:17; Isa. 40:28). God's reign is forever in time
(Ex. 15:18; Pss. 10:16; 29:10; 45:6). God's mercy endures forever for those who
are His (1 Chr. 16:34, 41; 2 Chr. 5:13; 7:3-6; Ezra 3:11; Ps. 100:5; 106:1 107:1;
118:1-29; 136:1-26). Likewise, God's righteousness is everlasting (Ps. 119:142-
160; Pr. 10:25; Isa. 51:8). God's commitment to those who are His will be
benefited from a salvation that lasts forever as well (Isa. 45:17; 51:6). A few
instances of *qedem* also indicate that the mountains, the people of Israel and God
as King are all ancient, from of old (Dtr. 33:15, 27; Ps. 74:2, 12). The N.T. words
(*aiōn* and *aiōnios*) continue the everlasting in time meaning. They both stand for
ancient as with or before the beginning of creation (Lk. 1:70; Jn. 9:32; Acts 3:21;
15:18; 2 Tim. 1:9). In this sense sometimes *aion* even stands for the world as the
continuing creation (Mt. 13:22-49; 1 Tim. 6:17). Our God is blessed forever (Rm.
1:25; 9:5; 11:36; 1 Tim. 1:17). May God's glory and dominion be forever (1 Tim.
1:17; 2 Tim. 2:10; 4:18; Heb. 1:8, 13, 21; 1 Pet. 5:11; 2 Pet. 1:11; 3:18; Rev. 1:6).
Additionally, *aiōn* conveys that God is alive forever (Rev. 1:18; 4:9-10; 5:14;
15:7). There are also two instances in which *aidios* develops everlasting chains of
judged angels and God's everlasting power (Rom. 1:20; Jude 6). This is the
Biblical evidence that portrays that God is an everlasting God.

---

[25] Christopher North, *The Second Isaiah* (Oxford: Clarendon Press, 1964), pp. 180-81.

Some will raise the problem that an eternal God cannot be alive because all the concepts of life with which we are familiar have change and thus sequence. This assumption ignores that as eternal, God is the everlasting source of all life, and it is also our experience that only the living give life. However the Biblical text develops that God is the living God more in the sense of interacting with the creation in time. That is "God is alive"[26] (*hāyâ*, zao) means that He interacts with the creation sequence in time unlike lifeless idols, which do not. The statement that God is alive (*hāyâ*) is synonymous with saying that God is soul (*nephesh*).[27] He is vibrant, active and acts in the midst of human situations. Special emphasis on the living (*hāyâ*) quality of God is developed within the former prophets of Samuel and Kings, and the latter prophets of Jeremiah and Ezekiel. *Nephesh* has a special emphasis in Jeremiah as referring to God. *Zao* has special emphasis in Hebrews warnings and hope. Perhaps the precarious situations and the obvious need to trust God highlights God as alive to meet the need. However, God is developed as alive from nineteen O.T. books and eight N.T. books. That God lives forever is developed as a contextual model to inform the believer that they will live forever with Him (Dan. 12:2, 7 and John 6:51-59).

So the Biblical presentation of God is that He is everlasting. There is no problem with such an everlasting God entering time to create, incarnate, present Himself as theophany, to interact with creatures in time, and to respond to what the creatures are doing as well. This is all part of God's everlasting relationship with creation, which in no way violates or alters His eternality. When issues of tense are raised (like Can God know now, or Did God do something, or Will He

---

[26] Num. 14:21, 28; Dtr. 5:26; 32:40; Josh. 3:10; Judg. 8:19; Ruth 3:13; 1 Sam. 14:39, 45; 17:26, 36; 19:6; 20:3, 21; 25:26, 34; 26:10, 16; 28:10; 29:6; 2 Sam. 2:27; 4:9; 12 5; 14:11; 15:21; 22:47; 1 Ki. 1:29; 2:24; 17:1, 12; 18:10, 15; 22:14; 2 Ki. 3:14; 4:30; 5:16, 20; 19:4, 16; 2 Chr. 18:13; Job 19:25; 27:2; Pss. 18:41; 42:2; 84:2; Isa. 37:4, 17; 49:18; Jer. 4:2; 5:2; 10:10; 12:16; 16:14-15; 22:24; 23:7-8, 36; 38:16; 44:26; 46:18; Ezek. 5:11; 14:16, 18, 20; 16:48; 17:16, 19; 18:3; 20:3, 31,33; 33:11, 27; 34:8; 35:6, 11; Dan. 6:20, 26; 12:7; Hos. 1:10; 4:15; Zeph. 2:9; Mt. 16:16; 26:63; Jn. 6:57, 69; Rm. 9:26; 2 Cor. 3:3; 6:16; 1 Thes. 1:9; 1 Tim. 3:15; 4:14; Heb. 3:12; 9:14; 10:31; 12:22; Rev. 7:2; 15:7.

[27] Lev. 26:11, 30; 1 Sam 21:35; Ps. 11:5; Pr. 6:16; Isa. 1:14; 42:1; Jer. 5:9, 29: 6:8; 9:9; 12:7; 13:17; 51:14; Ezek. 25:18; Amos 6:8.

accomplish what He promised, or God is compassionate in responding to our responses), one is no longer talking about the eternality of God but about the everlasting relationship which God has with the creation. Such discussions meaningfully describe the everlasting relationship, which God has with creation; such concepts would not be meaningful with regard to eternity since no temporal sequence and tense exists in eternity. The omniscience of God as it relates through God's everlastingness means that sequence would be known in God's relationship with creation and in that relationship tensed statements become meaningful for God. An example of this has to do with the Biblical statement of foreknowledge. That is, foreknowledge is an intimate knowledge which God has in His everlasting relationship with creation which because He knows it, actually determines what will happen long before we humans choose for it to occur (Acts 2:23; 1 Pet. 1:2, 20). Because of this, the concept of foreknowledge actually raises more complex concerns for the relationship of determinism and free-will, so I will handle it in the chapter, "God's Sovereignty and Human Free Will."[28]

The Bible (which is primarily develops the everlasting relationship of God to the creation) presents God as a Being interacting in time in tensed ways. Tensed statements would be inappropriate of eternity but are quite appropriate of everlastingness. The primary passage that the openness of God calls us to examine concerning this tensed language is Genesis 18. Proponents of openness would like to call our attention to statements like:

> The outcry of Sodom and Gomorrah is indeed great, and their sin is exceedingly grave. I will go down now, and see if they have done entirely according to its outcry, which has come to Me; and if not, I will know. (Gen. 18:20-21)

It looks like God will in the future of this statement obtain firsthand experiential knowledge that He does not in fact know yet, therefore the future is seen by them as open as to whether a requisite number will be righteous to save Sodom and

---

[28] Cf. Chapter, "God's Sovereignty and Human Free Will" in this book.

Gomorrah. At this point, the traditional sovereign view of God responds that this statement must be understood within the context of God already declaring that His purpose is to do something which Abraham understands to be judgment based on his response and not just the openness point that God progressively comes to know the evidence (Gen. 18:17, 20, 23). The traditional sovereign view will also respond that if God is as the openness view claims, then God does not know some present and past knowledge about the conditions of Sodom and Gomorrah. This point catches the openness view in an inconsistency, since openness proponents claim that God is omniscient about the past and present. At this point, we need to break in and point out that both traditions are using the text for their own purposes and ignoring the feature that Moses as the human author is emphasizing in this text. Texts are to be understood with their authorial contextual emphases and not by our biases of models to make sense of God or our existential context.[29] Moses (as author) has just underscored that nothing is too difficult for God, so impregnating Abraham's Sarah is no problem for God. Now with the possibility of the judgment of Sodom and Gomorrah looming large, the issue of this passage becomes *righteousness*. It is a subject that God raises by describing Abraham as being chosen to "keep the way of the Lord by doing righteousness and justice" (Gen. 18:19). Abraham, the would-be righteous one, then responds with a reply which focuses on the righteousness of God: "Wilt Thou indeed sweep away the righteous with the wicked?" The textual issue is then that the righteous God shows Himself to be righteous in a satisfying way for His righteous servant Abraham and Moses' readers who have the text, which selectively crops the account of the event to emphasize this righteous theme; "Far be it from Thee to slay the righteous with the wicked, so that the righteous and the wicked are treated alike. Far be it from Thee! Shall not the Judge of all the earth deal

---

[29] This hermeneutical method and the orientation to the authorial context to inform Biblical theology rather than the tradition of a theological hermeneutic is explained in Douglas Kennard, *The Relationship Between Epistemology, Hermeneutics, Biblical Theology and Contextualization*, pp. 124-48; 181-85.

justly?" So the interaction of Abraham focuses the issue on God's righteousness. God responds righteously, reassuring the righteous "If I find in Sodom fifty righteous within the city, then I will spare the whole place on their account." Abraham responds back whether God would save the city if the fifty righteous would lack five. The response goes back and forth between God and Abraham until God affirms that Sodom would be preserved if ten righteous would be found in her.   Chapter nineteen continues the account showing that at best three righteous could be found in that Lot and his two daughters are delivered Gen. 19:15-29; 2 Peter 2:7-9).   Even these three fall short of Abraham's pattern of righteousness as chapter eighteen and nineteen are compared for hospitality, obedience, and a focus on the preservation of self or others. Above all God shows Himself to be the righteous One Who preserves the righteous, while destroying the wicked. If we use this text for other than this textual emphasis we show that we are using it for our biases. This means that if we wish to get to know the everlasting God's involvement with the creation then we need to consider texts that develop this theme such as Psalm 139 or Isaiah 40-48. These passages will be developed in other chapters, herein.

God's relationship with the creation is shown by occasional comments in which He responds and interacts with events of the creation. For example, in Genesis 22 Abraham is tested by God to experientially verify whether God or the promise of God takes precedence in Abraham's life. When Abraham showed his obedience in attempting to offer Isaac, God responded, "Now I know that you fear God" (Gen. 22:12). It is an appropriate comment in responding to the situation but the fact of Abraham's obedience had been apparent for years. Additionally, there is a standard response in which God reacts to the situation of rampant idolatry as in Jeremiah 7:31; 19:5 and 32:35. After pointing out Israel's sin God identifies that such idolatry was not what He had commanded, and because these instances of idolatry and child sacrifice were so horrendous, God admits that these practices had not entered His mind. These comments should not be read as a lack of future knowledge on God's part. These "this had not entered My mind" comments come immediately following and parallel to the preceding comment that "this is not what I commanded," it should be read as a figure of speech emphasizing that the disobedience of Israel was way beyond the command of God. Likewise, some comments of God include "perhaps" as an indication that some Jews might get the prophetic point of their rebellion and repent as a remnant while Israel as a whole is heading for captivity in their rebellion (Jer. 26:3; Ezek. 12:3). The contexts around these "perhaps" comments include God's certain declaration that the captivity is coming quickly and that it would last seventy years (Jer. 25-26; Ezek.12). So God knows the future and interacts with the present in a way that shows that He is relationally committed to His creation.

God's relationship to creation as everlasting permits God to express change with respect to the changing creation and remain immutable with regard to His righteous character. God is the good and righteous source of all good, with no variation or shifting shadow in His character (James 1:17). We can count on God's consistent goodness so that we should not blame Him for temptations or sins in which we entangle ourselves. Because He has established creation this way means that our sin results in judgment (James 1:13-16). John Sanders challenges the claim that God knows the future with consistent purposes by his appeal to 1 Samuel 15:11.[30] In this verse God relates to Samuel that He regrets that He made Saul king for he has rebelled and been disobedient. This verse sets up the context in which Samuel must tell Saul of His rejection as king. This scene ends with Saul seizing Samuel's robe and tearing it, which Samuel turns into a metaphor for the situation: "The Lord has torn the kingdom of Israel from you today, and has given it to your neighbor who is better than you, and also the Glory of Israel will not lie or change His mind; for He is not a man that He should

---

[30] This challenge and others like it are developed at some length in John Sanders, *The God Who Risks: A Theology of Providence* (Downers Grove: Inter Varsity Press, 1998).

change His mind."(1 Sam. 15:28-29).[31]   The author's purposes of this selective
account of Samuel include showing the legitimacy of the Davidic Kingship.
Both these texts support this major theme. The Saul kingship sets up the practice
of a king in Israel, but God's grief as a response from the everlasting and
immutable character of God shows that God does emotionally respond to sin and
His divine consistent response is to reject the rebel in his unrepentant sinning
condition, and send him away in judgment. God in His everlasting relationship
with creation responds to the creation with emotion and consistent character and
purpose. However in the narrative this looks like divine blessing upon Saul while
he is faithful and divine curse in Saul's rebellion. It is to texts such as this that
openness points, which include statements of God's repenting. For example,
Genesis 6:5-7 presents an evaluation of humans prior to the Noahic flood that
recounts Yahweh seeing man's wickedness to such an extent that He is grieved in
heart and repents from His blessing to now destroy the world in judgment.
Certainly, Yahweh is consistent with His nature for blessing His creation until in
their disobedience they transgressed His standard (e.g. Gen. 2:17; 3:14-20; 4:7-
12). The text does not comment on this being a plan of Yahweh for it leaves it as
a description from the viewpoint of the changing historical narrative and such
phenomenological language is to be expected in a narrative account. Now that
man's thoughts were only evil continually, God's destroying judgment is to be
expected, and judgment comes with God's consistency in the flood.

     Our God is ontologically eternal and immutable as a Necessary Being,
while this same God relates to the creation once it begins in time with everlasting

---

[31] Other texts also show the consistency of God in carrying out His purposes whether
they be blessing grounded in His choice or a consistent response of rejecting into judgment. E.g.
Num. 23:19; Ezek. 24:14.

immutable character.[32] While the description of the eternality of God is atemporal as a dimension that providentially continues to supply life to our own creation, it is within God's everlasting relationship with the creation that God responds to us with blessing or curse, and mercy or wrath. When God enters time such as in creation, theophany, or incarnation, it is through God's everlasting relationship with creation, all the while remaining fully eternal within Himself.

---

[32] As stated earlier, it is in respect to Jesus Christ's everlasting immutable character that Hebrews 13:8 declares that "Jesus Christ is the same yesterday, today and forever." This helps us to see that there is real reassurance in the consistent character of Christ. This means that the kenotic view of the divinity of Christ emptying Himself of His divine attributes so that He could become incarnate that Satori proposed in 1831 is excluded as well as the evangelical softened version of a willing non-use of divine attributes which He continued to possess, for both options describe essential change which is impossible for an immutable being. For a further discussion of this see the chapter "A Few Philosophical and Biblical Theology Problems with Statements of the Trinity," in this book.

A Few Philosophical and Biblical Theology Problems
With Statements of the Trinity

A few years ago I was in Jerusalem's Old City visiting bookstores and seeing the sights when a book in a window caught my eye. The title was *You Can Take Jesus, I'll Take God.* It was a radical Jewish apologetic for orthodox Judaism against Christianity. As I read the book and other apologetic works by Jews and Muslims, one of the most emphasized areas they hammer Christianity on is in the coherence of the doctrine of the trinity. Most of their critique is accurate; Christians do not often describe the Trinity very well. In fact, I have heard statements trained professionals make that often have contradictions and incoherences within them. If a statement of the trinity is contradictory it is not worthy to be believed. We should make sure we understand and worship a God, whose concept is free of contradictions, for God is certainly not contradictory.

Trinity Defined

The traditional orthodox trinitarianism of the Christian church from earliest Fathers, medieval theologians, reformers and evangelicals maintains that God is one essence consisting of three coequal persons (Father, Son and Holy Spirit). The one divine essence or being or nature or substance is defined by the whole set of essential properties or attributes. Aquinas underscored that such essence has to do with What God is. Each persons is a distinct subsistence or (following Athanasius) a distinct hypostasis. Charles Hodge defines person as an

I

intelligent subject who can say "I" about itself and "Thou" to the other members of the trinity. Aquinas emphasizes "person" has to do with Who God is in relationship to the divine essence. I define "person" as *an instantiation of a spiritual nature as a moral end in itself in relationship to others*. This definition captures that the person (who) is identified with the divine nature (what) but does not exhaust the divine nature (there are other divine persons). This definition also recognizes that each person (who) of God is to be appropriately worshipped, glorified and served as God. Furthermore, this definition recognizes that each divine person is in an eternal equal relationship with each of the other divine persons even if those relationships economically (ministries of the Godhead) are reflected in ways that show economic subordination (modes of operation) while maintaining ontological (the being of the Godhead itself as it is) equality. The trinity thus has three persons (who's) in the one divine nature (what).

Early in the second century the *Letter of Barnabas* (2:9; 5:5; 6:14; 7:2; 12:2, 8; 19:7) affirms God is composed of Father, Christ the preexistent Lord and Judge, and the Holy Spirit. *Didache* 7:1 indicates this idea of trinitarian nature was the Christian norm. Theophilus (*To Antolychus* 2:15) coins the term *trias* to connote Father, Logos, and wisdom. Against the Gnostics, Irenaeus argues that one Creator and Redeemer God subsists as Father, Son and Spirit. The Ebionite (or contemporary Unitarian) concern was to preserve the one nature of God as king so the Logos is diminished to exist in God the Father as human reason exists in man. This Logos operative in the man Jesus adopted and deified Christ at his baptism. Such dynamic monarchianism derives the persons and the equality of the persons for the Holy Spirit is merely an impersonal attribute of the Godhead. Arius (or Socinians or English deists and contemporary Jehovah's Witnesses) move the adoption of the Son to a creation of the Son as a created god, the greatest of all creation. In a related view, Harnack identified Sabellious' attempt to preserve the one divine nature as modalistic monarchianism: one divine person acting out three subsequent roles, implying that the Father suffers the passion as he acts out the role of the Son. Tertullian coins the term *trinitas* to describe the one God (Father) unified in essence or substance (*substantia*) and with three distinct divine persons (*personae*)[1] stoically proceeding (*essential extentia*) from the Father as Son and Spirit. Tertullian saw Christ, however, subordinated as impersonal reason becoming a person at creation and the Spirit was seen as stoic ethereal matter grounding the whole creation. Origen maintained a trinity with one God who is primarily the Father revealing Himself through the stoic Logos concept God's Image. The platonically eternally begotten Logos, who is personal and co-eternal with the Father forms a unity with Jesus' humanity by overwhelming Jesus' neoplatonic human spirit and soul. Origen sometimes calls the Son second God, but together the Father and the Son eternally create the Holy Spirit to work among believers. The Son and Spirit are in degrees divine, possessing in a derived way all the characteristics of deity, and cooperate with the Father to mediate the divine life flowing from Him. Eusebius of Caesarea clarifies that both the first God and the second God (Logos) maintain the same substance (hypostasis), like a fountain bubbles over with its nature, leaving Jesus' flesh passive.

Athanasias is the first to clearly defend the eternal equality of the three persons in the one divine nature. The Councils of Nicea (325 AD), Rome (341 AD), Sardia (343 AD) and Nicene Creed (381 AD) reflect this understanding.

> We believe in one God, the Father Almighty . . . and in one Lord Jesus Christ, the only begotten Son of God, begotten from the Father before all ages, light from light, true God from true God, begotten not made, of one substance (*homoousios*) with the Father. . . . And in the Holy Spirit, the Lord and life-giver, who proceeds from the Father. Together with the Father and the Son he is worshipped and glorified (Nicene Creed).

At Nicaea *hypostasis* "entity" and *oysia* "existent" were identical while the Latin fathers see *substantia* and *oysia* as equivalent attributal descriptions of God.

---

[1] *Against Praceus*, 2, 5-7, 8 *Apology* 21.

Athanasius held that the Son was begotten by internal necessary, eternal generation not as an act of the Sovereign will; thus the Son was co-eternal with the Father. Before Athanasius and the Nicene Creed won the day, a number of councils considered expressions of similar substance (*homoioysios*) and a generation of the Son as by an act of the Father's will (Antioch 341 AD., 344 AD, Philopoplis 342 AD, Synods of Arles and Milan 355 AD). Patristic scholar Christopher Stead in *Divine Substance* (1977) defends that many viewed *homooysios* as the same kind of thing (Aristotelian second substance -- a genus like animal, not a particular like this horse). Others point out *homooysios* as embraced instead of *homoioysios* (which is better understood in this second substance view) argues that *homooysios* has the particular divine nature in view. By the Fourth Lateran Council (1215) *homooysios* is clarified to be a numerical identity as a refutation of Joachim of Fiore's view of its being a collective unity. In addition, Logos Christology as advocated by Athanasius, maintains a unified deity and a unified person of Jesus Christ who expresses solidarity with humanity by overcoming death for all identified with the new man Jesus in His resurrection. This view continued in Monothelitism (the view that Christ only has one will) under the influence of the Aeopagite but lost power when monothelitism was condemned at Constantinople in 681, and then Islam conquered this region. Lombard and Abelard continued to advocate this Logos Christology.

In Nestorian Christology each nature (divine and human) has its appearance (*porsōpan*) so that Jesus Christ is divided into appearances of humanity and divinity forming a conjunction rather than a unified person.

The Cappadocian Theologians (Basil the Great, Gregory of Nazianzus and Gregory of Nyssa were concerned that the three *hypostases* might dissolve into a platonically defined *oysia*, so they emphasized their Trinitarian formula as "one divine *oysia* in three distinct *hypostase*." By *oysia* they meant one invisible, divine nature in a simple God and by *hypostasis* they meant mode of being or personal center in social relation to others and unique characteristics. They distinguished three persons by mutual relations (Father is unbegotten, Son begotten, and Spirit spirited) and by activities (Father as source, Son as agent, and Spirit as consummation of all things). Against accusations that this was tritheism they defended that the persons never operate independently of each other since the same identical energy passes through all three. With regard to the incarnation, the divine nature and human nature interdepend fusing into a third entity. Luther embraced this fused unity of Christ's deity and humanity, providing a foundation for consubstantiation in the sacraments.

Augustine, in his essay *The Trinity* (399 AD and 419 AD), informed by platonism, maintains that each of the three persons (*personae*) possesses the entire essence (*essentia*) and is in so far identical with the essence and with each of the other persons in mutual dependence, interpenetration and indwelling. Thus, the distinction between persons is not substantial but only relational; the whole divine essence belongs to each of them through relational categories generating, generated and proceeding from both Father and Son. *Personae* for Augustine is relational rather than the later view of Descartes (1640) which sees person as the center of conscious self-reflection and self-determination. For Augustine, oneness of essence implies equality of perfections, unity of shared will, and oneness of operations. The three persons "are infinite in themselves. And so each is in each, all are in each, each is in all, all are in all, and all are one."[2] The Son is eternally begotten from the substance of the Father, where the Spirit proceeds eternally from the Father and the Son (*filioque*).[3] This *filioque* (from the Son) clause was expressly affirmed by Hilary, Augustine, Synod of Toledo (589 AD) and the Athanasian Creed and it became a major factor in the eleventh-century schism between East and West. The Spirit's procession differs from the Son's begetting in that the Spirit "came forth, not as one born but as one given."[4] This

---

[2] *The Trinity*, 6.12.12; 5.8.9; 15.5.8; also *Enchidion*, 38; *On Christian Doctrine* 1.5.

[3] *The Trinity*, 15.20.38; 15.17.29; 15.26.47.

[4] *The Trinity*, 5.14.15.

procession becomes understood less in a stoic way and more as a relationship. Furthermore, Augustine and Anselm are rare theologians who claim that the trinity is philosophically necessary within the divine eternal relationship to make sense of the attribute of love; three persons are eternally needed for God to realize the fullness of love: one to love, another to be loved and a third to be the bond of love. This argument continues to be championed by Richard of St. Victor (1173) and Swinburne (1988 and 1994). Anselm in *Why the God-Man* defends that the Son must have been incarnated and only the Son could have become incarnated. That is only one could be generated or else there would be grandsons. The only Son generated took up essential human essence alongside His essential deity.

Within an Augustinian orthodox understanding of trinity, Melito of Sardis first proposed, and the church accepted the proposal at the Chalcedon Council (451 AD) that Jesus Christ possesses both fully divine and fully human natures, within a unified person. Christ's two natures are without mixture, without change, without division and without separation. Aquinas continues this view emphasizing substance (nature defined by whatness) and person (as who) so that this hypostatic union of Christ entails one unified (who) and two natures (whats); deity and humanity. Calvin continues this view with Christ as a unified mediator.

The Protestant confessions articulate a consensus of the church concerning orthodox trinitarianism and Chalcedon Christology. For example, there is broad agreement between Lutheran *Augsburg Confession* (1530) at. I, *The Formula of Concord* (1577) art 12, The Anglican *Thirty-Nine Articles* (1563) art I, The Reformed *Second Helvetic Confession* (1566) art. 3, and the *Westminster Confession* (1646) ch. 2. The core of the latter statement reads:

> In the unity of the Godhead there are three persons, of one substance, power, and eternity: God the Father, God the Son, and God the Holy Ghost. The Father is of none, neither begotten nor proceeding; the Son is eternally begotten of the Father; the Holy Ghost eternally proceeding from the Father and the Son.

Evangelical theologians have regularly followed this view including: Turretin, Hodge, Shedd, Chafer, Berkhof, Thiessen, Erickson, and many others.

Some significant deviations from this orthodox position will be examined now. Schleiermacher approaches Christology from a phenomenological perspective whereby the noble humanity of Jesus adds divinity by pure expression of dependence upon the god in whom he trusted. To make sense of Philippians 2, kenotic Christology was first proposed by Sartori in 1831, that Christ self-limited His divinity to become unified with His humanity in the incarnation. Hegel proposed that the Trinity represented the dialectical process where Father is Universality (eternal being-in and of itself), the Son is particularization (Being-for another) and the Holy Spirit is individuality (a return from appearance into Self). Hegel also proposed a philosophical argument for the trinity because it is only possible to come to self-consciousness through projection of oneself onto something other than oneself; it was necessary of the Father to have the Son as other than Himself before coming to full self-consciousness to occur in the life of the Holy Spirit. Jürgen Moltmann and Eberhard Jüngel follow Hegel in this argument. Process theology identifies all of God with Father and the primordial nature as either the Son or the Father, the creative thrust with the Son, and the consequent nature as the Spirit. Many liberals and O.T. Biblical theologians identified the Spirit as a mere force extension of the Godhead. For example, Geoffrey Lampe and Maurice Wiles continue to define Spirit in that way. Many conservative evangelicals wishing to identify the Spirit as a legitimate person redefine the concept of person using composite psychology (prominent early in the 20th century) so that a "person" refers to an individual with intellect, emotion and will. Neo-Orthodox theology of Barth and Brunner so emphasize the economic trinity (the ministries of the Godhead) that the ontological trinity is neglected. In the wake of neo-orthodoxy, individuals such as Moltmann have championed social trinitarianism, a view that has entered into evangelicalism as claiming a continuation of the Cappadocian trinity.[5]   In social trinitarianism, "person" is defined in a post-enlightenment way as a self-aware individual. "Nature" is defined in one of two ways.   Nature is either 1) the shared set of properties corporately held by the group (no person needs all the attributes as long as they are exhibited in the group) or 2) the shareable set of properties individually necessary and jointly sufficient for membership in a class of beings. Either way, kenotic Christology is embraced and the divine nature for the incarnate Christ excludes the following traits: necessity, immutability, sovereignty, omniscience, omnipresence, omnipotence;   these traits may be merely excess traits nice for God to have.   Colin Gunton has split the difference between the traditional orthodox and the social trinity in framing God talk as of a post-Kantian phenomenological, economic, incomprehensible being in relationship with the concept of person as subsistence in relationship.[6]   He modifies his concept of person from the spatial relational one that he used for humans to a person model that would permit the mutual interpenetrating of *perichoisis* as illustrated by the relationship of electricity and magnetism in Faraday's equations.   All illustrations break down for trinity and Faraday's equations are no exception. With increased distance from the electrical source the magnetic effect diminishes, such that as a trinity illustration it would call into question the immutable omnipresence of God and divine persons.

Orthodox Trinity Restated

      The trinity entails: 1) one God (e.g. Dtr. 6:4; James 2:19) as indicated by one divine nature (What God is identified by, namely divine attributes). This means that while God is greater than our descriptions, our descriptions of God still do describe God as He is.   2) Three coequal persons (Who God is). Precisely

---

[5] For a helpful discussion of social and orthodox trinity compared see Ronald Feenstra and Cornelius Plantinga, *Trinity, Incarnation, and Atonement*, (University of Notre Dame Press, 1989).

[6] Colin Gunton, *The Promise of Trinitarian Theology*, (Edinburg: T&T Clark, 1997).

put "person" means *an instantiation of a spiritual nature as a moral end in itself, in relationship to others* (e.g. 1 Pet. 1:2-12; Matt. 28:19). The next three points identify that each of these persons is in fact the essential God.   3) The Father is one of those persons of God (e.g. John 6:27; Eph. 4:6). 4) The Son is one of those persons of God (e.g. John 1:1; Heb. 1:8). 5) The Spirit is one of those persons of God (e.g. Acts 5:3-4). This view of trinity is coherent because it is three of one thing (who's) and one of a different thing (what).

This orthodox trinitarianism has implications for the incarnation so that the incarnate Jesus Christ is a unified person who has two complete natures (whats): divine and human.   Following Chalcedon these natures are neither mixed, changed, without division nor without separation. Prior to the incarnation, where Christ adds humanity, the Son was only divine. Since the incarnation, both of the Son's natures must be included in any discussion. So that a question such as, "Could the Son sin?" is not fully answered without the following: as God the Son could not sin, as man the Son could have sinned, thus permitting authentic temptation, but as a unified person the Son did not sin. With regard to location: as God the Son is omnipresent, as man the Son is locally present and embodied, and as a unified person, so the Son may then answer from either omnipresence or His local presence with the sense that he is the same "I". With regard to knowledge: as God the Son is omniscient, as man the Son is finite and growing in knowledge to the extent that the Father permits, so as a unified person he may answer from either mind with the same personal referent "I". As such, most of the N.T. discussion of Jesus Christ strongly evidences His humanity (especially in the synoptics) and his unified person, with occasional glimpses of His deity (as He stills a storm or as the writer of Hebrews defends Him as superior to the angels).

This Trinitarian divine essence in relationship is illustrated in Jesus' prayer in John 17. Jesus prays to the Father to glorify the Son, something which would only really be appropriate for God. This glorification in John is identified at Jesus death-ascension event. It opens up the opportunity for Jesus to return glory to the Father as He has on earth already by completing the task of revealing the Father and providing everlasting life, in which Christ is the object of faith. Neither Father nor Son is kept essentially hidden for Jesus reveals divinity of the Father and Himself in what He says and does. Jesus has maintained a mutually giving relationship with the Father and has included the disciples as beneficiaries of revelation from the Father and Son such that the disciples realized that Jesus was sent from the Father with divine authority so that these disciples became obedient to Them, which further glorifies the Father as well. All the Father has, such as these disciples, are Christ's and all that Christ has is also the Father's. The context in which this prayer is expressed finds Jesus about to leave from being visibly present among the disciples, so He prays that the Father would carry on protecting the disciples in His visible absence of His humanity among them when He visibly leaves. Jesus prays for His disciples throughout every generation so that we would be protected by the Father, set apart by the Father's word, and that our love would emulate that of the Father and the Son for each other. The unity of the love relationship of the Father for the Son and the Son for the Father includes an intimacy of knowledge of each for the other and a mutual interpenetrating of each omnipresently throughout the other, which funds the oneness of purpose to love the other immutably from before the creation to beyond glory. This Trinitarian intimate *perichoisis* extends to us as we the disciples are indwelt by all the persons of the Godhead so that we too would intimately know God through His Word and be drawn into an intimate unity of purpose in loving others. This love relationship begins with loving the persons of God Who penetrate us and then extends to loving fellow humans as evidence of the divine love in us, so that they will know that we are Christians by our love.

A Few Problems

From this foundation I would like to examine a few philosophical problems in some Trinitarian models. These entail the following issues: 1) Contradiction fostered by a composite definition of nature and the attribute of simplicity; 2) contradictory definitions of nature and person; 3) contradiction fostered by mutable immutability; and 4) contradiction fostered by eternalizing of temporal processes.

Composite Nature and Simplicity

Many of the models define the nature of God by divine attributes and add the platonized attribute that God is simple. The definition of the nature of God as "divine attributes" identifies that each distinct attribute meaningfully refers to God as He is ontologically. For example, God is divisibly described by a complex of attributes such that He is: immutable, holy, righteous, omnipresent, omniscient, jealous and loving. These diverse attributes and others meaningfully describe God as each of the three persons. Often, appeals to Biblical texts defend that God is accurately described by this diverse list of attributes.[7] At times philosophical arguments are also embraced for God existing as a Maximally Great Being or powerful creator, with a complex of attributes that these concepts entail. Within a context such as this, at times the attribute of simplicity is also embraced of God.[8] Stump[9] defines simplicity as comprising four claims:

1. God cannot have any spatial or temporal parts.

2. God cannot have any intrinsic accidental properties.

---

[7] For example, Biblical texts marshaled to defend these attributes include immutable (Jas. 1:17), holy (Isa. 6:3), righteous (Gen. 18:25), omnipresence (Ps. 139:7-12), omniscience (Ps. 139:1-18), jealous (Dtr. 5:9) and love (1 John 4:8).

[8] E.g. Aquinas, *Summa Theologica*, vol. I, Pt. 1, Q3, A7.

[9] Eleonore Stump "Simplicity" in Quinn and Taliaferro *A Companion to Philosophy of Religion*, p. 250 and Stump and Kretzmann "Absolute Simplicity," *Faith and Philosophy* 2(1985), pp. 353-81.

3. There cannot be any real distinction between one essential property and another in God's nature.

4. There cannot be a real distinction between essence and existence in God.

Claim 1 is a normal conclusion based on the attributes of omnipresence and eternality, such that God is not spread out over space or time. Such a God could interact with every place and time because they are present to God.

Claim 2 presupposes the difference between intrinsic and extrinsic properties, and concludes that the ontological nature of God is immutable. That is, while God may be relationally presented as responding to His creation, God's ontological nature is made up of necessary intrinsic attributes. So God in and of Himself has no changing attributes, even though He relates to the creation in ways of blessing and curse that may appear to be different from our view-point.

Claim 3 identifies that God ontologically and mystically transcends language and description of His attributes, such that these attributes do not have any univocally distinct meaning from each other. Claim 4 is a special instance of this in that essence and existence are not univocally distinguishable either. It is at this level in claims 3 and 4 that a contradiction occurs for any who also claim that God has meaningfully distinct attributes (such as God's goodness and wrath, or God's transcendent holiness and imminence). Such a view of simplicity implies that God's nature is uncompounded, incomplex and indivisible. Ultimately the very affirmation of simplicity denies the complex attributal nature of God, so that there is a real contradiction.[10] God is either described by these attributes or He is not described by these attributes; a theologian gets into real contradiction when he says both. The Bible and philosophical arguments present God as having a nature accurately described by a complex of distinguishable attributes. One has little but

---

[10]For a longer defense that this is in fact a contradiction, cf. Alvin Plantinga, *Does God Have a Nature? (Milwaukee:* Marquette University Press, 1980).

a contradictory tradition following platonic philosophy to also try to maintain the attribute of simplicity. The most reasonable option would be to deny that God is simple with regard to nature. Furthermore, God as three persons in the trinity is a unified complex of persons. So, God is not simple regarding His personhood either; to view God as simple with regard to persons would be an affirmation of Unitarianism against trinity. If God is not simple with regard to nature or person then God is not simple.

Definition of Nature and Person

Contradiction again arises in one's description of trinity if terms like nature and person are defined to cover the same domain. If "person" and "nature" have overlapping meaning then "three persons" would mean that which overlaps would be *three* but simultaneously that which overlaps would be *one* because God has one nature. For example, if a divine person is defined as "an intellect, emotion, and will" then such a person's "intellect" would be "omniscience" and "will" would be "sovereignty." Thus a divine person would be defined as "omniscience, emotion and sovereignty." In the trinity there would be three of these omniscient, emotional and sovereign Ones. Yet often omniscience and sovereignty are descriptions of God's nature. Thus, there is only one omniscient and sovereign being. But such definitions of person (intellect, emotion and will)[11] and nature (complex of divine attributes)[12] produce a real contradiction claiming simultaneously three omniscient sovereign beings and one omniscient sovereign being. Richard Swinburne recognizes that he holds this view and that it produces

---

[11] One contemporary example of defining personality this way is C. C. Ryrie, *The Holy Spirit*, pp. 11-12. Richard Swinburne in *The Christian God*, pp. 126-27 defines person in a similar way as having beliefs of a certain complexity and being able to perform intentional actions of a certain complexity.

[12] One contemporary example of defining nature this way is C. C. Ryrie, *The Holy Spirit*, pp. 17-18. Richard Swineburne in *The Christian God*, pp. 154 agrees with this definition and on p. 186 he admits that such a definition renders such a trinity view as contradictory so he confesses that he translates *theos* inconsistently at times in a relational way to prevent contradiction.

a contradiction, so to prevent his view from being a contradiction he inconsistently translates *theos* at times in a relational way to prevent contradiction while at other times defining it in this traditional orthodox way. I don't think that Swinburne's inconsistency is worth emulating but we agree that this issue is a real contradiction and the concept of the trinity cannot be contradictory if it is to have meaning. This view of "person" with regard to the hypostatic union would consistently produce a description of Christ as having a unified intellect, emotion, and will. In such a view Chalcedon is denied, for the divine and human natures are mixed and change to unify intellect and will. Chalcedon would retain omniscience and sovereignty in the divine nature of Christ simultaneously with limitation of knowledge and submissiveness in Christ's human nature. The view that Christ only has one will as a unified person is a position the early church condemned at Constantinople in 681 AD as monothelitism.[13] To remedy this contradiction and condemned novelty requires leaving qualities of nature as reserved for nature, not imparting them into a definition of person. If someone was committed to including intellect, emotion and will within this definition of person then the simplest rehabilitation would redefine person as *an individual whose nature includes intellect, emotion and will.* This returns person to the definition range of a hypostasis or a who. An alternative rehabilitation could take one into a coherent social trinitarianism. However remaining within an orthodox trinitarianism keeps one consistent with Chalcedon and Constantinople; Christ would be a unified individual who had two distinct natures: the divine nature would be omniscient and sovereign, and the human nature would be limited (though growing) in knowledge, and submission. While I would not join Swinburne in appealing to the Freudian account of divided mind because it does not get to the depth of nature and it is tainted as psychosis, I do agree with his

---

[13] A contemporary example of monothelitism is John Walvoord, *Jesus Christ Our Lord*, pp. 119-20. He does not define person in his chapter on the person of Christ so he ambiguously maintains Chalcedon and monothelitism simultaneously. However, the two views are mutually exclusive with regard to will.

analysis that the divine mind would know omnisciently what the human mind would know but that Christ's limited human mind would not be able to grasp all His divine mind knows, and that the unified person of Christ could speak from either. Now, a practical issue is raised: should we define terms such as person by keeping them close to what a tradition has become or should we rehabilitate our definition of person in line with the issues that defined it originally? I think more precision is gained by returning to the earlier roots for it keeps one closer to both the Biblical emphasis and the patristic emphasis. My definition of person as *an instantiation of a spiritual nature, as a moral end in itself, in relationship to others,* attempts to reflect the Biblical and patristic emphasis. If a student needs a simpler definition for person, then define person as "who." There is repeated concern to identify a person as a nature in such phrases as "the Word is God" and "the Word became flesh." The closest word in the Biblical text to "person" is the holistic use of "soul" (*nephesh* and *psychē*)[14] which is identified as having a spirit or spiritual nature in both the Biblical text and in patristic anthropology. In both arenas there is concern that divine persons are to be obeyed, worshipped and served so they are a moral end in themselves at the level of supreme being. However, this definition attempts to define "person" for angels and humans as well, so it is best to leave "moral end in itself" in the definition and to allow the level of being to identify the appropriate moral implications. For example, a human person should not be worshipped, but rather respected, loved and not murdered. In the Biblical text and patristic Trinitarian discussion there is repeated concern for the divine persons being understood to be in an ontological relationship that has implications to the way they and we function in our distinct roles. It is from these Biblical and patristic emphases that my definition of "person" is formed.

---

[14] For explanation and defense of the holistic view of soul, see Douglas Kennard and Paul Holmes, "The Nature of Man: A Biblical Theology Approach," or Hans Wolff, *Anthropology of the Old Testament*, pp. 17-25, or James Dunn, *The Theology of Paul the Apostle*, pp. 76-78.

However, my definition brings precise clarity in other issues as well. For example, a human fetus has human DNA, sufficient to identify it as human. The Bible describes a fetus as being body and soul accessible and created by the Spirit to be loved, valued by God, and in an ontological relationship to God and parents (Ps. 139:13-15; 51:5; Ex. 21:22-25). Thus the fetus is a human person and should not be aborted because it has personal human rights (e.g. Ex. 21:22-25). However, many other definitions of person (such as intellect, emotion and will or self-aware individual) cannot defend a fetus as a person. When does the will evidence itself? After birth? When does the intellect evidence itself? In the last trimester or after birth? When is someone self-aware? Within six months after birth? The author has heard papers presented by evangelicals who defend a pro-choice stand because the fetus analyzed by these psychological definitions is not a person yet. Whereas many other evangelicals who define person as "intellect, emotion and will" are just inconsistent as they defend a pro-life stand.

Mutable Immutability

Immutability is often given as one of the divine attributes. This means that with regard to divine nature God is unchanging and unchangeable. For example, the Father is consistent in His bestowal of good gifts with "no variation, or shifting shadows" (Jas. 1:17) so that no one should blame Him for temptations when the temptations actually are conceived by the human himself. This divine attribute identifies that God does not change in His essential nature. It is not threatened by appearances of the phenomenon within the created order. For example, having allowed blessing to come to man, God now repents (consistent with His nature) and brings judgment upon mankind since they have gone too far in their sins (e.g. Gen. 6:5-7). Immutability does not exclude God presenting Himself as repenting or turning in response to agents' choices. Immutability has to do with the consistency of the divine character, rather than His presentation of Himself. For example, judgment to those for whom it is due and blessing to those for whom it is appropriate are consistent with God's character. Immutability does not require impassibility (unchangeability of divine emotions) for God is deeply relationally connected with His creation so that sin grieves Him deeply (e.g. Gen. 6:6). The faithful character of God with regard to His other attributes, such as righteousness and justice, permits God to have purposes not always known by others but at times communicated to those He has called into relationship (e.g. Gen. 18:17). Though God has purposed to do something (Gen. 18:17), Abraham reconfirms to himself that God is just by means of God's explaining Himself anthropomorphically. For example, God hears the outcry from Sodom and Gomorrah (Gen. 18:20-21). God anthropomorphically goes to Sodom to see if in fact the sin evidenced by the outcry is as bad as the claims. In this, God comes to know the actual condition of Sodom by fairly investigating it first hand (Gen. 18:21; 19:1-13). This growing in firsthand knowledge communicates to those in relationship with God that His justice is fair, while God has obviously known all along because His purposes from the start reflect an extensive knowledge of the conditions already (Gen. 18:17; 19:13). Divine immutability is not threatened by God's changing His stated framework of operation or in answering prayer (e.g. Gen. 18:22-32). The fact that God is willing to preserve Sodom from judgment if there are fifty or even ten righteous people in the place shows the consistent responsiveness of God to the appeals and concerns of His chosen people. Through it all God shows Abraham that He is consistently righteous and will judge justly. In fact, God often goes beyond the believer's requests to show Himself consistent; even when ten righteous could not be found, the righteous were rescued while the wicked perished (Gen. 19:17; 2 Pet. 2:9). Furthermore, while the believer suffers and it appears to him as though God has changed by removing His presence (Ps. 42:9) we may rest assured that God's presence permeates everywhere and His knowledge is exhaustive and it is upon this basis that the believer can bring his petitions to God (Ps. 139). God really *is* the immutable One who cares, knows it all, is everywhere and effectively answers our prayers.

Contradictions come for immutability when the change occurs on an ontological level with attributes of the divine nature rather than on an economic level of presentation of revelation. One of the most regular places where this kind of contradiction appears is when the divine nature of Christ is modified to form the hypostatic union, which occurs in different levels of kenotic Christianity. If Jesus Christ is immutable with regard to His deity (e.g. Heb. 13:8), then He needs to retain all His divine attributes without change. This means any giving up of some divine attributes (such as immutability, omnipresence, omnipotence, or omniscience) or self-limiting of these divine attributes is a real ontological change to this nature. For example, in such conditions at least the full empowerment of divine attributes is altered to a reduced empowerment within a self-limiting mode and that is real ontological change of those attributes and omnipotence (changed from full to limited empowerment of those attributes). So in a kenotic Christology's account of incarnation: an omnipresent Christ is no longer omnipresent, an omniscient Christ is no longer omniscient, an omnipotent Christ is no longer omnipotent, and an immutable Christ has in fact changed from full empowerment to self-limiting of those attributes. Such a kenotic view denies the Chalcedon formula by proposing real change in divine attributes (from full empowerment to limited empowerment) and maybe even a mixing of natures. This renders Christ mutable ontologically or mutable with regard to His essential attributes, which in fact is contradictory for any who also affirm Christ to be immutable with regard to His essential divine nature. Such a contradiction identifies that there is falsehood, not worthy to be believed.

The primary textual reason for such versions of kenosis (or emptying) are grounded in Philippians 2, but this text does not support such versions of kenotic Christology. Contextually, Paul underscores the need for Christians to be unified in love, mind and soul (Phil. 1:27; 2:1-2). This unity is obtainable by Christians only as they are intent on the purpose of being humble, regarding the other as more important than oneself. We evangelicals who are often enamored with our own personal interests need this reminder to embrace humility and unity. It is in this context that Jesus' incarnation wonderfully displays humility as an example for us to follow (Phil. 2:5). Jesus Christ existed in the form (*morphē*) of God with regard to His divine nature (Phil. 2:6). *Morphē* has to do with form or shape which in this instance is Christ's preincarnate divinity, which had no lack. So that Christ did not regard equality with God as a thing to be grasped, grabbed or held onto like a snatch and grab artist that would grab something not his and run; Christ fully possessed the divine nature without diminishment. Within this context of strength Christ empties (*ekenōsen*) Himself in some way appropriate to the emphasis of the passage (Phil. 2:7). However, the passage never says that Christ self-limited divine attributes, rather what is being developed is the human need for humility which Christ exemplifies wonderfully in his humanity (Phil. 2:3-5, 7-8). So, the emptying (*ekenōsen*) needs to be seen in light of Jesus' human nature, the form (*morphe*) of a servant in the likeness (*homoiōmati*) of men (*anthrōpos*, Phil. 2:7). It is the person Christ in His human nature that is humble; humility (*etapeinōsen*) has to do with this human condition (*genomenos*; Phil. 2:8). That is, instead of demanding the honor due His deity, His humanity became obedient even to a dishonoring death on the cross. That this humility is working in this humanity is further evidenced by death, (which humans experience) whereas God cannot die. In response to Christ's obedient human pursuit of dishonor, God highly exalted Jesus' humanity in His ascension (Phil. 2:9-11). The exalted human Christ has a Name which is above every Name. Eschatologically everyone will submit to Christ and praise Christ as Lord to God's glory. There is no self-limiting of any divine attribute here, rather, while Christ in His deity has every right to demand honor, Christ in His humanity demonstrates humility obediently pursuing a course of dishonor, which is rewarded by God's exalting Jesus as man to high honors in which God insists that others will also highly honor Him.

The presentation of Jesus Christ in the Gospels is mainly that of his humanity, birth, embodiment, growth in knowledge and ability, being tempted, aging, eating, admitting he does not know, being locally present, being hindered in ministry by demons and human unbelief, changing, dying, rising, and ascending. These changes of human nature do not contradict Christ's immutable divine nature of omnipresence, omniscience, omnipotence and glory. Usually Christ's humanity depends upon the Father for knowledge (Jn. 17:7-8; Lk. 10:21-22) and the Spirit for empowerment to heal and do miracles (Acts 10:38; Mt. 12:28, 31). Occasionally, Christ's deity shows through His humanity as in stopping the wind in the storm, which prompts the disciples to worship Him (Mt. 8:26-27; 14:32-33). Such is an approach to the gospels which, with the Chalcedon formula, admits that Jesus Christ is a unified person with fully divine and human natures which exist without mixture, without change, without division and without separation.

Eternalizing Temporal Process

Under the influence of neoplatonism the relationships within the Trinity were specifically delineated in an ontological way as eternal generation of the Son and eternal procession of the Holy Spirit. The pressing concern that neoplatonism brings to those relationships is that if these are essentially true then they need to be eternal truths within the ontological trinity (trinity as it is before creation). In such a view, "eternal" means "outside of time, without change, and perpetual." However, here is where the contradiction comes, because the atemporal concept of eternal is linked to a temporal historical concept of birthing. Generation is built from the word *genaō* which means birth as a historical instance. What would a perpetual beyond history birth as a historical instance mean, but contradiction? Does it mean eternal extrusion? Does it mean a stoic procession or essential extension? Whatever it means, the words chosen to express it deny each other: eternal demands a nonchanging, ahistoricity and *genaō* expresses historical birth that changes one to being beyond the womb. The particular version of *genaō* that is normally Biblically appealed to in defense of eternal generation is the word *monogenēs*, which means "unique birth." Non-Johannine uses of *monogenēs* mean, "only child," as in a family that has only one child (Luke 7:12; 8:42; 9:38; Heb. 11:17). Johannine use develops *monogenēs* as a unique historical birth of the revelatory Word, Jesus Christ, thus enabling Christ to reveal God through Christ's humanity. For example, John 1:14 describes the unique birthing process (*monogenēs*) as the incarnation of Christ's humanity in flesh so that He as the Word could reveal the divine glory historically through His humanity. The fact that the Word is God (Jn. 1:1) means that the uniquely born (*monogenēs*) God (divine One adding humanity in his birth) is uniquely enabled to explain the Father, which explanation took place in the historic incarnation prior to John's writing his gospel (aorist of *exērgeomai;* Jn. 1:18). This uniquely born Word (born for the purpose of revealing the Father) has revealed God and after the ascension (as John is writing[15]), the divine Word interpenetrating the anthropomorphic breast (*kolpon*) of the Father. The Father gives the uniquely born (*monogenēs*) Son of God (in His incarnation coming into the world) for men to believe in Him and thereby obtain everlasting life (Jn. 3:16, 18; 1 Jn. 4:9). Since the Biblical text emphasizes *genaō* and *monogenēs* to be the historical birthing of Jesus' humanity in incarnation, and eternal generation claimed to be taught from these passages is itself contradictory, it is best to reject the ancient tradition that Jesus Christ was generated before all ages in eternity. The generation of the Son is best seen, consistent with the Biblical text, as the historical birthing of Jesus' humanity within the incarnation process. Christ as

---

[15] *On*, the present tense of *eimi*, indicates a present relationship, but not a continued enwombment that would indicate that the unique birth in this context had not happened because, in fact, with the incarnation the unique birth occurs.

God is eternal, whereas His humanity was uniquely born in the historical incarnation event.

Likewise the procession of the Spirit is best seen as a historical process that occurs after Jesus Christ ascends, rather than an eternal procession motivated by stoicism or neoplatonism. The Biblical words for "sending" that procession describes are: "sending" (*pempsō*), "going out" (*ekporeyetai*) and "pouring forth" (*ekcheō*). While a stoic procession informed Tertullian's view of Trinity, we should make sure that our doctrines reflect the Biblical world view and not be attracted to foreign world views such as stoicism that might have helped frame the doctrine in the first place. The concept of sending (or procession) happens historically in time (as an economic relationship rather than an ontological relationship) indicating when the Spirit comes to continue Christ's ministry on earth. Thus eternal procession becomes a contradictory concept when it is informed by the Biblical text; "an eternal nonchanging ahistorical process occurs historically bringing about a change" is a contradictory concept. Furthermore, the Biblical text indicates that this procession happens historically when the Holy Spirit is sent to continue Jesus' ministry. John 14:17-18 indicates that the disciples with Jesus in the upper room have the Holy Spirit with them but there will be a change as Jesus leaves, for then the Holy Spirit will be in them. After Jesus leaves the Father will send (*pempsei*) the Holy Spirit to the disciples to remind these disciples about the things Jesus said to them when He was in fact with them (Jn. 14:25-26). The Holy Spirit will come after Jesus leaves, sent (*pempsō*) by Christ and going out (*ekporeyetai*) from the Father (Jn. 15:26). However, the Son must leave first and return to the Father who sent the Son and thus the disciples will have an advantage as Christ leaves, for the Son will send (*pempsō*) the Holy Spirit to them so that the Spirit might convict the world concerning sin, righteousness and judgment (Jn. 16:5, 7-8). The same economic relationship of being sent that the Son had, the Holy Spirit will have, and thus the Holy Spirit is another comforter like Christ. In Acts 1:8 the Holy Spirit has not been received by the disciples yet, so that they await His empowerment in the future. Christ finally ascends in Acts 1:9 leaving His disciples. On the feast of Pentecost the Holy Spirit fills the disciples and they have a dramatic empowerment to proclaim the gospel (Acts 2:2-4). God declares that in the last days He will pour forth (*ekcheō*) the Spirit on all mankind (Acts 2:17). Jesus Christ in His exaltation receives (*labōn*) the promise of the Holy Spirit from the Father and so Christ pours forth (*execheen*) this Holy Spirit phenomenon which the Jews present can see and hear (Acts 2:33). In the wake of this historical procession which happened at Pentecost, the Father sends (*exapesteilen*) the Spirit into believers' hearts prompting them to intimate prayer by which we cry out, "Daddy, Father" (Gal. 4:6). This condition of the indwelling Spirit who prompts believers to intimate prayer happens for all who belong to Christ, are adopted as sons by the Father and are co-heirs with Christ (Rom. 8:9, 15, 17). Since the Biblical text emphasizes procession to be a historical coming of the Spirit at Pentecost and eternal procession claimed to be taught from these passages is itself contradictory, it is best to reject the ancient tradition that the Spirit is from eternal procession. The procession of the Spirit is best seen, consistent with the Biblical text, as the historical coming of the Spirit on Pentecost. Within this economic sending [16] the Biblical text better aligns with a Western view that has the Holy Spirit sent by Father and Son; most of the sending words with regard to the Holy Spirit are used equally by the Father and the Son in the same way. [17]

Conclusion

If we are to understand, and worship, and teach about our God as Trinity, then let us do it in a way that is not unworthy (because it is a contradiction or

---

[16] Economic sending rather than eternal ontological procession (which was used by the Fathers to frame this discussion) float the filoque (from the Son) clause, and separate Eastern Orthodoxy from the Catholic West.

[17] Compare *pempso* in Jn. 14:25 and Jn. 16:5 with Jn. 15:26 and 16:7. Compare *ekcheo* in Acts 2:17 with Acts 2:33.

because it does not reflect the Biblical text). Let us make sure that our understanding, worship, loving, and teaching are both coherent and Biblical with the emphasis that God reveals concerning Himself.

ʾElōhı̂m, the Creator

The term *ʾēl,* which means "god," suggests power and authority. Some suggest that *ʾēl* derives from the root *ʾwl* (strong), others suggest *ʾeloah* (God), and others see the root *ʾlh* together with *ʾĕlōah* (implying fear).[1] Though there is disagreement in the etymology of the term, it is broadly recognized in its use to mean "god." Here in Genesis it is used to describe a profoundly powerful God in contrast to the other cosmologies of the ancient Near East. So the effective power and authority to create swiftly and effortlessly helps to inform the grandeur of this God *ʾel.* Many suggest that the plural, *ʾElōhı̂m,* extends these conceptions of power, authority, and majesty beyond which a singular name can do justice. For example, Eichrodt developed this as an overwhelming monotheism.

> A similar design led the writer of Genesis 1 to use the term *elohim* for the Creator God. By choosing this particular name, which as the epitome of all embracing divine power excludes all other divinity, he was able to protect his cosmology from any trace of polytheistic thought and at the same time describe the creator God as the absolute Ruler and the only Being whose will carries any weight.[2]

---

[1] An example of a brief discussion of this etymology can be found in Laird Harris, Gleason Archer and Bruce Waltke, *Theological Wordbook of the Old Testament* (Chicago: Moody Press, 1980).

[2] Walter Eichrodt, *Old Testament Theology,* vol. 1, pp. 186-87. There should be no development of trinity in these early chapters of Genesis, for if "plural" is to be taken as a plural of person it would mean "polytheism" in this early context of revelation and that is clearly not correct in a Pentateuch context in which monotheism dominates.

It has become popular in certain contexts to see *elohim* as God's court or angels. For example, Psalm 8:5 as understood by the LXX and Hebrews 2:7 takes *elohim* as angels. Job 1:6 and 2:1 presents the sons of *elohim* to be angels in God's court. However, this same author denies angels a role involved within the creation except that of worship while God creates the universe (Job 38:1-11). Furthermore, Isaiah in his development of the incomparability of Yahweh develops that He is the One, Who creates the universe and people as well; there is no one else (Isa. 42:5-9).[3] This brings us back to this context of Genesis in which no other than *elohim* is described as the creator. The creation is singularly done so effectively by One's speech. This is better understood in this Mosaic context as a single monotheistic God (Deut. 6:4), Who as the creator creates so effectively that the plural is best taken as a plural of majesty. This plurality of majesty may be viewed as carrying over into the pronouns that are used in grammatical agreement with *Elohim* like the 'Us' and 'Our' of Genesis 1:26 and 3:22.[4] So, no development of plurality of person is being developed by these texts, when they are easily explained by simple grammatical agreement. Perhaps the abundance of singular pronouns used with the plural *Elohim* makes a case for monotheism.

In ancient Near Eastern cosmology the creation accounts often involve a long period with deep conflicts through which a born god who would be king battles and destroys rival gods and the forces of chaos in order to remake them into the new creation. An example is seen in the *Enumma Elish*. In stark contrast, *Elohim* is neither born, or developing. Carroll Stuhmueller develops the unique theological entrance of this God, for He alone among all semitic creative gods undergoes no birth or metamorphosis.[5] God is complete in Himself and He

---

[3] Cf. Chapter on the incomparable Yahweh for further development of this point.

[4] There does not seem to be any other creator involved in Genesis or crafting the image of God as man. The second pronominal referent is in Genesis 3:22. Here the singular referent who is the judge is Yahweh Elohim. It is only after the judgment that a cherub appears on the scene. In other contexts, where the plural is clearly developing "God and His court," the variety of referents are clearly visible in the context before the plural pronoun is used, as in Isa. 6:8.

[5] Carrol Stuhmueller, "The Theology of Creation in Second Isaias," *CBQ* 21 (1959) 429-67.

stands transcendently apart from all that is created. This polemics both the Egyptian pantheism and the Mesopotamian dualism, which both are developing inferior gods. Our God is truly worthy of control because only our God truly created everything. God is presented as creating swiftly and effortlessly a whole creation with no threatening rivals within the creation. John McKenzie develops that there is no cosmic mortal combat with the risk of God's being defeated by a monster of chaos, but rather God is in His shop as a carpenter with no risk of being devoured by His chair (the created thing).

> Against this background, the Hebrew account of the origins can scarcely be anything else but a counter statement to the myth of creation ... The Hebrew author enumerates all the natural forces in which deity was thought to reside, and of all of them he says simply that God made them. Consequently, he eliminates all elements of struggle on the cosmic level; the visible universe is not an uneasy balance of forces, but it is moderated by one supreme will, which imposes itself with effortless supremacy upon all that it has made. By preference the author speaks of the created work rather of the created act, because he wishes to emphasize the fact that the creative Deity, unlike *Marduk*, has not had to win supremacy by combat with an equal.[6]

This chapter will especially draw together the parallel texts of Genesis 1 and 2 and Psalm 104 to develop a Biblical theology of creation from the O.T.

The structure of Genesis develops literary units with the hinge of the word "account" (*tôlᵉdôt*). For example, both Genesis creation accounts begin with the same grammatical structure: a summary of the whole creation within the unit, followed by three circumstantial clauses (which explore the attending circumstance of lack within which the creation makes sense). The fact that these circumstantial clauses of Genesis 1:2 and 2:5-6 depend on the main verb of the overview statement (Gen. 1:1 or 2:4) clarifies that grammatically there is no temporal gap or events between these textual statements.

---

[6] John McKenzie, *The Two Edged Sword* (N.Y.: Image Books, 1966), pp. 101-2.

There is no existing creation before the summary statement of Genesis 1:1. This summary creation event begins with the first two words connecting together by the alliteration of the *BRA* sound in the words "In the beginning" and "created." Or as Young develops. "This is a beginning that is characterized by creation, and this is a creation that is characterized by the beginning. Here it means 'the absolute beginning!'"[7] The word created (*bārā*) is an activity of God alone; it is never used of man. The result is always a definitive creation, something new and fresh. "The heavens and earth" is a merism of opposites presenting God as the creator of all.

A number of chaos metaphors are developed in the conditional clauses that set a conceptual framework in order to bring out the creation order. For example, the concepts of formless (*tōhû*) and void (*bōhû*) signify chaos and lack of order, as in a desert waste (Dtr. 32:10; Job 6:18) or after a devastating judgment (Jer. 4:23-26; Isa. 34:11). Perhaps the form of God's creation is given through God's activity of the first three days and then God fills the creation in days four through six, however here the two words operate as a hendiadys for amorphous chaos. Additionally, darkness is symbolic of evil and vulnerability throughout the Bible (eg. Ex. 10:21-22; 14:20), however in this context darkness is merely part of the designed time of day without light (Gen. 1:4-5, 18). Furthermore, the watery deep (*thm*) is not conducive to life and represents the abyss. This deep is what drowns Egypt, Tyre and everyone in the flood when it is released by God to fight sin with chaos/flood (Gen. 7:11; 8:2; Ex. 15:5, 8; Ezek. 26:19). God's way of deliverance for Israel was to pass through this deep on dry ground in the midst of the exodus into kingdom (Ps. 106:9; Isa. 51:10; 63:13). God's conquering over this chaos is a polemic against the Babylonian goddess *Tiamat* and other mythological conceptions of the sea of chaos (*yām*), which is occupied by the monsters of chaos (*Leviathan* and *Rahab*). Here God does not Himself sense any risk from the deep and later it can be seen as a creation sea out

---

[7] Young, *In the Beginning*, p. 24.

of which blessing may come (Gen. 49:25). The "*rûaḥ* of *Elohîm*" could join the chaos metaphors as a chaotic wind from God (Isa. 11:4; 30:28) without the battle imagery of *Marduk*'s use of the chaos wind to defeat *Tiamat*, but *Elohîm* is presented in Genesis 1 as God involved in creation, so it is best to take it as the monotheistic Divine Spirit involved in creation.[8] There is no life besides God, so the Spirit of God hovers like a mother bird over her brood with such movements as to cause her brood, the creation, to take flight (Dtr. 32:11); God has intimate contact with the creation to bring forth order. Waltke develops that there is no restrainer of the chaos as in the ancient Near Eastern myths and there is no threat or rival to God; the monotheistic God creates utilizing these chaos metaphors.

> The Spirit of God does not contend with a living hostile chaotic force but hovers over the primordial mass awaiting the appropriate time for history to begin. How can the chaos be hostile when it is not living but inanimate? It can only be shaped according to the will of the Creator.[9]

The pattern of creation follows regularly as: 1) an announcement (And God said), 2) command (let there be…), 3) report (and it was so), 4) evaluation (And God said that it was good) 5) temporal framework (And there was evening and morning, the … day). *Elohîm*'s creating by word implies sovereignty and extends far beyond *Marduk*'s magic by word as he was unable even to quiet *Tiamat* by word.[10] The evaluation of "good" (*ṭôb*) can be an aesthetic judgment of beauty (perhaps Gen. 6:2) but in this context it is an acknowledgment of purpose and order and blessing, thus the creation is fitting into God's sovereign design (Gen.2:9, 17-18; 3:5-6, 22). Sometimes, this evaluation comes in the middle of the day to structure levels of the creation. For example, the water, sky, and land are all separated into a structure on day two and three, the evaluation

---

[8] Do not read this as the Holy Spirit (as in a trinitarian understanding) for in the Pentateuch context monotheism is emphasized as a foundational stage of progressive revelation. The trinity is not clearly taught in the Bible until the N.T.

[9] Bruce Waltke, *Creation and Chaos*, p. 48.

separates these as a lower structure than that of vegetation. (Gen. 1:10).
Likewise, in the middle of day six, after the land beasts were created, the
evaluation occurs to identify man in the creation as a superior content of creation.
The fact that God creates only good reflects back onto Him as the Good God (e.g.
Mt. 19:17; Jas. 1:17). The days (*yôm*) of Genesis can be taken as the light part of
the day in contrast to darkness (Gen. 1:5), or as an age of creation (Gen. 2:4) but
the term day used with a number and described in the Hebrew way as dark of
night and then light of morning is best taken as a *solar* day (Ex. 20:11). So in
comparison to other ancient Near Eastern creation accounts the Biblical creation
moves swiftly to its completion in six solar days. These days in Genesis 1 set up
a loose parallel (of light, separated environs, and climax) between the structure of
days one through three and the contents of days four through six.

The creation of light does not occur prior to the creation as in other ancient
Near Eastern myths, where it is an attribute of their gods (e.g. *Apsu* and *Marduk*).
In this case light is created by God to dispel the chaotic darkness thus effortlessly
obtaining an immediate victory (Gen. 1:3-5). The separation of light from
darkness and the naming of them demonstrates *Elōhîm*'s sovereignty, as Von Rad
develops.

> The ultimate enunciation of this orderly cosmic arrangement and
> wholesome stabilization is the divine naming of the present
> darkness as night and the present light as day. The name given by
> God, is an expression of the essence and a seal of the way it will
> look henceforth. Thus the accent lies, not on the verbal naming,
> but on the calling into and fixing of the existence of creation. The
> precise translation, therefore is 'And God *appointed* the light as
> day...' But in the ancient Oriental view the act of giving a name
> meant, above all, the exercise of a sovereign right (cf. 2 Kings
> 23:34; 24:17). Thus the naming of this and all subsequent creation
> works once more expresses graphically God's claim of lordship
> over the creatures.[11]

---

[10] Compare tablet 2:117 or the sovereignty theme is developed by Nahum Sarna,
Understanding Genesis (N.Y.: McGraw Hill, 1966), p. 12.

Israel would remember the plagues (Ex. 10:21-24), how God brought thick darkness over the Egyptians but light among the Israelite huts. Light would represent good and salvation as dark represents chaos, evil and judgment. Psalm 104:1 contemplates that in this creation God wraps Himself about with a majestic garment of light. Israel would know that God was the way when they followed the light phenomenon through the wanderings, day and night. They would also see here that this same God is sovereign over both light and darkness; metaphors of goodness and evil were both present but in their proper place.

The parallel creation of lights on day four simply brings the word for lamps as visible from below as in the expanse of the creation (Gen. 1:14-19). If any of these lights were named it would conjure up pagan gods but here the word 'light' is meant to be prosaic and degrading, as to exclude polytheism. These are created objects; sun and moon are not named so that every tempting association may be avoided; the words sun and moon are also names for pagan deities, namely *Shemesh* and *Yareach*. The stars are briefly stated as created lights showing no place for astrology. These lights are established as functionaries in the creation for signs, seasons, days and years. *'Ĕlōhîm* has created these lights to fill His heavens showing again His sovereignty.

In days two and three God continues to bring separation to the creation (Gen. 1:6-10). This is first brought about by a firmly hammered or stamped barrier called firmament (*rāqî'a*).[12]   Psalm 104:2-3 describes the firmament

---

[11] Gerhard VonRad, *Genesis*, p. 53.

[12] Firmament is an extended surface, a solid expanse as if beaten out in a bowl. It is created by God, holding up the heavenly waters, so that the birds can fly in an open environment under its expanse (Gen. 1:6-8, 20). The sun, moon and stars are phenomenally seen in the firmament and as such the firmament declares God's glory through the created items seen through it (Gen. 1:14-15, 17; Ps. 19:2; Dan. 12:3). Praise is appropriate anywhere in this created sanctuary of the earth (that is within the firmament) that God has made (Ps. 150:1). The firmament continues to be presented in a solid way, for it is the structural expanse appearing as a crystal roof with God's sapphire throne sitting upon it (Ezek. 1:22-26; 10:1). This firmament might be a circular or a vaulted arch since Isaiah 40:22 claims God sits upon such a shape above the earth in the context of the clouds (cf. Job 22:14). Other images communicate this structural element in more fabric like as of a heavenly tent curtain or clothes, or with upper chambers with beams for support (Ps. 104:2-4; Isa. 40:22). This realist imagery is furthered by the use of *'arubah* (windows or lattice in a literal building Ec. 12:3; Isa. 6:8). The word for window however refers to the flood

structurally with beams to support the upper chamber holding up the waters and surrounded with a tent curtain. This barrier that holds up the heavenly waters from the waters below is joined by the rising of land that separates the land from the seas. Psalm 104:6-9 portrays the rising of the land and the fleeing of the waters as dramatically responding to God's thunderous rebuke which limits the earth's garment to its proper place. Something like this occurs again as the flood waters recede and the earth is once again brought up from the waters of chaos (Gen. 8). The simplicity of accomplishing these divisions by a word stands boldly as a claim for *Elohim*'s sovereignty; He rules over the domains of the pagan gods and separates and controls them. Once the waters are separated under God's sovereign control they become territorial markers and irrigation channels created by God to do His bidding as tools which water the plants and animals (Gen. 2:6, 10-14; Ps. 104:10-13).

The last division of form is God's creation of vegetation. It is described with an emphasis on its kind maintaining the God-given order and its fruit sustaining this God-given order. Bringing the vegetation from the inanimate earth identifies it with the earth in contrast to the ancient Near Eastern gods, who have been sidelined again. The speed at which *Elohim* creates the plants demonstrates God's sovereign power, as well as continues to polemic evolutionary views. This vegetation is primarily developed in these creation accounts to show God's generosity in blessing animals and man with food as a loving Father who crafts the environment for those who are His (Gen. 1:11-12, 29-30; 2:16; Ps. 104:14-17).

---

waters pouring through these heavenly firmament windows (Gen. 7:11; 8:2). Furthermore these heavenly windows may be either spiritually real or metaphorical as in the instances where a more generic judgment of entrapment, or blessing of deliverance from enemies or food coming from God (2 Ki. 7:2, 19; Isa. 24:18; Mal.3:10). Perhaps with the realist emphasis of firmament and windows, it is best to incorporate them as spiritually real dimensional phenomena that are visible only at selected instances like the angelic army surrounding Elisha whether his attendant could see them or not (2 Ki. 6:17). This spiritually real cosmology is a broadly accepted perspective in the ancient Near East, though the Hebrew framework does not reflect the polytheistic bias common among the other ancient Near Eastern religions.

Then God created the animals. The creation of the animals involves both
the spoken word and the intimacy of personal creation, which indicates a higher
form of existence. These animals are created as "living creatures" or more
appropriately as "living souls" (*napheshîm,* eg. Gen. 1:20, 24, 30; 9:10, 12, 15).
In Hebrew, the word soul is not a special human psychological or spiritual
quality, but *nephesh* refers to a wholistic living, willing being. These souls are
enumerated as the swimming things, flying things, livestock, crawling things, and
wild animals. It is this animal pattern of wholistically being a soul that is then
applied to man as well in creation (Gen. 2:7). As such souls, these animals and
man experience the blessing of God in fertility. Once again the pagan myths are
polemicized, for fertility comes from the Creator, Who designed them to be
fruitful, multiplying and filling the earth (Gen. 1:22-25). The fact that animals are
souls identifies them to be responsible agents, who should and do receive
consequences for their sins. For example, the snake involved in the temptation is
judged (Gen. 3:1, 14-15). Additionally in the Noahic covenant animals and
humans alike who kill a human are to suffer capital punishment (Gen. 9:5-6).
Likewise in the Law, the ox that gores a man to death is to be killed as well as the
owner of the ox if the ox had a prior propensity to gore people (Ex. 21:28-29).
The fact that animals are souls also means that they have limited rights as well,
such as being rescued if they fall into a pit even on a Sabbath day (Mt. 12:11–12).

The greatest polemic of the false gods with regard to the animals is the
way *tannînîm* or sea monsters occur in the account (Gen. 1:21). Psalm 104:26
mentions them by name as the *Leviathan.* For the Cannanites, the *tannînîm,*
called *Leviathan,* are ominous chaos rivals that have preceded *Baal,* which he
must confront in warfare at the beginning; *Baal* must conquer these with much
effort to bring order to the creation. However, in the Biblical account, the
tannînim or *Leviathan* are God's bath toys; thus no rival at all and the order of the
creation is well under way before they are briefly mentioned in passing as created
by *'Elohîm.* When compared to God, these puny creatures are created by God to

play in God's seas. The *tannînîm* experience the blessing of God's fertility along with the rest of the animals. In response to this much of the creation account Psalm 104 breaks forth in petition and song for the glory of the Lord and the destruction of the enemies of God (Ps. 104:31-35).

God is seen as the definitive Creator. In contrast to the other cosmologies God is seen in these Biblical accounts of creation as more powerful in His accomplishment of the creation. The Biblical text portrays God as a greater sovereign than the other cosmologies that require their gods to express huge effort in order to accomplish their attempts to rule. Perhaps the repeated reminders of the creation's being good reflect on God as good or the source of goodness. These features in which God demonstrates Himself in Genesis 1 are then reflected in minute form through the image of God, which pictures God.

Man is the climax of God's creation. This is evident by the parallel structure to vegetation as after the pronouncement of good on their respective days (Gen. 1:10, 25). Additionally, the divine announcement of resolution preceding man's creation shows unique handling of this creation. Furthermore, the repetition of *bara* in Genesis 1:28 indicates the highpoint of the creation. Cassuto also makes the case that the change from narrative to poetry accentuates man as the noblest of God's creatures.[13] Certainly the image of God and the intimacy with which God creates indicates that man is God's superior creation.

Image (*ṣelem* and *eikōn*) and likeness (*dᵉmût* and *homoiōsis*) are synonyms which convey a copy or a duplicate. Such a concept would not be thought of in this ancient Near Eastern context without accentuating the physical representation. Humans are statues or representations of God. In the ancient Near East the setting up of the king's statue was equivalent to proclaiming that his domain was over that sphere in which the statue was erected (e.g. Dan. 3:1ff.).[14] For example, when in the thirteenth century B.C., pharaoh Rameses II had his image carved out of rock at the mouth of the river *el-Kelb,* on the Mediterranean

---

[13] Cassuto, *Genesis*, p. 57.

north of Beirut, the image meant that he was ruler of this area. The fact that God has set man up as His statues and man has dispersed around the globe in obeying God shows that *Elōhîm* is sovereign over the whole earth. Wherever we meet a fellow human, God is sovereign there as well. One obvious implication to this as an image of God is the utter foolishness of crafting an idol, because such lifeless things do not represent the living God nearly so well as the living image does. As representations of God we have the task of being His representatives, to do his will. *Elōhîm* has been strongly developed in this context as the creative and sovereign One. There is no surprise that the blessings for the image of God reflect these attributes of God through humans being fruitful, multiplying, filling the earth so that they can subdue and rule the earth (Gen. 1:26-28; 9:1-7). To accomplish these blessings which demonstrate God, we are the image of God individually and, as male and female together, we are corporately the image of God. Of course, each of the persons involved in the procreative task is evidencing a minute picture of God's creative task. In fact, the concept of image in this context also can be seen as sonship (Gen. 5:1, 3; Lk. 3:38). The concept of son of God in the ancient Near East is used of kings. Furthermore, the terms subdue and rule (*rādā* and *ḳābash*, Gen. 1:26, 28) are forceful terms that speak of trampling on others in conquest or vine press to force these others to serve. The naming of the animals and woman by Adam argues that man is in fact operating as an ancient Near Eastern sovereign, for kings have the right to name others and thereby demonstrate that these others are under their dominion (Gen. 2:19, 23; Dan. 1:7). After the fall the terms subdue and rule are never undone, but as humans become contorted by the lure of sin, restrictions that limit man's excesses are seen instead (e.g. Gen. 9:2-6). Man remains viewed in contrast to the creation as a little lower than God with glory and majesty so that he can rule over the works and creatures of God's hands (Ps.8:4-8).

---

[14] Wolff, *Anthropology of the Old Testament,* pp. 160-61.

The creation account in Genesis 2 emphasizes God in the role as Father creating the environment for His son Adam with the provision for place, resources, occupation, blessings and an arranged marriage. Man should recognize that the resources lovingly enable the occupation, which God has for man. The occupation itself has man expressing his care for the orchard (which is what an ancient Near Eastern garden is). Normally the ancient Near Eastern garden was surrounded by a hedge or a wall to set it off from the outside world (Gen. 2:8; 3:23). The fact that God is met in the garden hints that the garden is sacred space (Gen. 2:8; 3:8-9).[15] In the ancient Near East the meeting place of heaven and earth was on a mountain where a sacred stream ushers forth, which similar description further hints that the garden is sacred space (Gen. 2:10). When humans are finally excluded from the garden, the garden is then seen as holy in comparison to the surrounding area. At that point they are met by *cherubim* at the gate back to the garden, which creatures are associated in the ancient Near East with royalty and temples, thus further hinting that the garden is sacred space (Gen. 3:24). The words referring to the care of the garden focus man toward the sacredness of his task as serving God. For example, "cultivate" (*ʿabad*) elsewhere in the Pentateuch expresses the idea of servant to God, which is the highest role a man can have (Gen.2:15; Ex. 3:12; 10:3, 8, 11, 24, 26). Likewise, the word "keep" (*shāmar*) is used elsewhere in the Pentateuch as obeying God's commands (Gen. 2:15; Ex. 15:26; 16:28; 19:5; 20:6, 8). These words hint that man's responsibility in chapter two may be more priestly in order to balance the creative and regal thrust of chapter one, but all these roles can be subsumed within the role of man's being the son of God. Humans have relationship to God accessing this

---

[15]For development of this theme see Gordon Wenham, "Sanctuary Symbolism in the Garden of Eden Story" in *Proceedings of the Ninth World Congress of Jewish Studies* (Jerusalem: World Union of Jewish Studies, 1986). Additionally Jon D. Levenson, "The Temple and the World," *Journal of Religion* 64(1984), pp. 275-98 develops the creation narratives as viewing the cosmos as a temple. Furthermore, Kathryn Gleason, "Gardens in Preclassical Times" *Oxford Encyclopedia of Archaeology in the Near East,* ed. E. Meyers (N.Y.: Oxford, 1997), 2:383 develops the close relationship that temples tend to have with gardens in the ancient Near East.

relationship as priests and sons. Humans reflect God in miniature as creative and ruling.

To enable these roles, God arranges a marriage for Adam. In fact the only thing of the two creation accounts that is declared not to be good is that man is alone. The Hebrew for "alone" (*bad*) means without aid or helpless; it does not mean psychologically lonely. The point is not man's need for a companion but that he cannot do the tasks such as procreation without the woman's aid. The woman becomes a helper (*ʿezer*), like God who assists in these tasks (Gen. 2:18, 20; Ps. 121:1-2). Because she is a helper corresponding (*kᵉnegdô*) to man she is to be seen as a duplicate or corresponding copy of himself. The descriptions of the woman further develop this similarity. The rib (*ṣēlāʿ*) actually means a side portion as in barbequed ribs that have meat and bone together. Adam recognizes that they are made of the same flesh and bone, so that he poetically names her woman (*'ishā*), which contains the name man (איש) within it (Gen. 2:23). In the commentary for Israelite readers, arranged marriages enable the man to leave or forsake a oneness with one's parents in order to cleave or physically join to each other in loyal love, ushering in sexual intercourse and progeny. This drive for marriage can be seen as an outworking of the original union of one flesh of man and woman in the creation.

With the close of the creation account in Genesis 1 there is the development of sacred time, which serves as the temporal climax for this first creation account, structured as it is by the repeated temporal framework (Gen. 2:1-3). God stopped (*seboth*) creating and set this day apart as a day in the calendar, which reflects God's stopping the creation. Later as the sign of the Mosaic covenant for Israel this sacred seventh day of creation is incorporated as the rationale for the Sabbath day (Ex. 20:8-11; 31:12-17).

The second Genesis creation account continues to explain the origin of temptation, sin and judgment (Gen. 3). This account provides a narrative that reflects the historical account but also is selective in recounting the process of how temptation works so that Israelite readers and now Christian readers might not follow into the way of temptation. The account also provides a view of God as He responds to this temptation and sin that is instructive about human relationship with Him. The fact that man and woman are both naked and not ashamed shows that they are at ease with one another without any fear of exploitation and potential for evil in contrast to the tensions that will come as a result of the fall. There is however a word play which shows that in their naked (*arûmmîm*) innocence the snake[16] was particularly shrewd (*arûm*) to take advantage of them (Gen. 2:25-3:1). For example, this particular snake is described as a beast with unusual craftiness such as being able to talk and there is no mention that Eve is surprised, nor that other snakes need to have these abilities, but then again other animals might have had some of these abilities then; the text

---

[16] The tempter is a snake, which will crawl on its belly, not a Satan that is rarely developed in the O.T. Many in Christendom see an age old struggle with Satan and man heavily developed out of the O.T. as in Greg Boyd, *God at War* (Downers Grove: InterVarsity Press, 1998). No Biblical text places Satan in the Genesis 3 account. Revelation 12:9 and 20:2 develops that Satan has a long standing conflict with the woman Israel and her son Christ. John 8 develops Satan as a murderer from the beginning (*arxes*), in which beginning is used in the near context as the beginning of Jesus' ministry (John 8:25, 44) and the subject immediately preceding this statement is how the religious leaders have been seeking Jesus' life (John 8:40, 44, 59). Romans 16:20 is a metaphorical allusion for future blessing of the Roman Christians and not a comment on the players of the fall. Ezekiel 28 does not mention Satan or describe what relation the described event has to Genesis 3. However, it does describe a cherub in the garden of Eden in a beautiful nonfallen condition and there is one cherub on the way to the tree of Life but no mention of one behind the snake (Gen. 3:23-24; Ezek. 28:12-14). Snakes (*nāhāsh*) in Moses' theology of the pentateuch are affirmed as good channels of the work of God (like a blessing to Dan, Moses' rod, and the healing bronze snake) as well as threatening crawling animals (Gen. 3:1, 14; 49:17; Ex. 4:3; 7:15; Num. 21:6-9; Deut. 3:15). Evil is not invading on the back of one greater than man, but rather a subordinate snake as an expression of the creation is seen as rebelling against man who is the miniature sovereign. So where does this resilient tradition of Satan as behind the snake come from? Jeffrey Russell in *The Devil: Perceptions of Evil from Antiquity to Primitive Christianity*. (Ithaca: Cornell University Press, 1977, pp. 207-9) claims that the first century pseudopigraphal works *The Books of Adam and Eve* and the *Apocalypse of Moses* are the first to identify Satan as tempting Adam and Eve in the garden. Russell (pp. 218-20) explains that there is a consensus among historians that this is the effect of Iranian Zoroastrianism on these texts. Under this influence, Judaism identified the *Ahriman* myth (a dualistic god of evil which takes the form of a snake to destroy happiness by the two men eating some fruit (*Zendavesta,, Th.*3: p. 54-55, 62) and a chief angel Sammael described in the pseudopigrapha text *Wisdom of Solomon* 2:24. I don't think that we want to identify with a view that has Zoroastrian myth as its root as seen through the lens of rejected Jewish sectarian writings. So this author sees no clear text that places Satan as involved with the temptation and fall of humans.

just does not say how extensive animal reasoning and communication happened to be in that forum. There had been some hint in the creation account that humankind's miniature sovereign role would be resisted by the choice of such forceful terminology as *rādā* and *kābash* (Gen. 1:26, 28). Evil is not invading on the back of one greater than man but rather a subordinate snake (an expression of the creation) is seen as rebelling against man who is the miniature sovereign. The temptation is a pre-modern event, so as an event it needs to be taken together without dividing it up into seconds or parts as if they could stand alone. The whole narrative recounts our fall into sin. The temptation begins with a subtle distortion questioning God's generous freedom given to Adam and Eve to eat freely from the trees of the garden (Gen. 2:15; 3:1). Eve betrays her lack of knowledge[17] of God's word by overemphasizing God's strictness ("nor touch it"), minimizing the freedom (the infinitive absolute "eat freely" becomes you "may eat"), and weakening the penalty (the infinitive absolute "surely die" becomes "lest you die" Gen. 2:15-16; 3:3). In such a vulnerable condition of inaccurate knowledge of God's word, the snake responds by denying God's word, especially with regard to denying judgment. Such comments judge God's nature with a bias toward disobedience, and in God's place the snake promises good things that are half true with a horrible double meaning (Gen. 3:4-5). As the snake moves from the focus of the narrative, the temptation continues with the woman (Gen. 3:6). It is the lure of the world that thrusts the temptation home. There is a progression from the external description of physical practicality and beauty to internal desire (a longing for wisdom perceived to be helpful from a twisting independent mindset). Once in the act of sin, sin involves others with it, so she gave to her husband with her and he ate. Their eyes were opened as the snake had said, but with a twisted perception that rendered them ashamed of their nakedness and

---

[17] The text does not explain whether she had been told correctly or whether it is a lapse in her memory. The text merely points out the proper point of view and by contrast her slightly askew view of it reflected here. Either way she reflects an incorrect knowledge of the tree and its fruit.

pathetically tried to cover it up (Gen. 2:25; 3:7). Fig leaves look like they will cover more than they actually do; they dry quickly; and they have fuzz on them that itches.

In the setting of the sacred space of the garden, God manifests Himself to man intimately by walking and talking with man face to face (Gen. 3:8-9). However, having sinned man forfeits this privilege of intimacy by fleeing in fear and is thus expelled from the holy garden to common soil (Gen. 3:8-10, 23-24). Still, humans are able to maintain some relationship with God but so few do so. It takes until Enosh is born before men begin to call upon the Lord in prayer (Gen. 4:26). Additionally, Enoch and Noah are unique in recovering this intimacy of walking with God (Gen. 5:22; 6:9). The choice of relationship with God seems to be available, but the record shows that we humans chose either sin or distraction with other things[18].

Unfortunately, the record also shows that humans increasingly gave themselves over to sin. With the taking of the forbidden fruit, it was then shared with others (Gen. 3:6). This act of sin is extended by Cain in his submitting to the dominance of the beast of sin (Gen.4:7). However Adam and Eve had shame in their sin (Gen.3:10-13). Cain also had shame in his punishment (Gen. 4:13-14). In bragging about his double murders, Lamech is a harbinger of our era with the loss of shame even when the crime is found out (Gen.4:23-24). In such a condition as this, sin eventually dominated the earth. The description of man's sin prior to the flood is one of the most pungent statements of total depravity, "the wickedness of man was great on the earth, and that every intent of the thoughts of his heart was only evil continually" (Gen. 6:5).

The sovereign God fights chaos with chaos by instituting futility within the created order, as evident in the divine oracles of judgment (Gen. 3:14-19; Rom. 8:20-21). This futility permeates all relationships: 1) intimacy with God breaks down, 2) humans are exhausted in their work now that the ground is cursed, 3) marital relationship exists with tension between woman's quest for liberation[19] and male dominance, 4) there is increased pain in child bearing, 5) there is enmity between human and snake relationships,[20] and 6) snakes are cursed to crawl in the dust. This futility leaves the blessings (be fruitful, multiply, fill the earth, subdue, and rule) intact, but now mingles them with the experiential knowledge[21] of evil, such as increased pain in childbirth and increased effort in accomplishing labor (Gen. 1:28; 3:5; 9:1-7). Likewise, humans still retain the initial tasks such as cultivating the ground but now in a manner that subjects them to futility with thorns and thistles and much labor (Gen. 3:17-19, 23). Even the extreme measures of God's utilizing the waters of chaos to attack the sin-dominated condition of the earth renders the remnant as preserved in blessing and work (Gen. 9:1-7, 20).

One of the most devastating features of this chaos futility is that of death. Soul (*nephesh*) is a synonym to life, so it is chaotic that souls die. God warned Adam that in the day that he would eat from the forbidden fruit he would surely die (Gen. 2:17). God's oracle of judgment speaks of Adam eventually dying and returning to dust (Gen. 3:19). Adam responded to this pronouncement of death as a ray of hope of release from futility and therefore named his wife Eve, the mother of all living (Gen. 3:20). God further barred their way to the tree of life, which had been available before, but now was beyond their reach so that humans would not be caught in the teeth of sin perpetually (Gen. 3:24). This life is a kind

---

[18] Compare the successes of the two genealogies of Genesis 4:17-26. Seth obtains prayer while Cain's line obtains city making, metallurgy, and other distractions.

[19] The word "desire" in Genesis 3:16 should be taken as the near context takes it in Genesis 4:7 "desire to dominate and conquer" rather than the distant context of Song of Songs 7:10 "desire of that husband for his wife."

[20] This prefigures the Israelite experience with the snake attacks of Numbers 21:6. Thus Genesis 3:15 is not a first statement of the gospel for snakes and humans are described here, as developed in note 13. The word for seed (*zera'*) is a collective referring to plural descendents of snakes, and humans (compare with other Genesis *zera'* texts like Gen. 15:3-5).

[21] The tree of the knowledge of good and evil was the test portal through which humans could enter into the experience of curse among the blessing. The second literary unit has three mentions of curse (Gen. 3:14, 17; 4:11) to mirror the three statements of blessing mentioned in the first literary unit (Gen. 1:22, 28; 2:3).

of walking death as well. However, when sin begins to dominate murder ensues (Gen. 4:8, 23). The repeated death knell sounds through out the genealogy of Adam with the phrase "and he died" (Gen.5:5, 8, 11, 14, 17, 27, 31). With sin burgeoning to total depravity all souls are killed in the global flood except those in the ark (Gen. 7:21-23).

Within the increase of chaos, 'Elohîm still provides hope. For example, God's questioning that reveals sin limits the swift plunge toward total depravity. Additionally, Adam took the oracles of judgment to still provide hope as he named his wife Eve (Gen. 3:20). Furthermore, God provided clothes to take care of human nakedness in a manner that did it better than the pathetic cover up of fig leaves (Gen. 3:21).[22] However as sin increases, hope is primarily available for those who have a relationship with this living God. Enoch walking with God, found himself removed from this sinful earth to be translated to be with God (Gen. 5:24). Likewise righteous Noah in his walking with God obtained God's favor to continue God's created earth's souls (human and animals) through God's deliverance via the ark (Gen. 6:9; 8:1). God's covenant with Noah and all life provides hope that no use of the waters of chaos in a global flood will ever come again; God has put this weapon of war down with a promise (Gen. 9:8-17).

'Elohîm has defined Himself intimately through His power to create and rule His creation. Thus God is intimately involved in the narrative of His own creation. However, this narrative is an open one in which God continues to foster life, struggle, hopes, and death.

---

[22] There is no development or teaching evident in this verse about sacrifice or atonement so it is inappropriate to see gospel here. Some of the ways God helps are just very practical, and clothes that last are a generous gift of God.

YAHWEH, The God of the Exodus

Moses hid out in the wilderness burying himself in shepherding and family for forty years until the cry of Israel's bondage rose up to be heard by God. The author in Exodus 2:23-24 is piled up terms of hardship (sighed/bondage/cried out/cry for help/bondage/groaning) to show the rationale for why God will heed Israel's cry in the oppression at that particular moment. Likewise, the hints toward salvation loom large as God heard, and remembered His covenant with Abraham, Isaac, and Jacob. This salvation spun its way into *sight* by repeating different players who *see* in the context, beginning twice with God seeing the condition of Israel (Ex. 2:25 *r'h*). The angel of the Lord[1] appeared (niphal of *r'h*) in burning bush, as a foretaste of the theophanic fire (Ex. 3:2-3; 13:22). The burning bush is quite impressive since it is mentioned five times here. Moses had to turn aside to see (*r'h*) this sight and Yahweh saw (*r'h*) him turn aside to look (Ex. 3:3-4). Engaging in conversation God called out "Moses, Moses." To which Moses replied "Here I am." Out of the holy fire God spoke, "Do not come near here; remove your sandals from your feet, for the place on which you are standing is holy ground." God's very presence rendered the place holy or set apart. God

---

[1] Some argue for the angel of the Lord to be the preincarnate Christ, but in no text in which the angel of the Lord appears is it ever developed in that way. Rather, the angel of the Lord appears in contexts of monotheism like this one in which He is identified as Yahweh the monotheistic God of: Abraham, Isaac, and Jacob (Ex. 2:24; 3:2, 14-15). Reading the N.T. trinitarian ideas into the earlier stages of the progressive revelation of the O.T. eisegetically abuses what the O.T. text is emphasizing; the God of Abraham, Isaac, and Jacob is faithful to rescue His people by beginning the exodus.

identified Himself as the God of Abraham, Isaac, and Jacob, to which Moses responded with further hiding of his face (*pānîm*). God responded that He has seen (*r⁴h* Ex. 3:7,9), heard the face (*pānîm*) of affliction and is aware of the sufferings of Israel under the oppression of Egypt. So, God has come down to deliver the Israelites from the power of the Egyptians, but He will do this through the agency of Moses as representative on the scene to lead Israel out of Egypt to the Promised Land.

Moses' response to this call was that of inadequacy; "Who am I that I should go to Pharaoh to lead Israel out." God's relational response was that He will be *with* Moses, which as a phrase is reminiscent of the religious commitments of Abraham and Joseph (Gen. 21:22; 39:2, 21; Ex. 3:12). A reassuring sign was provided for Moses in the promise that when he has led the people out of Egypt, they will worship God at this very mountain where the burning bush occurs. However, such a sign requires Moses to trust God to be faithful to His word, since the sign was in the rescue of the people.

Then Moses' response was to claim ignorance. That is, in going to the sons of Israel, how shall Moses refer to the God of their fathers? The name of this God as Yahweh is defined by relationships in Exodus 3:14 from the "to be" verb (*'ehᵉyeh*) "I AM WHO I AM," and "I AM has sent me." This verbal name is either the Qal imperfect emphasizing God's presence as the unchanging one who can be counted on as present aid (as in the rescue of Israel from Egypt), or the Hiphil imperfect emphasizing that God will always be there to create and provide what is needed.[2] This memorial name then emphasizes God's presence in very practical ways to meet Moses and Israel's needs, especially in the exodus. This

---

[2] Grammatically, the verb could be either option. There is no development of the aseity or the Greek philosophical concept of eternal existence of God in this verse, rather a much more practical idea is being presented which reflects God's commitment to Moses, Israel, and the divine plan to carry out the exodus. Some also conjecture that this naming of God in Moses' call is the first instance in which the name Yahweh is used, but this is unlikely with Moses mother Jochebed having the name of Yahweh imbedded within her own name (Ex. 6:20). Some others conjecture that this statement in Exodus 3:14 is a refusal to answer Moses, but taken together with verses 15-22 answers Moses quite fully, explaining what Moses now must do.

God is further identified as the God of Abraham, Isaac and Jacob, which shows His continuity with His Abrahamic covenant promise (Gen. 15:13-16) and His compassion at this time (Ex. 2:23-24). That is, while God is a responsive God to the crying needs of Israel in Egypt, the program of their slavery, including the length of time of their slavery, was completely worked out in advance for it to include Moses at this time in this call. So, God admitted that He was indeed concerned about Israel and the oppression that they had to suffer in Egypt (Ex.3:16). This concern motivated the exodus from Egypt for Israel to be gathered into the Promised Land of blessing. This message has different faces to it. To the Jewish elders the whole program was to be developed in a reassuring manner, while to the Pharaoh the partial truth of requesting a retreat to the wilderness for sacrifice and worship was to be the proposal (Exodus 3:16, 18 is parallel to the Genesis 47 request to worship Yahweh). Because of the resistance of which the king of Egypt raised, God struck Egypt with miracles so that Pharaoh would let Israel go. However, Israel's exodus would be so victorious that they would plunder the Egyptians of their goods.

Moses' response to God's promises was to lack faith, though it is put in the ploy of "what if they do not believe me." God's gracious answer in relationship is to begin showing these available miracles such as: Moses' staff turning to a snake, Moses' hand becoming leprous, and Nile river water becoming blood (Ex. 4:2-9). Moses' response to the staff becoming a snake was fear (Ex. 4:3). The Jewish people's response was faith in the promised rescue of God when they saw these miracles (Ex. 4:30-31). Pharaoh's response was rebellion and the demand for more bricks (Ex. 5).

Moses further showed his unbelief by making excuses for himself as inarticulate. This claim needs to be appreciated within a context of Moses having grown up in the court of Pharaoh and the examples throughout Exodus and Numbers where Moses does not seem to have any such heaviness of mouth or tongue. Moses later will whined that he has uncircumcised lips (Ex. 6:12, 30).

God graciously reminded Moses that as creator He is the one Who gives or removes speech, so actually this excuse further calls into question Moses faith in the creator God who is now relating to him with full knowledge of the articulate mouth that He has created for Moses.

At this point, Moses evidences insubordination with his claim, "Please, Lord send the message by another." In this relationship, Yahweh had had enough excuses so out of anger he stopped Moses there with the permission that Aaron could speak on his behalf, but that Moses would still tell Aaron what to say.

Finally Moses responds in obedience and returns to Israel to be the vessel of Yahweh's rescue. As he does so however, he continues to evidence some unbelief in not having circumcised his son as the Abrahamic covenant required (Gen. 17:12-14). It is only on the basis of Moses' wife's fast action that their son was kept alive when Yahweh met them on the way to kill the son. The Lord let the boy live in response to her quick circumcision of the lad.

The function of the plagues has to do with informing Pharaoh, who does not know (Ex. 5:12) so that he might know the unique pervasive power and ownership of Yahweh (Ex. 6:7; 7:5, 17; 8:10, 22; 9:14, 29; 10:2; 11:7; 14:4, 18). Many of the plagues attack different aspects of Egyptian religion, showing it to be impotent compared to the power of Yahweh. For example, the Nile river was thought in Egyptian cosmology to be the blood stream of Osiris as it flowed with water. However, as Yahweh caused the Nile to flow with blood, it is as though Osiris is hemorrhaging from mortal wounds through Yahweh's internal battle within the supposed pantheon of the gods (cf. chart, 'Yahweh's plagues in Egypt' on pages 113-14 in this book). Since Egypt is thought to be at the top of the political heap, so the Egyptian gods are thought to be the most powerful. However, each god is bested in its own domain by the sovereign God Yahweh. This is the consistent practice of Yahweh, showing Himself to be the only sovereign and the only One of ultimate power.

Likewise, when it comes to the conquest the same point is made by Yahweh over the pantheon of the gods of the land. The Canaanite gods were thought to be especially powerful in their own geographic area but the conquest shows them to be impotent as well. Additionally, Baal, the god of fire is known for riding the storm clouds from the Carmel mountain heights but he is unable to bring his own weapon of fire to the very slopes of Carmel as Yahweh did in 1 Kings 18, consuming the whole drenched sacrifice with heavenly fire. So Yahweh shows all other rivals to be impotent.

However, more than the Egyptian religion is polemicized, for the plagues destroy Egypt, rendering its people desirous of paying Israel to go. The plagues are a strong divine curse in the Abrahamic covenant, reciprocating curse as Pharaoh has tried to curse Israel. The plagues are Yahweh's tool to harden Pharaoh's heart and to pulverize Pharaoh into impotence (with the final blow drowning Pharaoh's army in the Red Sea), giving the fledgling Israel a toe-hold in the land. Likewise, the conquest also conquers enough of the land to obtain real control over the hill country. Israel was to be ever-vigilant to take the rest of the land, which finally under David was substantially obtained. Yahweh repeatedly shows Himself to be the only real God of power.

From the standpoint of Yahweh Who is there to provide deliverance for Israel, there is no equal to the sovereign monotheistic God. From this context of exodus and conquest, Yahweh presses His will upon His people Israel as a suzerain in a bestowal of the Mosaic covenant as it is formed in the pattern of an international treaty (Ex. 19-Lev. 27; Dtr.; Josh. 24). The major point of this suzerainty treaty is that Yahweh is declared to be king and Israel is mandated to remain loyal under allegiance to this reigning God.

However, Israel was not often faithful to covenant. In fact, at the very instance that Moses was on Mount Sinai receiving the covenant and tabernacle design to reflect proper worship, the people under the leadership of Aaron had prostrated themselves before a golden calf in idolatrous worship to Yahweh (Ex.

32). Yahweh is so incensed with these rebellious people He told Moses to go down "because your people have become corrupt." In relationship with Israel He shows his anger by not wanting to be in relationship with them. He told Moses "I have seen these people and they are a stiff-necked people. Now leave me alone so that my anger may burn against them and that I may destroy them. Then I will make you into a great nation." This is appropriate wrath on God's part since He has imposed a suzerainty treaty upon Israel with the ramification that if they disobey then covenant curse will come their way. This is a prime instance of Israel's disobedience. Moses sought the favor of Yahweh his God by saying, "O Yahweh why should Your anger burn against Your people, whom You brought out of Egypt with great power and a mighty hand? Why should the Egyptians say, 'It was with evil intent that he brought them out, to kill them in the mountains and to wipe them off the face of the earth'? Turn from your fierce anger; relent and do not bring disaster on your people." Moses is reminding God that the whole issue of Who He is, is at stake in the narrative of how He now responds to His own chosen people. However, the issue goes deeper than this, in that Yahweh is a God of promises, which He has made repeatedly. "Remember Your servants Abraham, Isaac, and Israel (the very one by which the people are named), to whom you swore by your own self: 'I will make your descendants as numerous as the stars in the sky and I will give your descendants all this land. I promised them and it will be their inheritance forever.'" Yahweh has had a deep commitment to accomplish this very exodus. When Yahweh made this oath to which Moses refers, Yahweh identified the very time frame (400 years) and the very generation (the fourth from Abraham) in which He will bring the people into this promised land (Gen. 15:13-16). The angry judgment, which God was inclined to do in suzerain relationship to His rebellious people, is not available to Him because Yahweh has bound Himself by an oath in the Abrahamic covenant. This type of oath normally sees that whoever traveled between the pieces of split animals is bound to keep what He promised or else the fate of the animals, that is death, will be his fate but Yahweh was the only one who went between the pieces (Gen. 15:17-21).[3] Yahweh's existence and character is on the line; will Yahweh be honest and keep His oath? It is a tension between Yahweh's faithfulness to the Abrahamic covenant and the suzerainty treaty, which He is just putting into place. The Abrahamic covenant preserves the national entity to go into the Promised Land at this juncture. The Hebrew *nhm* does not make any comment on the changeability of mind like some English texts do but rather simply that Yahweh repents of the apparent course of action that He had revealed, namely judgment on Israel, as an expression of suzerainty treaty covenant curse. Yahweh repents and does not bring this disaster upon His people as He had threatened. Moses goes down to the people and has the Levites go throughout Israel killing the idolatrous people and then calls the people to repentance. Moses begs Yahweh to forgive their sin. However, Yahweh reminded Moses that "Whoever has sinned against Me, I will blot out of My book." This showed that the suzerainty treaty is still binding Israel to judgment but that Yahweh will find repeated ways of executing this covenant curse which will essentially preserve the nation so as to also realize the Abrahamic covenant blessings as well. Yahweh then again re-commanded Moses to lead Israel to the Promised Land and reassured him that the angel of Yahweh will still go with them. The people repented at this instance but God still executed His plague against them because of what they did at the golden calf. So the tension internal to God and the covenants which He made with His people was satisfied without diminishing either.

The continuing narrative through Exodus, Numbers, Deuteronomy and Joshua shows that Israel eventually did get to the Promised Land and took possession of it. However, narratives (like real life) are often messier than ideal systems of theology. So repeated testings of Yahweh are met by Yahweh through an array of resources to meet   the needs   of Israel and to judge the rebellious

---

[3] In Jeremiah 34:17-19 there is an example of this kind of oath being violated by Israel and they forfeit their lives in covenant curse when the captivity takes place.

people. God provides quail, manna, water from rocks, leprosy, a budding rod, consuming fire, gapping chasm, capital punishment, and victory in battle. Throughout all this narrative Yahweh shows Himself to be deeply committed to the relationship He established with Israel and consistent with His covenants which govern this relationship. That is the nature of narrative; one sees God as He relates, initiates and responds to those whom He is relating to in the narrative. Yahweh, the God of the exodus, brought the people Israel into the Promised Land, showing that He is dominant in accomplishing His plan. It is almost as if it is a unilateral move on God's part, but He shares the journey with Israel through joys and judgments. One of the greatest contributions that narrative theology contributes to theology as a whole is the deep commitment that Yahweh has to relationship with His people. This is also very different to the fickle gods of the ancient Near East who have neither this level of consistency to any people nor any covenant relationship. Yahweh shows Himself as engaged in depth of relationship and faithful to His purposes and commitments. Yahweh is king. He accomplishes His will, and He does so in relationship with His people.

Yahweh's Plagues in Egypt

The plagues show Yahweh so that pharaoh might know the pervasive power and ownership of Yahweh (Ex. 6:7; 7:5, 17; 8:10, 22; 9:14, 16, 29; 10:2; 11:7; 14:4, 18).

Text	Plague	Egyptian God's Polemized	Effect	Pharaoh
7:14-25	Nile & Water to Blood	Khnum-guardian of Nile sources Hapi-spirit of Nile & bringer of fertility Osiris-god of underworld, Nile was his bloodstream	Stench & Can't Drink	Heart Was Hardened
8:1-15	Frogs Overrun	Hele/qet- a frog goddess of fruitfulness and wife of: Khnum-symbol of resurrection and fertility	Repulsively Overrun & Death Stench	Remove Them and Go; He Hardened His Heart
8:16-19	Great Swarms	Kheper [a]-in form of beetle he symbolizes daily cycle of sun, Magicians are impotent to reproduce	Annoyance	Heart Was Hardened
8:20-32	Fly Swarms	Uatchit manifested self by Ichreumen fly depositing egg on living so larvae could feed	LXX: Blood Sucking Godfly, Egyptians Wasted, Israel Untouched	Remove Them and Go; He Hardened His Heart
9:1-7	Animal Plague	Ptah accociated with Memphis, had an Apis bull as a sacred animal Hathar-goddess of Joy (with cow ears) Khnum-Ram god Amon- king of gods and parton of Pharaoh's with ram's head or ram with crown Geb-god of earth, pictured as or with a goose. Isis-queen of gods (with ram or cow's horns)	All Egyptian Livestock Die, Crippling Transportation, Agriculture and Worship; Israel Exempt	Heart Was Hardened

Yahweh's Plagues in Egypt

The plagues show Yahweh so that pharaoh might know the pervasive power and ownership of Yahweh (Ex. 6:7; 7:5, 17; 8:10, 22; 9:14, 16, 29; 10:2; 11:7; 14:4, 18).

Text	Plague	Egyptian God's Polemized	Effect	Pharaoh
9:8-12	Boils On Man & Beast	Sekhmet-lion headed goddess had power to bring epidemics to an end Serapis-god of healing Imhotep-god of medicine Magicians were impotent to stand before Moses	Incredible Pain	Heart Was Hardened
9:13-35	Killing Hail & Fire	Nut-sky goddess	Men & Beast in Field Died; Israel Exempt	Repentance Until Plague Was Lifted, Then Heart Was Hardened
10:1-20	Locust	Feared locust god Serapia-protector from locusts	Ruined Egypt & Crops	Rebellion; Heart Was Hardened
10:21-29	Darkness (Khamsin Sandstorm from Wind?)	Re-sun god and king of gods Nut - sky goddess and protectress of the dead	All Commerce Stopped; Israel Exempt	Repentance Heart Was Hardened
11:1-11 and 12:29-36	Death of First Born	Osiris-king of gods Re-sun god, both foster life and retain the dead in their kingdom Possibly Taurt-goddes of maternity and protective household deity	Despoiling Egyptians of Silver & Gold; Grief & Loss of lives; Israel Exempt Through Passover	Heart Was Hardened But Broken Pharaoh Sends Israel Out of Egypt

Psalm 139: A Hymn and Lament to the Omniscient and Omnipresent God

Psalm 139 is one of the clearest and boldest Biblical texts addressing the omniscience and omnipresence of God with implications to God's sovereignty and our prayer. W. A. Shelton calls it "one of the grandest psalms in the entire collection, if not, indeed the best of them all," and says of it, "Its tone is high, and its conception of the personal and highly spiritual nature of God rises to glorious heights...It is the O.T.'s highest conception of the relationship of God to the individual soul."[1] Every aspect of life is known by and controlled by God from David's procreation to any attempt to escape Him, so David affirms his hatred of God's enemies and calls upon God to prove his loyalty. As with most psalms the development is rather generic, encouraging anyone who finds herself in a similar situation to David to pray and own this psalm as her own as well. It is so wonderful to pray our theology and to see its deep personal implications with God so deeply involved in our lives.

The psalm begins and ends with an enclusio that echos with a repetition of the same words (vv. 1-3, 23-24). These repeated verbs are search (ḥāqar), know (yādaʿ), way (derek), and purposes or anxious thoughts (rēaʿ in vv. 2 and 17, and synonym śarʿappāy in v. 23). At the start of the psalm this divine knowledge

---

[1] W. A. Shelton, "Psalms LXXIII-CL," in *The Abingdon Bible Commentary*, ed. F. C. Eiselen, E. Lewis, and D. G. Downey (Nashville: Abingdon Press, 1929), p. 595.

becomes the basis of God's control but by the end of the psalm these sentiments become reassuring requests in prayer.

In verses 1-6 David expresses that God knows all about him.   In synonymous parallelism God searches me (*ḥăqartanî*) with words used elsewhere of spying out the land, prospecting and legal investigation (Deut. 13:15; Judg. 18:2; Job 28:3). The Lord's knowledge of David is as though He has completed an thorough investigation of His servant. Using the figure of merism of opposites for sitting and rising, and travelling and resting, God is acclaimed to know all about David (vv. 2-3). The discernment of the Lord is communicated through the verb of winnow (*zērîtā*). This winnowing or sifting of David's thoughts and intents is either from afar as a spatial metaphor or from before as in prescience "long ago."[2] Either way we take that metaphor, David clearly states that God knows it all (thoughts, intents, acts, and character) before David would speak (v. 4) so God is not limited to an open future but penetrates to know the future in advance. The process of the Lord's knowledge is painstakingly sifting, which results in the Lord's being intimately acquainted with all my ways. David further emphasizes the comprehensiveness of God's knowledge through the phrase "all my ways" which is a common metaphor for a person's actions, undertakings and moral behavior.

This form of knowledge is overpowering and involves control for David's life (vv. 5-6).[3] With this knowledge the Lord has surrounded (*ṣartani*) David, as evident in its root which is elsewhere used of besieging a city (e.g. 2 Chron. 20:1). This control of God's knowledge is further developed as "You put Your hand on me," which as a phrase is only elsewhere in the Biblical text in Job 9:33 where it refers to Job's desire for someone to exercise authority over both himself and God so that he would gain an impartial hearing. So both metaphors express in synonymous parallelism that God's knowledge controls him. David reflects that

---

[2] B.D.B., s.v. *rahoq* 2.b., p. 935 and compare Isa. 22:11.

such knowledge is overpowering in its control, beyond his abilities (*pil'iyyāh...mimmenî*), rather than merely incomprehensible.[4]   With the issue being that of control, David admits that he cannot prevail against it (*lō' 'ûkal lāh*) and it is insuperable (*nisg^ebāh*) as with impregnable walls of a fortress. With God being all knowing and controlling, there is no escape from this omnipresent God.

In verses 7-12 David develops that God is present everywhere so that he cannot hide from God. In synonymous parallelism David announces his theme of hiding from God's presence or face. This theme is developed over the next three verses to indicate that there is no place to escape. Using merism, David considers God as present in heaven where the throne room of God is normally thought to occupy, but also even in the opposite deep pit of the land of the dead where God is not normally thought to be, God is there as well. Likewise to travel from East to West as fast as the dawn travels will still not let David escape from God. As with God's penetrating sheol the place of the dead, so the depth of the sea is associated in Hebrew thought forms with chaos, which are normally seen as beyond God's presence, but even there God is present and controlling. God's control is evident in "Even there thy hand will guide me and Thy right hand will lay hold of me" (v. 10). Whether David contemplates the darkened environment of sheol or the chaotic environment of the depth of the sea or the oppression of evil in this life, he considers that light is as darkness and darkness is a heavy weight crushing him. Even this darkness would not prove too dark for the Lord, Who penetrates it and sees through the darkness as if there is no barrier or fog at all.

The Lord knows everything about David and controls him with this knowledge. David cannot escape God's controlling Knowledge even in the chaos

---

[3] The openness commitment to libertarian free will and the denial of prescience is grounded in a commitment to reject the kind of control that God's knowledge of the future brings, however an openness God does not fit this Biblical text with its divine controlling knowledge..

[4] B.D.B., s.v. *pālā'* p. 810 and compare Jer. 32:17; and Gen. 18:14, while reading *kethib* as in Judges 13:18.

and depth of suffering in this life, because David can conjecture no place of escape in which God would not also be as well. However, God exercises even greater control than this in His creating and planning of David's whole life. This is evident by verse 13 beginning with the conjunction *ki,* which should best be taken in a causal way. That is, because David has been created and had his life planned by God, David is even more under God's control from which he cannot escape.

God intimately created and determined David's life (vv. 13-16). God created (*qānîtā*) David's inward parts. Actually, the word for inward parts refers to kidneys but in Hebrew thought this word describes the highly sensitive organ of self-thought. The less visible is being emphasized with the inner parts of David being created within his mother's womb.[5] The womb environment is compared to sheol as being hidden from view, except from God Who can see clearly into this secret place. In such an intimate secret place God sees our embryonic nature, our bones and our inner parts; so as a craftsman God is perfectly equipped to form us. God is personally involved as a craftsman weaving (*tᵉsukkēnî*) in meticulous fashion the tapestry that is David. The verb skillfully wrought (*ruqqamtî* in v. 15c) is parallel to this weaving idea.[6] H. W. Wolff concludes that "everything that grew in his mother's womb is the work of the great weaver (*skk*); skin and muscles are seen as the fabric."[7]

Beyond the intimate sight of David in the time of his being created, God compared it with a previous written plan for all the days of his life. There are several other references to a book of God in the Old Testament and in ancient Near Eastern literature akin to a tablet of destiny.[8] This figure refers to

---

[5] The fact that David's mother's womb is involved, and other texts present the origination of David's life in the sex act (Ps. 51:5) shows some measure of human cooperation along with the divine creation process.

[6] For similar meaning compare its use in Job 10:11

[7] H. W. Wolff, *Anthropology of the Old Testament*, p. 96.

[8] For O. T. references compare these examples: Isa. 4:3; Ezek. 2:9-10; Dan. 12:1. For ancient Near Eastern examples and discussion, see H. Ringgren, *Religions of the Ancient Near East*, trans. J. Sturdy (Philadelphia: Westminster Press, 1973), pp. 108-9.

foreordination of his whole life before he had even begun to live any of it. The future is not open if God knows it so intimately that he has planned it and then created David to fit within these complete plans of David's days. There is some possible ambiguity in the antecedent of the pronouns (kullām) "all of them" and (bāhem) "among them." If the pronouns refer to the embryo then David is affirming that the Lord blueprinted or foreordained the development of his embryo in the womb with a full plan for David's life. If the pronoun is to be understood proleptically to refer to "days" then David is affirming the foreordination of the days of his life, that is, either how long he would live (cf. Job 14:5) or by metonymy what would happen during the course of his life (cf. Jer. 1:5). Either way, the future is not open, for God has planned at least a few things concerning David but it may include everything. Thus, the reason David can affirm that the Lord knows his every thought, word, and deed is that He knows them beforehand (vv. 1-4, 16). The reason that he cannot escape from the knowledge and consequent control of God is that the Lord has formed his life and foreordained the course of his life. Likewise, the reason that David responds with such awe about the Lord's thought and purposes (vv. 17–18) is that it proves how precious and constant are the Lord's thoughts about him.

It is God's thoughts and purposes concerning David that are by the huge volume and intimacy amazing to David, so he expresses his awe to the Lord (vv. 17-18). When he awakes, probably from meditation[9] God is still intimately with David in presence and in knowledge. This anecdotal awareness of God's sovereignty, omnipresence, omniscience, and imminence raises the issue as to how David will respond. David's response is that of loyalty to God in prayer in light of these divine attributes

David exhibits his loyalty by opposing God's enemies and submitting to a divine search that will lead to everlasting life. The petitionary response first

---

[9] While there are other views about awakening in resurrection or from sleep induced from counting all these divine thoughts, I think awakening from contemplation fits best, e.g. M. Buttenweiser, *The Psalms*, pp. 537-40 and compare Jer. 31:26.

negatively asks God to slay the wicked, especially those who surround David in his dark times (vv. 19-22). Such a petition ushers into a warning for these murderous men to depart from David's context. David explains his rationale for this petition on the basis that these violent lawbreakers are ultimately against God as His enemies and that part of David's loyalty is to hate those who hate God. David's animosity towards God's enemies is seen in the backdrop of a kind of holy war that stays loyal to God's cause even if it should cost opposing the lawbreakers. From the response of repudiating the enemies of God, David now turns to a positive petition for God to undertake a search of David's motive and ways for the outcome of everlasting life (vv. 23-24). This positive petition ends the enclusio with which the psalm began and thus completes the exploration of God's omniscience by asking God to turn His exhaustive knowledge back on David as a tool for God to rehabilitate David in God's ways. David's anxious thoughts refer back to the thoughts and motive that God already knows (vv. 2, 23). The trying of David's anxious thoughts is as in testing and purifying metals, is an expression on David's part to not have any lack of complete loyalty to God. An example, which David petitions to be rooted out of his life is any association with the way of pain, perhaps toward others or a way that might bring pain back upon David as a divine discipline. In contrast David wishes to be led by God into the everlasting way or the longstanding way of blessing.[10]

In summary, having repudiated the enemies of God (vv. 19-22), David asks God, Who knows him thoroughly (vv. 1-4) because He created him (vv. 13-16), and from Whose knowledge there is no escape (vv. 7-12), to examine his motives and thoughts to keep him from deviating from the ancient path of favor and blessing (v. 23-24).

---

[10] The concept of everlasting is often seen as the age-old path (e.g. Jer. 6:16; 18:15). At this point it would tend to contribute to the psalm as communicating the proven age-old way of blessing. At this point in the stages of progressive revelation it is better not to see this as a reference to the fuller N.T. concept of everlasting life, which in the N.T. will include resurrection from the grave.

Incomparable Yahweh

The prophet Isaiah develops God as King. Yahweh is explicitly demonstrated to be king through the words *adon* and *melek*. The word *adon* is built off *adhan* and *adhath*, onomatopoetic words for father and mother.[1] The word is mainly used of earthly lords in the O.T. but at times it is used of God "to emphasize Yahweh's rule over all the world."[2] When *adoni* is used it is a distinctive title for God, meaning Lord over all.[3] Parallel to this usage is the epithet *melek*, which was used frequently of Yahweh as the One who reigns. The term is often used of Yahweh's reign over Israel reflective of their covenant relationship (Isa. 8:21; 33:22; 41:22; 43:15; 44:6). The verb is employed in an eschatological sense when God rules during the Kingdom age (Isa. 24:23; 52:7). In contrast to the earthly kings who die in their temporality, *adoni* continues as the everlasting king over all (Isa. 6:1, 5). In fact, the concept of God's holiness (*qadosh*) in Isaiah has to do with His being set apart to this distinct category of everlasting transcendent king.[4] In the vision Isaiah spends few words to describe God except to focus on His distinctive regal glory. When Isaiah sees this vision

---

[1] Eissfeldt, *adhon; adhonai*, TDOT, p. 59; cf. Ugaritic texts CTA, 23 [SS] and 24 [NK].
[2] Ibid, p. 61-62.
[3] Ibid, p. 63, 72; cf. Th. C. Vrizen, "Essentials of the Theology of Isaiah," *Israel's Prophetic Heritage*, p. 132. The suffix is an honorific or intensive plural of rank which strengthens the meaning of the root. Kenneth Barker, "Lord," *Wycliffe Bible Encyclopaedia*, p. 1048.
[4] Unlike Rudolf Otto *The Idea of the Holy* (pp. 6, 25), who develops the concept of "Wholly Other" as a negative idea of what man is not, holiness is better understood as a positive concept of separate to whatever is being emphasized in the context. In Isaiah six God's holiness is His everlasting transcendent kingship.

and hears the glowing ones (*serāphĭm*) call out God's holiness, Isaiah recoils in terror of his sin. Such fear and reverence is the proper response when confronted with the transcendence of Yahweh (Isa. 6:2-3, 5; 8:13). Yahweh's holiness is then communicated through the glowing coal by the glowing one who carries it to Isaiah to touch his lips and make Isaiah appropriate to carry the message of judgment.

The ancient Near Eastern concept of king included six major functions of which Yahweh fulfills them all. In the ancient Near East, the king was a mediator, representing the gods to the people, and a priest representing the people before the gods.[5] The people viewed the king as the "deputy of the supreme god," and for the Hittites and Egyptians the king upon death became a god.[6] The king maintained justice as judge and thus spoke the law as the absolute, the sovereign lord in his empire.[7] He was the commander-in-chief of the military in his role as warrior.[8] As shepherd he tended his people providing protection, provision, and guidance. He also maintained well-being and harmony in society and nature. In Israel the king provided all these roles except that of priest. Yahweh provides all these functions as king overall. Yahweh, Himself, as Israel's king, represents the divine will to the people primarily through the established covenant relationship and specific prophecies which remind them of their obligations and blessings. Yahweh is in covenant relationship with Israel and responds as their king and judge with covenant lawsuit (*rĭb*) concerning their sin (Isa. 1-39).[9] "Yahweh takes his place in court; He rises to judge the people. Yahweh enters into

---

[5] Kenneth Barker, "The Office and Functions of Ancient Kingship."

[6] H.G. Guterbock, "Authority and Law in the Hittite Kingdom," *Authority and Law in the Ancient Orient, Supplement to Journal of the American Oriental Society,* no. 17:23; Albrecht Goetze, *Kleinasien* in *Handbuch der Altertumswissenschaft,* 3:95.

[7] Viktor Korosec, *Hethitische Staatsvertrage* in *Leipzige rechtswissenschaftliche Studien,*60, p. 51.

[8] Goetze, p. 86; Korosec, p. 51.

[9] For a description of the patterns of covenant lawsuit see: Herbert B. Huffman, "The Covenant Lawsuit in the Prophets," *JBL,* 78:285-6; Kristen Nielson, *Yahweh as Prosecutor and Judge,* pp. 15-17, 27-32, 62-83; James Limberg, "The Root *rib* and the prophetic Lawsuit Speeches," *JBL,* 88:297, 301; Charles Fensham, "Common Trends in Curses of the Near Eastern

judgment against the elders and leaders of His people"(Isa. 3:13-14). As divine warrior God carries out this sentence of judgment. The title Yahweh Sabaoth reflects the militancy of God as warrior leader of the armies of Israel, angels, and the whole creation (Isa. 48:2; 51:15).[10] The term *sabaoth* is from the form meaning "soldier or army" and "characterizes God as the Lord who makes all things possible. What appears to men as totally improbably and impossible he can do at any time, as Lord of all things."[11] Yahweh is also the Great Shepherd over Israel and the nations enabling His people to hope for a new exodus of regathering them from dispersion into the land, to pasture them safely and even enable them to lie down relaxed knowing that they are protected from any wild beast (Isa. 14:30; 34:6; 40:11; 49:9-10; 63:11).[12] Compared to Yahweh the other kings in Isaiah are impotent and fleeting, for the only successful kings in Isaiah are Yahweh and His anointed.

C. J. Labuschagne develops the incomparability of Yahweh as of supreme importance especially with those qualities that distinguish Yahweh from other god concepts.[13] Incomparability is a polemic theme and an affirmation of loyalty in ancient Near Eastern documents, but no section has so prolonged a development and depth of polemic for the incomparability of Yahweh as the section of Isaiah 40-48.

Yahweh is the living and true God (Isa. 37:4, 17; 57:15). Yahweh repeatedly says through the prophet, "I am Yahweh, there is none else, there is no God beside me" (Isa. 45:5-6, 14, 18, 21; 44:6-8; 46:9). This stress on monotheism contributes to the incomparability theme in that there are no other existing Gods, nor does Yahweh have an equal. For example, idols cannot be

---

Treaties and Kudurru- Inscriptions Compared with Maledictions of Amos and Isaiah," *ZAW*, 75: 155-75.

[10] J. P. Ross, "Jahweh Seba'ot in Samuel and Psalms" *Vetus Testamentum,* 17:76.

[11] Otto Kaiser, *Isaiah 1–12* (Philadelphia: The Westminster Press, 1972), p. 41.

[12] Walter Eichrodt, *Theology of the Old Testament* (Philadelphia: The Westminster Press, 1961) I: 236-7; also L. Durr, *Ursrug und Aushau der isr.-jud.,* p. 406.

[13] C. J. Labuschagne, *The Incomparability of Yahweh in the Old Testament* (Leiden: E. J. Brill, 1966).

favorably compared to Yahweh for they are the work of men's hands and thus
totally dependent upon men for their existence and form (Isa. 40:18-20; 44:9-20).

> Yahweh cannot be portrayed by an idol or by any likeness in the
> creation which he has made (40:18ff.). Yahweh is Lord over the
> gods who are being represented in various forms (40:19-20). For
> this reason he is incomparable.   The worthlessness of the
> Babylonian gods is shown by the fact that they can be reproduced
> in various forms (40:25).[14]

The idols come from common trees, which serve as the source for firewood (Isa.
44:14-20). These idols are of no significance.

> Isaiah has a sarcastic term for naming the idols, 'elihim; this,
> though not of the same terminology as el, yet reminds of it, but
> by making out of the word a diminutive, represents the pagan gods
> as 'godlets,' or (etymologically taken) as 'good-for nothing-ones.'
> The false god fails to measure up to the conception of full deity
> (2:8, 18, 20; 10:10ff.; 19:1, 3; 31:7).[15]

In this same vein, Yahweh calls the idol worshippers before Him in judgment
(Isa. 41:21-24). In His accusation He demonstrates they are unable to do that
which is characteristic of deity.   Then He further demonstrates that they are
unable to do any thing at all: "Do something, whether good or bad" (Isa. 41:23).
To which Yahweh concludes that these false gods are nothings; they do not exist.
They cannot accomplish anything. "But you are less than nothing and your works
are utterly worthless. He who chooses you is detestable" (Isa. 41:24). From this
basis the idol worshippers should be ashamed. Those who make idols are nothing
(Isa. 44:9). They are ignorant, with blinded eyes and a deluded heart (Isa. 44:18-
20).

Yahweh is incomparable in that while idols are time-bound, Yahweh is far
superior, being beyond time and everlasting with time. Yahweh is the first and

---

[14] Joseph Mihelic, 'The Concept of God in Deutero-Isaih,'*Biblical Research,* 11:36.
[15] Geerhardus Vos, *Biblical Theology, Old and New Testaments* (Grand Rapids: ₹
Eerdmans, 1948), p. 236.

the last, before Whom no being was formed and after whom nothing will exist (Isa. 40:28; 41:4; 43:10ff.; 44:6;48:12). When this is coupled with His consistent intervention in history it leads to a concept of immutability of His nature.[16] "What is expressed here is not the permanence of an always existent divine being, but the contrast between god and history in its totality ('and with the last I am still he')."[17] This contrast includes a strong polemic against all other gods who are temporal. The merism (first and last) declares that Yahweh is the only God Who is from everlasting to everlasting (Isa. 43:10). In contrast, in Mesopotamia, Egypt, and Canaan, the gods grew old and younger ones came along and replaced them. There is no hint of this concerning Yahweh in Isaiah. These declarations of Yahweh's transcendence over the world and time provided a basis for comfort within Judah's captivity.

> Men only learned to value Yahweh as the eternal, immortal God, when they had brought home to them in the most painful manner the transience of the nation, an experience which caused many to question even the living power of the national God. During the Exile, therefore, there are frequent references to the eternal God, whom the stars obey, and before whom this fleeting world cannot but tremble (40:28; cf. 60:19); to the everlasting King, who puts the false gods to shame; to the eternal Governor, exalted over the world and time (26:4). With this intense emphasis on the transcendence of God eternity was also naturally included within his attributes.[18]

Christopher North even defends that Yahweh is contemporary with all history.[19] For the Hebrew, history had a beginning in creation and it would have a consummation. Yahweh stands apart from this in a different dimension, which allows Him to extend beyond the bounds of time and exist during time. That is, Yahweh's involvement with time is not the same as the concept of time, which

---

[16] Eichrodt, I: 192.
[17] Claus Westerman, *Isaiah 40-66* (Philadelphia: The Westminster Press, 1969), p. 65.
[18] Eichrodt, I: 183.
[19] Christopher North, *The Second Isaiah* (Oxford: The Clarendon Press, 1964), pp. 180-81.

people possess. Isaiah uses mixed tenses, which seem to imply that the past, present, and future are all present to Yahweh. North explores this concept with passages such as Isaiah 48:4-5 which says, "I *knew* how stubborn you *are*" and "therefore I told you long ago," before the nation existed. No eternality of Yahweh is worked out in detail but there are a few hints in that direction as an advance over the everlastingness of Yahweh. Yahweh is contemporary with all history. "Ever since anything came to pass, there am I" (Isaiah 41:4; 48:16).

Yahweh is also the creator in ways that show His incomparable superiority. For example, Babylon had gods associated with sun (*Shamash*), moon (*Sin*) and all planets and stars were identified with named deities who governed different aspects of life, be it: national, royal, natural or daily life. In this polemical challenge Yahweh alone creates all of these heavenly objects which had been taken to symbolize Babylon's pantheon (Isa. 42:5; 44:24; 48:12-13; Ps. 89:11-13). Then Isaiah develops Yahweh's sovereignty over them in leading them forth, naming them and bestowing on them His vigor and strength, which leaves no star lacking (Isa. 40:25-26; Ps. 147:4). Isaiah is bold in affirming that the God of the captive people "created" the stars, whom their captors worshipped as gods. Yahweh is alone as creator of heaven, earth, and man (Isa. 27:11; 40:28; 44:24). This means that He is sovereign as the potter is for the potsherd and as parents are for their baby (Isa. 45:9-10). Thus Yahweh is in absolute control of all things (Isa. 45:5-13); there is no other god.

Yahweh as creator serves to identify that Yahweh is the one who intervenes in history (Isa. 40:25-31; 45:7-25; 48:12-3). "Yahweh is great, and that our Lord is above all gods. Whatever Yahweh pleases He does, in heaven and earth" (Ps 135:5-6). Only One with supreme creative power could comprehensibly direct the events of history and overcome all obstacles placed in the way of the salvation of His people. Isaiah, more than any other prophet, has a comprehensive conception of God's activity in the whole history of Israel. Yahweh's incomparable greatness over the rulers of the earth is evident in His transcendent throne being above the heavens in contrast to the temporary reign of earthly rulers (Isa. 40:21-24). He uses these earthly rulers, such as Cyrus, to accomplish His purpose because He is the creator of all and none can oppose Him (Isa. 45:11-13; 51:12-16; 52:1-6). Yahweh is the only God and thus creates light and darkness, prosperity and disaster; there is no room for a dualism or a supposed rival (Isa. 45:5-6). In Yahweh's victory over the nations His supremacy in history is evident. "If the impotence and untrustworthiness of Egypt had been demonstrated in this crisis and the might of Assyria had been humiliated before the power of Yahweh, then there was no other god who could vie with him or pretend to share his supremacy."[20] Yahweh is He who intervenes in history showing Himself as the only supreme being; all gods are impotent. Labuschagne writes concerning Isaiah 46.

> It is interesting to note that the prophet regarded as the primary difference between Yahweh and the idols, the fact, that Yahweh actively carries and saves (verse 4), while the idols have to be carried 'as burdens on weary beasts' (verses 1 and 7), unable to save (verse 7; cf. 45:20), unable to move from their place (verse 7).[21]

In fact, Babylon's idols cannot save themselves from captivity (Isa. 46:1-2). Yahweh the sustainer of Israel shall rescue it in the end (Isa. 46:3-4). The idols cannot act but Yahweh does what He pleases (Isa. 46:5-11).

Yahweh not only controls history as it happens, He fulfills it before it occurs through His prophetic pronouncements. In Judaism a prophet had to have complete accuracy of his prophecy or he could be considered presumptuous and thus be stoned (Deut. 18:17-22). This ability and requirement of complete accuracy leaves Yahweh as the only One who can predict the future accurately, even with details. Yahweh is thus supreme such that no one and nothing can be

---

[20] John Mauchlie, *Isaiah 1-39*, p.39.
[21] Labuschagne, p. 112.

favorably compared with Him.   Labuschagne develops this in commenting on
Isaiah 49:9.

> Yahweh proclaims His incomparability: 'I am God, and there is
> none like me, declaring the end from the beginning and from
> ancient times things not yet done.' For Deutero-Isaiah this quality
> of Yahweh affords clear proof that He is utterly distinct from the
> gods and that He is the only true God (cf. also 44:6 and 41:23).
> Yahweh's ability to declare the future, which Deutero-Isaiah
> associates with His incomparability (cf. also Jer. 10:7), is
> consequent upon the fact that He has revealed Himself as the all-
> wise Controller of history. Yahweh not only regulates human
> history, but also determines what is yet to be. Here we meet the
> idea of Yahweh's intervention in history carried to its ultimate
> conclusions, the most outstanding attribute of the incomparable
> God spanning past, present and future.[22]

Yahweh is the vocal God in contrast to the dumb idols. Yahweh makes prophecy
that is fulfilled both in the book and now in the historical record (Isa. 46:9-10).
Kenneth Barker explains that Yahweh's sovereignty is the dynamic reason why
Yahweh can declare His incomparability, "since Yahweh's rule extends into the
future-indeed, he reigns forever-he can predict what will happen (41:4; 43:10;
44:6-8; 45:21-22; 46:9-10)."[23]   Yahweh puts the idols on trial and challenges
them to produce fulfilled prophecy. The conclusion is that they are silent, unable
to speak, let alone predict. Those gods are false (Isa. 41:26, 28-29). Yahweh next
takes up His own challenge (41:8-9).

> I am Yahweh; that is my name!
> I will not give my glory to another or my praise to idols.
> See, the former things have taken place, and new things I declare;
> Before they spring into being I announce them to you.

The background for Yahweh's boldness is the fulfillment of the intricate prophecy
throughout the book.   For one example, Yahweh demonstrates His

---

[22] Labuschagne, p. 114.

incomparability and supremacy by declaring that He will raise a king from the East named Cyrus, who will liberate His people Israel from the Babylonians (Isa. 41:2-4; 45:1ff.). Presumably, Yahweh uses Cyrus' free agency to choose to reestablish Israel as well as His own sovereign choice. This occurred in 539 B. C. with the conquering of Babylon by Cyrus (king of the Medes and Persians). No other person could foretell the coming of Cyrus; only Yahweh was able to foretell his coming and make his victorious conquest of the nations possible. This predictive accuracy continues in Jesus' ministry as well. While Peter is protesting that he will if necessary die with Christ, Jesus predicts that Peter will deny Him three times before a cock will crow that very night (Jn. 13:37-38; 18:15-18, 25-27). Again presumably, Peter freely chose to deny Jesus, then to repent in grief, which enabled Jesus to recover him graciously for ministry (Mt. 26:69–75; perhaps Jn. 21:15-9 three questions paralleling the three denials).

The prophet's role as the "called" (nābî) by Yahweh is to speak for Him. The malāk are the messengers of God. They are officers of the heavenly court sent by Yahweh to tell His people the message in the same way as a Near Eastern royal messenger would.[24] Since Isaiah received the message from God it was expounded with divine authority. Usually the message is quite clear and is communicated to the audience who need to repent. At times signs and reliable witnesses to signed documents are used to help confirm the certainty of the prophecy as unforgeable and thus increase the faith of those who hear the prophecy. When the prophecy did not go to the group described within the prophecy (such as Isaiah's prophecy against Assyria or Babylon) then the prophecy is as good as accomplished when its time will come. In such conditions judgment is certain. However, if the word of Yahweh is given directly to the person to be judged this may imply that a prophecy is conditional upon their response. For example, Isaiah tells sick Hezekiah, "Thus says Yahweh, set your

---

[23] Kenneth Barker, "Toward a Theology of Satan," p. 8.
[24] John Holladay, "Assyrian Statecraft and the Prophets of Israel," *Harvard Theological Review* 63:31.

house in order for you shall die and not live" (Isa. 38:1). Yet when Hezekiah
turned his face to the wall and prayed to Yahweh reminding Yahweh of his
faithfulness and weeping bitterly, Isaiah was sent back to inform Hezekiah, "Thus
says Yahweh, I have heard your prayer, I have seen your tears; behold I will add
fifteen years to your life" (Isa. 38:4-5). That is what seemed unconditional as a
prophecy because it went to the person who could repent and deal with it, actually
had an implied condition within it as the word from Yahweh. This is not alone
since other examples such as Jonah's prophecy also show its conditional nature
when the Ninevites repent upon hearing of the impending judgment and the forty
days pass without God bringing the judgment upon them (Jonah 3:4-10).
However, much of the prophecy in Isaiah comes with the proviso that Israel will
not be turned back (Isa. 6:9-13). That is, though Isaiah had earlier offered
redemption for his people they were unresponsive and finally went over the line
of certain captivity. The Isaiah six vision is changing the openness to heal to the
certainty to judge. The prophecy that comes to Israel thereafter comes with
certain judgment, thus without any condition. The prophecy that is proclaimed
against the other nations, such as Babylon, gives no evidence of the other nations'
having received these messages, so that they stand as unconditional prophecies
from Yahweh.

Many would see that the concept of the divine word has empowerment
inherent in the word. One of this author's professors, Isaac Rabinowitz, explained
this view from Isaiah 55:10-11.

> The author of these verses obviously believed that the "word of the
> Lord" -- a phenomenon, be it noted, comparable in palpability to
> rain or snow -- was such that, once introduced ("sent") into the
> world, it had the capacity of acting to fulfill itself at some
> subsequent time, to make its communicative or expressive
> signification 'come true' as accomplished fact.[25]

---

[25] Isaac Rabinowitz, *Toward a Valid Theory of Biblical Hebrew Literature*, p. 319; also:
John Mckenzie, 'The Word of God in the Old Testament,' *Theological Studies*, 21:183-206;
Wesley Fuerst, ' The Word of God in the Old Testament,' *The Lutheran Quartely*, 10:316; O.
Grether, *Name und Wort Gottes im Alten Testament*, pp.103-7 describes the Word of God as a

In this view the Word of God is power laden, which irresistibly achieves its end. Such an empowered word is common among Israel's neighbors as well. For example Marduk proves his kingship in heaven by speaking a word of power which annihilates a robe and then recreates it.[26] Additionally, in a hymn to the moon-god Sin, it is said "When thy word settles down on the earth, green vegetation is produced ...The word makes fat the sheepfold...The word causes truth and justice to be."[27] Likewise, an Egyptian hymn speaks of *Amon Re-Atum-Har-Ashti,* who spoke with his mouth and there came into existence all men, gods, and animals.[28] Isaiah has similar speech concerning the power of Yahweh's word as a polemic against the silence of the idols and false gods (Isa. 41:17-29; 42:9; 44: 6–8; 45:4). Yahweh pronounces weighty declarations of judgment against nations (Isa. 13:1; 14:28; 15:1; 17:1; 19:1; 21:1, 11, 13; 22:1; 23:1). These words of judgment overtake the group Yahweh addressed (Deut. 28:15; Isa. 9:8; Zech. 1:5-6). This is similar to Yahweh striking the earth, setting it ablaze, and slaying the wicked with His breath (Isa. 11:4; 30:33). What Yahweh says will be fulfilled because His purpose of destruction or deliverance is revealed through His speech (Isa. 1:19-20; 21:16-17; 24:3; 25:8; 40:5; 44:24-28; 58:14) and He does not take back His word (Isa. 31:2). Likewise the sure word of divine promise (particularly about Yahweh's coming to deliver and restore His beleaguered people) will endure forever to be fulfilled (Isa. 40:6-8). In Isaiah the word is not an actual essence in itself but finds its effectiveness in the powerful will of God for which it

---

missle with a time fuse; Walther Eichrodt, *Theology of the Old Testament* (Philodelphia: The Westminster Press, 1967) vol. 2, p. 69 insists that words, once spoken, remain effective or even dangerous "for a long time, like a long-forgotten mine in the sea, or a grenade buried in a ploughed field," E. Jacob, *Theology of the Old Testament,* p. 127 speaks of it as a "projectile shot into the enemy camp whose explosion must sometimes be awaited but which is always inevitable;" O. Procksch, " The Word of God in the Old Testament," within G. Kittle, *Theological Dictionary of the New Testament,* 4:93; Walter Roehrs, "The Theology of the Word of God in the Old Testament," *Concordia Theological Monthly,* 32: 264; a helpful summary of these views is surveyed by Anthony Thiselton, "The Supposed Power of Words in the Biblical Writings," *Journal of Theological Studies,* 25:283.

[26] *Enuma elish,* iv. 22-26.

[27] J. B. Pritchard, ed., *Ancient Near Eastern Texts Relating to the Old Testament,* p. 386, "Hymn to the Moon-god."

[28] Ibid., p. 371, col.ii, "Hymns to the Gods as a Single God."

is the audible expression and thus together they change the course of history. The effectiveness of Yahweh's word rests upon God Who stands behind His word and accomplishes it. This pattern is evident in Isaiah 48:3 where Yahweh speaks, "I foretold the former things long ago, my mouth announced them and I made them known; then suddenly I acted, and they came to pass."

Yahweh Sabaoth is the warrior par excellence. He takes the outfit of a warrior with breastplate of righteousness, helmet of salvation, His garments of vengeance to execute His judgments, and the cloak of zeal because whatever He does He does effectively and whole-heartedly (Isa.59:16-17). With this preparation Yahweh will raise the battle cry and triumph over His enemies (Isa. 42:13). Through His arm of power He conquered over Rahab and the primordial forces for chaos (drying up the waters of Teham), showing in a polemical form that Yahweh is the sovereign warrior who conquers all opposition from the earliest beginning (Isa. 51:9–10). Likewise, through His arm of power He works salvation for Israel (Isa. 52:10; 59:16; 63:5, 12). In addition He will repay wrath and retribution to His enemies according to what they have done (Isa. 59:18).

It is Yahweh and not Ba'al who rides swiftly on the clouds as His chariot (Isa. 19:1). He comes; the nations fear. They melt before Him. He brings their plans to nothing and defeats Egypt, Babylon and Assyria (Isa. 13:2-5; 19:1-4; Rev.17-18). He uses human armies and supernatural means. Isaiah 63:1-6 describes that ultimately, Yahweh will bring the judgment against the enemies as He establishes His eschatological kingdom.

> Who is this coming from Edom, from Bozrah, with His garments stained crimson? Who is this, robed in splendor, striding forward in the greatness of his strength? 'It is I, speaking in righteousness, mighty to save. 'Why are your garments red, like those of one treading the winepress? I have trodden the winepress alone; from the nations no one was with me. I trampled them in my anger and trod them down in my wrath; their blood spattered my garments, and I stained all my clothing for the day of vengeance was in my heart, and the year of my redemption has come. I looked, but there

was no one to help, I was appalled that no one gave support; so my own arm worked salvation for Me. I trampled the nations in my anger; in My wrath I made them drunk and poured their blood on the ground.'

The eschatological victory is guaranteed because of Yahweh's omnipotence, irresistibility, and righteousness. Such a commitment to righteousness is on such a pure and deep level that wrath and anger are appropriate divine responses of God to the creation, which warrants this level of judgment.

In Isaiah 54, Yahweh promises Israel, His bride, who had been chastened by expulsion, to take her back into his favor and forever to show her the loyal love that is entailed in their marriage union. To convey these truths with appropriate accurate force Yahweh claims and demonstrates emotions of anger, loyal love, and compassion that connects Him as feeling deeply for His beleaguered people.

> In a surge of anger I hid My face from you for a moment, but with everlasting kindness I will have compassion on you, says Yahweh your redeemer. Though the mountains be shaken and the hills be removed, yet My unfailing love for you will not be shaken nor my covenant of peace be removed, says Yahweh, who has compassion on you (Isa. 54:8, 10).

From this love and compassion, Yahweh provides profound comfort for His people (Isa. 40:1-2). The thought of them is always before Yahweh (Isa. 49:13-16). The new covenant is an expression of Yahweh's faithfulness to Israel and His servant (Isa. 49:7; 61:8). Yahweh delights in restored Israel as a bridegroom over His bride (Isa. 62:5). This loyal love is so compassionate that Isaiah breaks out into praise of Yahweh's greatness.

> I will tell of the kindness of Yahweh,
> The deeds for which He is to be praised
> According to all Yahweh has done for us–
> Yes, the many good things He has done

For the house of Israel,
According to His compassion and many kindnesses (Isa. 63:7).

Yahweh is incomparable as the God Who exists, predicts, acts, creates, intervenes in history, feels emotions deeply, judges the rebellious and redeems His people. Yahweh has no equal! No one even comes close!

God's Sovereignty and Human Free Will

In approaching the issues surrounding God's sovereignty and human free will there are a number of definitional issues that set the tone for each position. For example, Biblically the words "God is sovereign" simply means that God is king in an ancient Near East sense and thus will effect his will. However, how much of His will can be determined to be accomplished and in what manner is at the heart of the issue. Likewise, the way that free will is defined often identifies how a person positions himself on the spectrum between the options of: 1) everyone is always free with responsibility being unavoidable, and 2) no one is ever free which identifies that responsibility is impossible. At either end of the spectrum, incompatibilists make their commitment for either freedom of choice or determinism, because in their opinion these two cannot be brought together meaningfully. The incompatibilist defines free will in a manner that tends to pick up the following four features:

1. Authentic choice
2. That effects a change
3. For which you are responsible
4. And could have done otherwise.

In our contemporary situation Christian philosophers often embrace this incompatibilist option and affirm free will but the majority view within the heritage of orthodox Christianity has been to affirm some sort of compatibilism, embracing both freedom of choice and determinism. Often this compatibilist stance is held very ambiguously with descriptions on the heavenly gates as reading from one side "Whoever wills may come" and from the other side "Only the elect of God enter here." This mystery form of compatibilism often embraces the preceding definition of freedom of the will, which in fact contradicts with their definition of determinism. This mystery approach need not flee into ambiguity or contradiction so readily if it can clarify its definitions and nuance its answers. This paper will sample the range of options in the spectrum of freedom and responsibility in order to sensitize the reader to these issues and then explore compatibilism for a noncontradictory resolution of freedom and determinism that clarifies their relationship in a nicely nuanced way.

On one end of the spectrum is existentialism. Here determinism applies only to things, not to human consciousness. The essence of human consciousness is freedom itself and thus responsibility is unavoidable, as Sartre said "because freedom is condemned to be free."[1] Laurie Anderson playfully sings this perspective "You were born, so you're free; Happy Birthday." However, freedom exists not just in the abstract but also in the concrete as freedom to change or to do in the situation.[2] "Thus I am absolutely free and absolutely responsible for my situation. But I am never free except *in situation*."[3] However, absolute freedom does not mean that I can change the situation without regard for the other, "the Other's freedom confers limits on my situation, but I can *experience* these limits only if I recover this being-for-others which I am and if I give to it a meaning in the light of the ends which I have chosen."[4] The rock group "Rush" testifies to choosing free will and reminds us in their song "Freewill" that "if you choose not to decide that you still have made a choice."

---

[1] Jean-Paul Sartre, *Being and Nothingness* (New York: Washington Square Press, 1956), p. 652.

[2] Sartre, p. 650.

[3] Sartre, p. 652.

[4] Sartre, p. 675.

Libertarianism is a popular philosophical option on the freedom side because it allows for some events not to be caused but rather be the results of free choice and moral responsibility. Normal libertarianism is defined by the commitments to: 1) incompatibilism (an agent acts with free will only if the act is not determined by anything outside the agent), and 2) the principle of alternative possibilities (an agent acts with free will only if he could have done otherwise). This view is illustrated and argued by Daniel Dennett in *Elbow Room*, and Peter Van Inwagen in *An Essay on Free Will*.[5]   They insist on free will because the alternatives would be like being in prison, or being hypnotized or being paralyzed, or being a puppet, and most do not find these to be attractive options because these illustrations of determinism tend to remove normally recognized personal traits from humans. Dennett develops a few of these personal traits under the idea of freedom.

> We all take deliberation seriously, and would hate to learn that we are deluded to do so. We plan for the future; we lie awake nights gnawing at the bones of indecision, worrying about what to do and why; we promise ourselves that we will be more circumspect in the future. If we find ourselves on a jury, we try especially hard to pay close attention to the evidence presented, so we can render a responsible verdict. Is all this worry and work wasted? Is it somehow a sham or delusion? Many people are afraid that it is, if determinism is true.[6]

We believe that our plans and efforts effect a change or make a difference in some way besides raising our blood pressure. We deliberate as if our futures were open with real opportunities. This allows for humans to have limitations as determined by the circumstances in which we find ourselves. For example, we may be free to decide to paint our house and which rooms to paint which color but we are determined to need to open a paint can to get the paint out of the can as we begin

---

[5] Daniel Dennett, *Elbow Room: The Varieties of Free Will Worth Wanting* (Cambridge: MIT Press, 1985) and Peter Van Inwagen, *An Essay on Free Will* (Oxford: Clarendon Press, 1983).

[6] Dennett, p. 101.

to paint. Likewise, we may feel as though the earth is a restrictive jail limiting our movements by gravity holding us down as well as making our paint drips fall one direction but it is very different in that there is no obvious jailer. In this, conscience and character are not really deterministic features because they undergo moral development which reflects the heritage of choices which we have made. Thus, decisions based on character and conscience are merely reflecting earlier decisions which we have made. Christian libertarians remind us that the Bible has a lot of commands and promised blessings if we complete these plans. For example, the poor in spirit who associate with Christ are to be viewed as blessed "for theirs is the kingdom" and likewise the gentle who associate with Christ "shall inherit the earth" (Mt. 5:3, 5). Furthermore, Jesus described the decisions which people make in coming to Him as making a difference in their lives.

> Everyone who comes to Me, and hears My words, and acts upon them, I will show you who he is like: he is like a man building a foundation upon the rock; and when a flood rose, the torrent burst against that house and could not shake it, because it had been well built. But the one who has heard, and has not acted, is like a man who built a house upon the ground without any foundation; and the torrent burst against it and immediately it collapsed, and the ruin of that house was great (Lk. 6:47-49).

Such authentic choice among multiple options presented as available to them which choice effects a change for which they are responsibly rewarded, can be understood as real free will. Likewise, it looks as though some aspects of God's will are not realized when the human will expresses itself since God is "not wishing for any to perish but for all to come to repentance" and the ungodly are destroyed (2 Pet. 3:7, 9). Often this presents God as within time and involved in the affairs of humans in a way that looks like He limits His power so that humans can actually choose and He lets them go as they choose.[7] Another way to resolve

---

[7] Bruce Reichenbach's presentation is an articulate example of this resolution in Basinger ed. *Predestination and Free Will* (Downers Grove, Inter Varsity, 1986), pp. 101-24.

these scenarios limits God's knowledge to the events that are past history, or to what He can bring about Himself or conjecture about the future.[8] In this view, omniscience means that the temporal God knows all that can be known and since future decisions which have not been decided cannot be known (even by foreknowledge) without removing them from free will, no one knows them until they are actually decided in time.

Eleonore Stump wishes to position herself in a modified libertarianism that gives up the principle of alternative possibilities.[9] To accomplish this modified libertarianism she proposes a Frankfurt story which she modifies from John Mark Fisher as follows:[10]

> Suppose that a neurosurgeon Grey wants his patient Jones to vote for Republicans in the upcoming election. Grey has a neuroscope which lets him both observe and bring about neural firings which correlate with acts of will on Jones's part. Through his neuroscope, Grey ascertains that every time Jones wills to vote for Republican candidates, that the act of his will correlates with the completion of a sequence of neural firings in Jones's brain that always includes, near its beginning, the firing of neurons a, b, c (call this neural sequence 'R'). On the other hand, Jones willing to vote for Democratic candidates is correlated with the completion of a different neural sequence that always includes, near the beginning, the firings of neurons x, y, z, none of which is the same as those in neural sequence R (call this neural sequence 'D'). For simplicity sake, suppose that neither neural sequence R nor neural sequence D is also correlated with any further set of mental acts. Again for simplicity's sake, suppose that Jones's only relevant options are an act of will to vote for Republicans or an act of will to vote for democrats.
>   Then Grey can tune his neuroscope accordingly. Whenever the neuroscope detects the firing of x, y, z, the initial sequence, so that it isn't brought to completion. The neuroscope then activates

---

[8] Clark Pinnock presents an articulate example of this in Basinger ed. *Predestination and Free Will*, (Downers Grove, Inter Varsity, 1986), pp. 143-62.

[9] Eleonore Stump, Papers and discussion at the Wheaton Philosophy Conference Oct 21-23, 1999 entitled "Alternative Possibilities and Responsibility: The Flicker of freedom," and "Free Will."

[10] Stump, "Alternative Possibilities and Responsibility: The Flicker of Freedom" pp. 5-6, cf. John Mark Fisher, "Responsibility and Control," *Journal of Philosophy* 89 (1982) p. 26.

the coercive neurological mechanism which fires the neurons of neural sequence R, thereby bringing it about that Jones wills to vote for Republicans. But if the neuroscope detects the firing of a, b, c, the initial neurons in neural sequence R, which is correlated with the act of will to vote for Republicans, then the neuroscope does not interrupt that neural sequence. It doesn't activate the coercive neurological mechanism, and neural sequence R continues, culminating in Jones's willing to vote for Republicans, without Jones's being caused to will in this way by Grey.

And suppose that in (G) Grey does not act to bring about neural sequence R, but that Jones wills to vote for Republicans without Grey's coercing him to do so.

It certainly seems as if Jones is morally responsible for his act of will to vote for Republicans, and yet it also seems true that it was not possible for Jones to do anything other than willing to vote Republicans.

It is from this scenario that Stump concludes for a libertarianism that maintains a commitment to incompatibilism while jettisoning the commitment to the principle of alternative possibilities. The author asked Stump the question, what if the patient Jones and the neuroscope fired the R neural sequence simultaneously without either being prior to the other, wouldn't there be authentic choice and moral responsibility in this new scenario? Stump was unwilling to allow for this compatibilist option, identifying that she still is a modified libertarian. However, I wonder if such a Frankfurt story does not indeed permit an authentic choice and responsibility when the neuroscope does not in fact provide anything that Jones' choice in fact provides.

On the other extreme of incompatibilism, fatalism identifies that whatever happens is necessary and unavoidable because there is only divine control. For example, the earliest Islamic tradition is built on a strong belief of uncompromising fatalism, "Allah has willed it."[11] By the beginning of the eighth century some Muslims began to question this dogma, particularly from the members of *Kadariya* sect. In reaction to their questioning, a sect of extreme

---

[11]Robert Kingdon, "Determinism in Theology: Predestination" in the *Dictionary of the History of Ideas*, vol. 2, p. 29.

predestination formed called *Djabriya*.   They argued that man bears no responsibility of any kind for any of the actions which seem to come from him. This makes man merely an automaton, which idea was too extreme for most Muslims.   A variety of intermediate positions generally prevailed but the mature position in Islam orthodoxy, today, still endorses a strong measure of determinism.   Tom Robbins parodies this fatalistic position in his novel, *Even Cowgirls Get the Blues*:

> For Christmas that year, Julian gave Sissy a miniature Tyrolean village. The craftsmanship was remarkable. There was a tiny cathedral whose stained-glass windows made fruit salad of sunlight. There was a plaza and *ein Biergarten*. The *Biergarten* got quite noisy on Saturday nights. There was a bakery that smelled always of hot bread and strudel. There was a town hall and a police station, with cutaway sections that revealed standard amounts of red tape and corruption. There were little Tyroleans in leather britches, intricately stitched, ...There were ski shops and many other interesting things, including an orphanage. The orphanage was designed to catch fire and burn down every Christmas Eve. Orphans would dash into the snow with their nightgowns blazing. Terrible. Around the second week of January, a fire inspector would come and poke through the ruins, muttering, "If they had only listened to me, those children would be alive today.[12]

Notice how the repetition of the orphanage drama year after year (echoing Nietzsche's idea of eternal recurrence, in which everything happens again and again) seems to rob the little world of any real meaning. It is the repetition of the fire inspectors lament year after year that makes it sound so hollow.

Akin to this vertical determinism is a horizontal determinism of hard determinism. In hard determinism causality is necessary as the sufficient reason. If God is involved in hard determinism it is more as a master act that set up a semi-deistic model to run its own horizontal deterministic course. Mechanical

---

[12] Tom Robbins, *Even Cowgirls Get the Blues* (New York: Bantam Books, 1976), pp. 191-92.

determinism excludes human responsibility for everything is programmed into the mechanical world. Classical Newtonian physics is built largely within a hard determinism. Like a billiard ball universe that has objects moving, one can calculate which forces and which balls now at rest have caused the present movement and what the movement will become in time until they are stopped by friction or a pocket in which gravity removes them from this plain. Even the relativistic universe of Einstein operates in hard determinism but the billiard ball particles' size has merely shrunk to the microscopic electron or photon traveling no more than a maximum light speed if the billiard table is a vacuum, or expanded to the huge size of stars and galaxies which can gravitationally bend the path of light traveling by it. In 1901 Edington observed that light from a distant star bent during a solar eclipse as it traveled by the sun and the moon. In 1961 Frish and Smith compared the life span of mu-mesons traveling near the speed of light as compared to those they were able to stop in their bubble chamber on top of Mt. Washington and at the sea shore. They observed what Einstein had predicted; time was slowed down at fast speeds because the fast moving mu-mezons lived longer than the stationary ones. Even Heizenberg's uncertainty principle is operating within a billiard ball universe of hard determinism except that the available tools to find the location of an electron can only (practically speaking) find either the velocity or the location, but not both at the same time. To find the location of a microscopic particle requires bombarding the particle with a series of microscopic particles during which each ricochets identifying the location of the particle. The problem is they each impart some new change in velocity to the test particle thus rendering the velocity of the test particle unknown to the experimenter. To find the velocity of a microscopic particle requires directing only one microscopic particle at the test particle, it ricochets so that the velocity will be able to be computed, however the location is unknown since the experimenter only has one ricochet to use. Heizenberg recognized that on this microscopic scale the indeterminacy was only a practical experimental phenomena and not real indeterminacy. It was with Neils Bohr's quantum mechanics that the deterministic universe was sometimes superceded by a real universe of indeterminacy as the electrons shared space in the electron cloud or unpredictably jumped between electron clouds emitting or absorbing energy as they change their relation to the nucleus. At any given point in time the experimenter could have only a statistical probability that an electron was within a particular cloud, he could not be sure. This quantum indeterminacy is appealed to by libertarianism to show the inability of a horizontal hard determinism excluding authentic choice.[13] However, even though (on a microscopic level) quantum physics with its unpredictability was no longer within hard determinism, often on a macroscopic scale or on a probability level, determinism was a reasonable assumption because the microscopic indeterminacies of quantum cancelled each other out when considered macroscopically. Likewise, in the 1980's and 1990's the scientific community had a fling with chaos theory before they realized that what looked random on one level of analysis (i.e. velocity) produced a very predictable pattern on another level of analysis (i.e. acceleration) and that there were mathematical ways to describe the relationship between them (such as integration or differentiation). These days, chaos theory is more accurately referred to as complexity theory; the reasonable assumption of a hard determinism has simply become a more complex hard determinism. However, hard determinism attempted to move to animals and humans with fields like behaviorism and social engineering. Pavlov could make his dogs salivate at predictable times. Many psychologists find warrant for their theories by the indirect verification provided by those patients who recover through their counsel. However, the psychologist's patients do not always do what the psychologist expects and sometimes they do not take her counsel. On a personal level, a human is deciding between attractions that the options provide. Are the tools of moral production too complex to produce predictable behavior or are there moral

---

[13] E.g. Eleonore Stump in discussions with the author.

agents involved in the process that do not chose the option we might like them to choose? How well has social engineering's prison system reformed its prisoners which society sends it? Might prisoners also have a will and might the prison system be treating them like responsible agents to be punished for their evil deeds? In court, is it the society that is sentenced to rehabilitate or the prisoner who is judged? If the prisoner is viewed as the responsible agent to be punished then hard determinism does not apply to people.

Luther's view in *Bondage of the Will* works a hybrid of hard determinism of flesh and Satan as combined with a divine fatalism which either keeps men bound in their sins or else rescues them by God's grace. Luther holds to the bondage of the will by our human condition as flesh under sin that we find ourselves in this side of Adam's fall. The fact that man is flesh (as Romans 8 describes) indicates that the non-Christian is full of pride and self assertion preventing him from achieving genuine love of men or God. While Adam sinned willingly and freely in the fall, we are born with a will to sin so that as a non-Christian a man is inescapably inclined to sin and chooses sin voluntarily within this inclination of his nature.[14] God imprisons man's will to man's own sinful nature and to Satan as a sentence for original sin, condemning man to forfeit his original freedom to do good. Man is bound by his own sinful nature but each man is responsible and legally guilty for his own sin because it is his own nature and will that chooses these sins.[15] The guilt is man's own because God has given him the Law, but man constantly acts contrary to the Law. In this moral condition man cannot escape by natural powers such as discipline to produce love, purity and humility (for these are not obtained by practice but by new birth).[16] Even though man has lost every capacity to do good in matters concerning his relationship to God, there remains a passive capacity so that he can be grasped by

---

[14] Martin Luther, *Werke,* 18:693; 39:378-79 also John Calvin *The Institutes of the Christian Religion*, 2:1–3.

[15] Luther, *Werke,* 16:143; 18:693; 39:379.

[16] Luther, *Werke.* 10:92-93

grace and God's Spirit and be recreated for everlasting life.[17]   The decision of
who will be saved and who will be damned is solely and actively God's, so that
His will is unconditional in His determinism of the fate of all men.[18]   Luther
expresses his view in flamboyant vivid statements as he circles around the central
themes of justification by grace in Christ.   Through humanistic analysis, Calvin
frames his view more consistently as double predestination, primarily arguing
from Ephesians 1:4-5 that divine choice to place us in Christ is accomplished
before the foundation of the world; this means that it is accomplished by God
without any regard for our own worth.[19]   The Christian is a new creation whom
God has created from the sinner so that as a justified sinner he now can live the
life of faith that the Spirit prompts.[20]

The whole debate over predestination came to one of its historic climaxes
early in the seventeenth century under the disagreement of two Calvinist
professors.   Jacob Arminius, who had studied in Geneva with Calvin's successors,
tried to modify Calvin's doctrine in order to reduce its harshness and create some
role for human responsibility.   The views of Arminius were most succinctly stated
after his death in a five-point *Remonstrance* drafted by his followers in 1610.
This document urged a libertarian option as follows: 1) that God's decree of
salvation is conditional, benefiting only those who by an act of will accept and
persevere in faith; 2) that God's universal love is reflected in the fact that Christ
died for all men, although only believers are benefited; 3) that man can truly do
good, after he is born again through the Holy Spirit; 4) that man can perversely
resist God's offer of grace; 5) that the faithful receive divine assistance in leading
the good life, but only if they want this assistance and do not remain inactive.
The *Remonstrance* provoked a bitter controversy in which Francis Gomarus led
the attack.   The controversy spread beyond The Netherlands to other countries

---

[17] Luther, *Werke,* 18:636.
[18] Luther uses Romans 9-11 as the basis for God's double predestination, as evident in
Works, 35:378.
[19] Calvin, 3:21–22.
[20] Luther, *Lectures on Romans*, 15:128, also Calvin 3:19.

where Calvinistic influences were strong. The controversy was temporarily settled in a general synod of representatives of all the Reformed churches, held in Dort, 1618-19. The Synod of Dort was dominated by the Gomarists, so it adopted a five point retort to the *Remonstrance* called the five points of Calvinism: 1) Total depravity– man in his natural state is so totally corrupt and helpless that he is incapable of even desiring salvation; 2) Unconditional election–God's predestination decrees derive solely from His decisions, and do not in any way depend on the beliefs or the behavior of individuals; 3) Limited atonement–Christ died for the elect alone, not for all mankind; 4) Irresistible grace–once God begins to save a person this person is helpless to resist, and automatically is saved; 5) Perseverance of the saints–God so assists His elect to adopt the correct beliefs and to live the proper way of life that it is impossible for them to fall from grace. This is sometimes called TULIP, an acronym based on the initial letters of the five points. This deterministic formula limits man's freedom and exalts God's sovereignty on every point. However, despite Gomarus' urgings, the synod refused to adopt a clear supralapsarian formula (in the divine decrees predestination of some to life and others to death was antecedent to God's prescience of the creation and the fall), but settled on one with infralapsarian elements (God's election of some to everlasting life was consequent to His prescience concerning the fall of man and thus was a remedial measure).

Augustine holds a compatibilist view that has since become known as soft determinism. Augustine defended philosophical free will in his case against Manicheism and the problem of evil. In a context like this, human free will permits God to judge sin.[21] Yet the free will never determines itself without a motive.[22] No one except God has the power to determine what ideas enter a person's mind but the will remains free because it agrees with or rejects what has come to mind. God not only gives such gracious motives but knows in advance how man's free will shall respond. In this, foreknowledge has no more influence

---

[21] Augustine, *Epist.* 214, 2.

on the future than memory has on the past.[22] Augustine changed his emphasis from free will to sovereignly initiated grace in 396 A.D. when he was elevated to bishop. In *de praedestinatione sanctorum* I, 2 he responded to some of Simplicianus' questions such as, Why did God hate Esau in an attempt to explain the meaning of Romans 9:10-29? Augustine sees God as absolutely sovereign so that no act of virtue is performed without a gift of God's grace since He is the unique source of all good.[24] This grace is explained by him as being like offering candy to a baby who then runs to it because he is so attracted to it.[25] Augustine writes that God provides the natural grace as an internal providence that prepares efficacious motives for the will of all and more narrowly providing grace-enabling Christian virtues of which faith is one.[26] He then goes on to say that Man possessed free will before the fall. In the wake of the fall man's free will remains but the corrupted human nature on its own only provides the free will with options of inclinations to do sin.[27] The one who believes does so because in the elect the will is prepared by God.[28] Thus after this preparation the will can theoretically refuse, but it will not refuse because God knows how to prepare it by the choice of His grace. When the will receives the efficacious grace of faith the will gives its consent fully.[29] Furthermore, in baptism original sin is effaced and forgiven so that it is no longer a sin for the one baptized, leaving us with our own inclinations and deeds.[30] In this manner, if two men are equally tempted, there is no other reason why one resists the temptation while the other falls than the free choice of their wills.[31]

---

[22] Augustine, *Opus imper. Contra Jul.* I.41.

[23] Augustine, *de civ. Dei* 5.9.1-4; *de lib. arb.* 3.3.6-8; *in Joannis evan. tract.* 53.4.

[24] Augustine, *Expos. Rom.* 55, 60, 61; *de nuptiis et concupiscentia* II, 4, 12; *Contra Julianum haeresis Pelagianorum defensorem* V, 20, 40.

[25] Augustine, *In Joannis Evangelium tractatus* 26, 5.

[26] Eugene Portalie, *A Guide to the Thought of Saint Augustine.* Chicago, 1960, p. 196.

[27] Augustine, *de nat. et grat.* 3, 3 cf. n. 18; *de grat. et lib. arb.* 2, 4; *Contra duas epistolas Pelagianorum ad Bonifacium Papam* I, 2, 5; III, 8, 24; IV, 3.

[28] Augustine, *de praedestinatione sanctorum ad Prosperum et Hilarium* 5,10.

[29] Augustine, *de gratia Christi,* 7-10, 8-11.

[30] Augustine, *Contra duas epistolas Pelagianorum ad Bonifacium Papam* I, 13, 27.

[31] Augustine, *Epist.* 186, 9, 33.

Semi-Pelagianism or, more accurately, the Massilion controversy, rejected the Augustinian predestinationism of *de praedestinatione sanctorum* I, 2. For example, John Cassian exclaimed "He is truly free who has begun to be your prisoner, O Lord." Cassian was trying to remind the Christians of the need to cooperate with God's transforming power. This served as a mild expression of Pelagian views, which saw man as able to will the kingdom attributes on his own because God had commanded him to do so. In the wake of these views, Pelagianism was mildly censured in 415 A.D. at Jerusalem and Dsiospolis, and then strongly condemned at Ephesus in 431 A.D.

The Westminister Confession of Faith maintains a compatibilism of divine determinism with free will among humans only in the initial and glorified states. The determinism is briefly put in the discussion of providence.[32]

> God, the great creator of all things, doth uphold, direct, dispose, and govern all creatures, actions, and things, from the greatest even to the least, by His most wise and holy providence, according to his infallible foreknowledge, and the free and immutable counsel of His own will, to the praise of the glory of His wisdom, power, justice, goodness, and mercy.

The Westminster Confession also sees free will as initially a gift of God, corrupted by mankind, hindering them in their sin and only redeemable by God's grace in the state of glory.[33]

1. God hath endued the will of man with that natural liberty, that it is neither forced, nor by any absolute necessity of nature determined, to good or evil.
2. Man, in his state of innocency, had freedom and power to will and to do that which is good and well pleasing to God; but yet mutably, so that he might fall from it.
3. Man, by his fall into a state of sin, hath wholly lost all ability of will to any spiritual good accompanying salvation; so as a natural man, being

---

[32] *The Westminster Confession of Faith*, ch. 5.
[33] Ibid. ch. 9.

altogether averse from that good, and dead in sin, is not able, by his own strength, to convert himself, or to prepare himself thereunto.

4. When God converts a sinner, and translates him into the state of grace, he freeth him from his natural bondage under sin, and is spiritually good; yet so as that, by reason of his remaining corruption, he doth not perfectly nor only will that which is good, but doth also will that which is evil.

5. The will of man is made perfectly and immutably free to do good alone in the state of glory only.

Jonathan Edwards follows Locke in defining free will as the power a person has to act in accordance with his will or to choose and to act as he pleases.[34] The reverse of such freedom of the will would be constraint (which forces a person to do contrary to his own will) or restraint (which hinders man from doing according to his will). So for Edwards free will can be summarized as:

1. authentic choice,

2. which effects a change,

3. for which you are responsible,

4. and you act without psychological compulsion even though it may also be determined by another.

Following Augustine, there is a teleological necessity of a determiner behind the will, such as God or motive, to choose as the cause to produce effects upon itself.[35] With God as omniscient in His foreknowledge, God is the determiner of all that happens and there is a practical necessity for everything that happens.[36] This omniscient foreknowledge is amply demonstrated by Biblical prophecy

---

[34] Jonathan Edwards, *Freedom of the Will*, (New Haven: Yale University Press, 1957), 1:1, p. 137; 1:5, p. 163; 2:1, p. 172-73.

[35] That is, the will does not choose alone or it would be a contradictory infinite regress of will and there must be a sufficient reason for the will choosing such as in a motive or divine choice that grounds it or starts it moving. Edwards, 1:2, p. 141; 2:2, p. 176-7s7; 2:3, p. 182-3; 2:4, p. 186-87.

[36] Edwards, 2:1-12, p. 239-69.

being fulfilled. The practical necessity is required by the fact that God's mind knows everything in a necessary or nonchanging way and that which is known by God to occur, must occur. At this point, Edwards also embraces something like a Newtonian hard determinism because every act of the will must have a cause not merely in the vertical sense but in the preceding consequent cause, as in a series of billiard balls transferring their momentum down a row.[37] Since Adam's sin, humanity continues to reverberate with sin and the moral inability to be blameless.[38] Humans are still blameworthy even though they are sincere because their will is not indifferent but reflects the mix of virtues and vices that are present therein and so acts freely.[39] The essence of a virtue or a vice (dispositions of the heart and the acts of the will), lies not in their cause, but in their nature.[40] So that, God who determines all events (including sins) for His holy and glorious ends is not the author of sin (which is the moral choice for evil); the human moral agent is the author of sin and especially Adam (who by perfect accident chose sin, beginning the billiard ball sequence of depravity).[41] Since the moral choice is also the human's to make, as an expression of the image of God in man, then humans retain freedom of the will and moral responsibility for their choice as well.[42]

Anselm maintained that free will is a power of preserving the voluntary rectitude; man though fallen still possesses this potential to choose, thus having free will. However, no power is capable of actualizing potential unaided. If the potential is to be actualized it must be actualized by God's *concursus*.[43] This teaching fostered the thirteenth century doctrine of *concursus simultaneus*. In this view there is a non-exclusive redundancy of theistic determinism with viable human free choice and responsibility. To help resolve this relationship Anselm

---

[37] Edwards, 2:13, p. 270-73.
[38] Edwards, 3:3-4, p. 295-311.
[39] Edwards, 3:5-7, p. 312-33.
[40] Edwards, 4:1, p. 337-42.
[41] Edwards, 4:9-10, p. 397-414.
[42] Edwards, 1:3-5, p. 149-67; 4:4, p. 357-64.
[43] Anselm, *de lib. arb.* 3.

appeals to the concept of necessity in foreknowledge in a different way than Edwards. Anselm recognizes that since God foreknows all that will happen as it will happen then the events will necessarily happen. However, these events necessarily happen voluntarily.

> I might say: "It is necessary that you are going to sin voluntarily" or "It is necessary that, voluntarily, you are not going to sin"–just as God foreknows. But these statements must be construed to mean that something prevents the act of will which shall not occur, or compels that act of will which shall not occur, or compels that act of will which shall occur. For God, who forsees that some action is going to occur voluntarily, foreknows the very fact that the will is neither compelled nor prevented by anything. Hence what is done voluntarily is done freely. Therefore, if these matters are carefully pondered, I think that no inconsistency prevents freedom of choice and God's foreknowledge from coexisting.[44]

Anselm resolves the tension by recognizing that many events are contingent events dependent upon the human free will. Viewing God's foreknowledge as knowing in response to the human choice as through a "subsequent necessity, does not compel anything to be."[45] Since God eternally foreknows in simplicity there is no logical sequence of this divine knowledge and choice. Often Anselm retains Augustine's notion of God's providential grace that woos and lures human wills to decide in particular ways, but it is not as prominent as Augustine has it. Anselm really has a cooperative simultaneity or a nonexclusive redundancy of the divine and human wills.

Thomas Aquinas embraces the view of compatible simultaneous causes with a non-exclusive redundancy of theistic determinism and viable responsible free choice.[46] Theistic determinism is affirmed as the ultimate causal ground upon the choice of God's will. Thomas writes, "We must hold that the will of

---

[44] Anselm, *Foreknowledge and Freechoice,* section 2 in *Readings in Medieval Philosophy* edited by Andrew Schoedinger, (New York: Oxford University Press, 1996), p. 205.
[45] Anselm, sect. 2, p. 206.

God is the cause of things, and that He acts by the will, and not as some have supposed, by a necessity of His nature,"[47] and again "The will of God is the universal cause of all things, it is impossible that the divine will should not produce its effect."[48]   The rationale for this is that God is the first agent so that effects are wrought in their cause after the manner of their cause before the creation is made and, according to Psalm 113:11, God does all that He wills. "Now God wills some things to be done necessarily, some contingently, that there might be an order to things, for the building up of the universe."[49]   An example of this determinist divine choice of contingent things is evident when God wills good which by implication has evil attached to it such as natural defect or punishment.[50]   God does not will sin, it is merely the implication of the good He wills.   "It is necessary that the type of order of things towards their end should preexist in the divine mind, and the type of things ordered towards an end is, properly speaking, providence."[51]   In God's omniscience He immutably knows all things, even the future contingent things as contingent.[52]   God actively chooses the elect out of His goodness for their salvation, and the reprobate for their damnation on account of their sin.[53]   Thomas finds Biblical justification for this active double choice of God in Romans 9:22-23 and 2 Timothy 2:20.[54]   So the order of predestination and the specific individuals of predestination are certain; yet the compatible free choice which is the effect of predestination remains contingent.[55]   "Man has free choice, otherwise counsels, exhortations,

---

[46] Aquinas, *The Summa Theologica* Pt. I. Q 23. Art. 6. I answer that and Q 83. Art. 1. Reply Obj. 3.

[47] Aquinas, *The Summa Theologica* Pt. I. Q 19. Art. 4. I answer that.

[48] Aquinas, *The Summa Theologica* Pt. I. Q 19. Art. 6. I answer that.

[49] Aquinas, *The Summa Theologica* Pt. I. Q 19. Art. 8. I answer that.

[50] Aquinas, *The Summa Theologica* Pt. I. Q 19. Art. 9. I answer that.

[51] Aquinas, *The Summa Theologica* Pt. I. Q 22. Art. 1. I answer that.

[52] Aquinas, *The Summa Theologica* Pt. I. Q 14. Art. 13. I answer that, and Art. 15 I answer that.

[53] Aquinas, *The Summa Theologica* Pt. I. Q 23. Art. 3. I answer that, and Art. 4. I answer that.

[54] Aquinas, *The Summa Theologica* Pt. I. Q 23. Art. 5. Reply Obj. 3.

[55] Aquinas, *The Summa Theologica* Pt. I. Q 23. Art. 6. I answer that and Art. 7. I answer that.

commands, prohibitions, rewards, and punishments would be in vain."[56] Additionally, "we have free choice because we can take one thing while refusing another, and this is to choose."[57] Unfortunately man's free will has chosen to sin and this will alone is a sufficient cause for sin being accomplished.[58] Because of Adam's and our own sin man is depraved in mind and operates in a kind of ignorance so that we do not properly value the things and options about us, so on our own we do not properly choose. Man needs divine grace from God as the First Mover to will or to do any good whatsoever.[59] This divine grace serves as final cause through which the human will serves as the efficient cause transformed by God so that intrinsically Christian character and acts can be chosen by the Christian's free will. Man is completely unable to produce everlasting life, to rise above sin, to embrace and maintain Christian virtue unless God graciously renders it so.[60] With God's gracious deterministic choice, the Christian freely chooses the Christian virtue and everlasting life that attracts his will. Both God's choice and man's choice are included in a nonexclusive redundancy of wills compatibly held together.

I propose a compatibilist resolution of the problem which is closely aligned to Aquinas' and Anselm's framework, with less Aristotelianism. For example, divine causation is not limited to being a first or final cause, rather it is more a redundant efficient cause. In this model I embrace the definition of free will which we teased out of Locke and Edwards, namely, that the will is properly designated as free since the will has:

1 authentic choice,

2 which effects a change,

3 for which you are responsible,

---

[56] Aquinas, *The Summa Theologica* Pt. I. Q 83. Art. 1. I answer that.

[57] Aquinas, *The Summa Theologica* Pt. I. Q 83. Art. 3. I answer that.

[58] Aquinas, *The Summa Theologica* Pt. II. Q 75. Art. 2. I answer that and Art. 3 I answer that.

[59] Aquinas, *The Summa Theologica* Pt. II. Q 109. Art. 2. I answer that.

4   and you act without psychological compulsion even though it may also
     be determined by another.

Abundant commands, exhortations, rewards, and judgments in the Biblical text
identify that humans have authentic choice that effects a change for which we are
responsible with no evidence of psychological compulsion.   For example, the
poor in spirit who associate with Christ are to be viewed as blessed "for theirs is
the kingdom" and likewise the gentle who associate with Christ "shall inherit the
earth" (Mt. 5:3, 5).   Furthermore, Jesus described the decisions which people
make in coming to Him as making a difference in their lives.

> Everyone who comes to Me, and hears My words, and acts upon
> them, I will show you whom he is like: he is like a man building a
> foundation upon the rock; and when a flood rose, the torrent burst
> against that house and could not shake it, because it had been well
> built. But the one who has heard, and has not acted, is like a man
> who built a house upon the ground without any foundation; and the
> torrent burst against it and immediately it collapsed, and the ruin of
> that house was great (Lk. 6:47-49).

Such authentic choice among multiple options presented as available to them,
(which choice effects a change for which they are responsibly rewarded) can be
understood as real free will in the philosophical sense.   Thus human free will is
best understood to retain its contingent sense, open to new choices, changes and
outcomes.

    This perspective leaves us within the framework of compatibility of
sovereignty and free will because there is a nonexclusive redundancy of the
sovereign will and the human free will. One can think of these redundant causes
as compatible because they are both efficacious and need to be analyzed within
their own character.   In the classroom I illustrate this redundant causality by
speeding an eraser toward the floor. What made it go down? My hand and

---

[60] Aquinas, *The Summa Theologica* Pt. II. Q 109. Art. 2, 5, 7-9. I answer that.

gravity sent it to the floor for they both operated on the eraser to bring about the very same effect that the eraser would descend at a particular rate. If either was not there the eraser would still have descended at the same rate but both causes brought about the same effect. This example shows the philosophical possibility of an active determinism being compatibly connected with free will. Now any illustration will have limitations as it illustrates a particular aspect of the issue. In our world erasers do not themselves have will even though this can show the compatibility of redundant causes. Another picture might involve, say, a Christian hypnotist employed as entertainment. You might think that this is outrageous so you have to take this event in. So you purpose to go to the event but because you feel a little awkward about the event you decide to try to evangelize someone afterward at the restaurant across the street. Unknown to you, when the hypnotist first arrived on campus, he had requested a student directory and set about choosing people to whom to give suggestions. As it turns out he chose to have you try to evangelize someone at the restaurant after the meeting is over. When the hypnotist stages his performance, it is a grand time with your roommate barking like a dog and other activities all in fun. So when your name is called you go up and the suggestion (made while you are hypnotized) is given. When the meeting is over you have a deep compulsion to evangelize someone at the restaurant across the street. Here both wills cooperate together for the same effect retaining a legitimate free will because you made an authentic choice without the feeling of external compulsion and someone might get saved from this night of evangelism with you being rewarded for your faithfulness. This illustration shows that redundant wills can be compatibly intertwined within a soft determinism without abusing either but does not show that God in fact works this way. A better illustration is that of the Biblical authors writing Scripture. For example, as Peter writes 2 Peter at such a time that his death is coming quickly, he expresses his heart about reminding his readers of their salvation and their need to live virtuously in light of this (2 Pet. 1: 5-15). He follows this with his own testimony of what he has seen at the transfiguration. So Peter is using his personal word, experience and content choice as he writes this Scripture. However, we recognize what Peter goes on to say, that Scripture is produced by the active inspiration of the Holy Spirit Who breathes His word into the text and moves the writer wherever He wishes the Scripture to go (2 Tim. 3:16-17; 2 Pet. 1:20-21). Now that divine determinism is being considered in these illustrations the compatibility has more guarantee to reflect both wills even though the mechanism of direct determinism or soft determinism is not clarified in the texts. The character of Peter is reflected in what he says as well as the inerrant divinely authoritative message which we need to apply as from God. However, the divine activity is not just compatibly involved in such encouraging ways; even in the most heinous sins God is compatibly involved with the sinner in the sin, yet He remains righteous. For example, killing Christ would be included among the most heinous sins. The sovereign determinism of the killing of Christ is twice developed in parallel as foreknown and predetermined by God (Acts 2:23). Then in the same breath (evidencing that it is a compatibilism) Peter twice develops in parallel that the Jews killed Christ by the hands of lawless men, namely Romans. This was a non-coerced choice of rebellion that brought about the effect of the death of Christ for which they were responsible, since Peter calls them to repent from this opposition. The religious leaders' choice for rebellion continues to be compatible with its sovereign orchestration as evident in the way both statements continue to be held within the disciple's prayer (Acts 4:27-28). Both the divine determinism (in what seems to be a fatalism) and the free choice compatibly brought about the Jew's sin even though God did not sin in this event.

God's sovereignty is Biblically claimed in countless ways. Yahweh is the king Who continues to reign overall while the earthly kings reign over miniature plots for a moment (Isa. 6). Yahweh presents Himself as a suzerain or great king through the form of documents of revelation (namely: Exodus-Leviticus, Deuteronomy, and Joshua 24). When suzerain Yahweh challenged Egypt, the most powerful nation of that time, Yahweh destroyed Egypt and their pantheon of gods in order to lead Israel out to the promised land. Yahweh is the incomparable One Who is superior to all and thus accomplishes His will of judging sinners and rescuing those He has chosen (Isa. 40-48). As sovereign Yahweh predicts and guarantees that these predictions will come to pass for there is no rival to God (Isa. 44:6-8). When the history of the world runs its course God's kingdom will again conquer indicating that He continues to reign (e.g. Dan. 2:45).

God's sovereign choice includes everything within the decree as divine initiation determining what would come to pass. This is a view of meticulous providence on God's part. Paul in Romans 9 explains the process of God's determinism as dependent and initiated by Him so that the Christians do not have to fear being overwhelmed by evil. God overwhelmingly conquers for the Christian even as some are dying a martyr's death so that their inheritance with Christ is guaranteed. God's purpose is initiated by Him in promise before any choice could be made by the participants "in order that God's purpose according to His choice might stand, not because of works, but because of Him who calls" (Rom. 9:6-13). Since it is God's sovereign initiation which determines whether an individual or a nation is saved and blessed or actively rejected for curse, the determinism of their fate is set without their works even though their works are involved in playing out the dramatic narrative. Quoting Malachi 1:2, God declares "Jacob I actively loved, but Esau I actively hated" to indicate that the choice stands determined by God Who has set their fate. This is a harsh statement but it is the only meaningful one which makes sense of the question in the next verse, "There is no injustice with God is there?" (Rom. 9:14). God initiates and determines the action for such a question to be raised. God is the One Who has mercy or compassion to include in blessing so the choice does not depend on the will of man or the activity of man but on God as the initiator (Rom. 9:15-16).

Options such as Molinism[61] or Arminianism do not reflect that God is the initiating determiner as this passage portrays. However, the determinism is not merely of the good of mercy but also the active exclusion of curse as illustrated by the hardening of Pharaoh. The verse quoted in Romans 9:17 is the one in Exodus 4:21 in which God predicts and informs Moses that He has raised Pharaoh for this destruction in order to demonstrate His sovereign determination in the salvation of His people. This sovereign determination is the emphasis in the Exodus context as illustrated by the majority of instances in which God is declared to harden Pharaoh's heart (Ex. 4:21; 7:3; 9:12; 10:1, 20, 27; 11:10; 14:4, 17). There are other verses in the context that could be taken as divine determinism but these listed unquestionably emphasize God as the initiator and determiner of Pharaoh's fate. On the divine side, the hardening of Pharaoh may be viewed as within active divine direct causality but on the question of his not letting Israel go free, this direct causality becomes the means of a soft determinism motivating Pharaoh's continued resistance. However, this determinism works compatibly with human choice, for Pharaoh is recorded to take an active hand in hardening his heart in a few instances as well (Ex. 8:15, 32; 9:34). These two sides of divine determinism and compatible free will fit well within the redundant compatibilism strategy. In Paul's context the sovereign determinism is the feature being emphasized; "So He has mercy on whom He desires, and He hardens whom He desires" (Rom. 9:18). Unless one recognizes this strong sovereign determinism as what is happening in this context, the next verse's question does not make sense: "For why does He still find fault?" for "Who resists His will?" (Rom. 9:19). The answer keeps the determining initiative

---

[61] Louis de Molina developed the Molinist account that God can exercise providence based on His middle knowledge or knowledge of contingent truths over which he has no control. The contents of God's middle knowledge include counterfactuals of creaturely freedom, conditionals that enable Him to have knowledge of how any creature who does or might have existed would freely act in any situation in which that person might have been created and left free. For Louis de Molina such a God with middle knowledge could respond in advance to what would freely happen so that He could alter the outcome by choosing an option that the human agents would freely choose which was harmonious to His will.

with God, "Who are you, O man who answers back to God? The thing molded will not say to the molder, 'Why did you make me like this,' will it? Or does not the potter have a right over the clay, to make from the same lump one vessel for honorable use, and another for common use?" (Rom. 9:20-21). In a similar context exploring the features of salvation such as predestination accomplished within the heavenly benefits, Paul reminds his readers that God works all things after the counsel of His will (Eph. 1:11). This determinism is exhaustive including everything, for in this context the salvific determined events are seen as within a greater "all things" of God's sovereignty.

God's determination of sins and evil does not make God Himself evil because occasionally God explains His rational to be of good purposes which evidence that God is good. The supreme example of this kind of explanation is the prologue to the book of Job which identifies that Job's suffering takes place as a demonstration to Satan that at least Job serves and worships God without requiring God to reward him (Job 1:9-12; 2:2-6). There is however no evidence that Job actually knew that His suffering happened for a lofty purpose like this. God instead barraged Job with a volley of questions that left him with the sovereignty and omniscience of God when compared to Job's puniness. God did not tell Job why he was suffering, Job just must submit to Him. At other times, we do not have enough knowledge to judge Him so that we must live with the tension of unexplained things which seem incongruous (Rom. 9:14, 19-22).

God's plan and desires do not always line up. God determines His plan (*boylē*) and brings it about (Lk. 7:30; Acts 2:23; 4:28; 13:36; 20:27; Eph. 1:11; Heb. 6:17). The difference between God's plan and human plans (*boylē*) is that God's character guarantees an immutable plan that is not thwarted, while human plans can make no such guarantee (Lk. 23:51; Acts 5:38; 27:12, 42; 1 Cor. 4:5). In fact, God's plan overwhelms the human plans in arranging the historical circumstances or in judgment. God's desire (*boylomai*) allows for an emotional inclination reflecting God's empathy which to some extent effects His determinative will. For example, Jesus' prayer for the willingness of the Father to let the cup of God's wrath pass from Him is answered in the affirmative by resurrecting Christ (Lk. 22:42).[62] Likewise, it is the Holy Spirit's desire that directs His distribution of spiritual gifts (1 Cor. 12:11). Furthermore, God desired to show His unchangeableness concerning His promise, so He underscored it with an oath (Heb. 6:17). Finally, God's desire is that no one would perish. The eschatological judgment may seem later than what we might be inclined to expect, however it will come as He decides in His timing (2 Pet. 3:9).

God foreknows (*proginōskō*) means a prior determining relationship with a person or event before entrance onto the temporal scene. Usually, God is the one who knows in advance in a manner that has Him grounding their salvation (Rom. 8:29; 11:2; 1 Pet. 1:2). This form of divine knowledge is an anthropomorphism characterizing God from our vantage point of within time. Occasionally, the Biblical text refers to foreknowledge as simply prior knowledge. This is consistent with classical Greek use (Acts 26:5; 1 Pet. 1:20; 2 Pet. 3:17). However, when God is the One who has this foreknowledge then it determines the person or event to occur (Acts 2:23; Rom. 8:29; 11:2; 1 Pet. 1:2, 20). In these occasions with God as the foreknower such foreknowledge should not be thought of as merely knowing or implying sequence. While no Biblical text explores whether this foreknowledge is comprehensive, it is reasonable to conclude in favor of comprehensive knowledge of the future on the basis of the chapter on the nature of necessity and the anecdotal expressions from the exposition of Psalm 139.

As a necessary being, God does not have sequence within His essential nature. Both the ontological argument and the cosmological argument propose

---

[62] This prayer is answered in the affirmative because Hebrews 5:7 identifies that the Gethsemane prayer was "heard" by God and such a prayer being "heard" means that it is answered positively as it was asked (e.g. 1 Jn. 5:14-15).

that an actually necessary being exists which we will call God.[63] This necessary being is always existent immutably and eternally. This level of immutability and eternity means that there is no sequence within God. There is no chronological experience of God to immutably change from non-being to being in a certain way.[64] Furthermore, the knowledge He knows He has always known without variance. God would know all there is to be known for the whole of time as an eternally present experience, without change. However, this does not cause God to be opposed to knowledge held by His creation, for He would always know what every feature of the creation knows from the creation's perspective in space and time while also knowing simultaneously from His unique vantage point. For example, He would eternally know my knowing of the past and my fears of the future from my vantage point and the perspective of every created thing in addition to His unique additional perspectives. In our Einsteinian relativistic universe we may have problems defending simultaneity of events but God would know simultaneity because He is not limited by our finite empirical ways of knowing. However, this does not render eternity to be static, for Boethius defines eternity in a more determining manner as the complete possession all at once of illimitable life.[65] The complete possession is an atemporal sourcing that does not change and is not limited but brings about all that has changed in its expressions of finiteness. This means that eternity is the source for all power and life, as previously described under omnipotence above. So eternity is not primarily to be known for its static comprehensive determining knowledge but for the life

---

[63] For further explanation and defense of these arguments and the implications for the nature of necessity see the chapter, "The Nature of Necessity: A Case for Classical Theism in Opposition to the Openness of God Model" in this book.

[64] This means that the kenotic view of the divinity of Christ emptying Himself of His divine attributes so that He could become incarnate that Satori proposed in 1831 is excluded as well as the evangelical softened version of a willing nonuse of divine attributes which He continued to possess for both options describe essential change which is impossible for an immutable being. For a further discussion of this see the chapter, "A Few Philosophical and Biblical Theology Problems with Statements of the Trinity" in this book.

[65] Boethius, *The Consolation of Philosophy,* Book V, Prose 6; and *De trinitate,* chapter 4 in E. K. Rand ed., *Boethius: The Theological Tractates and The Consolation of Philosophy* (Cambridge: Harvard, 1973).

revealed to have come from God in His revelational creation. Because God initiates the whole of the creation (including all of its details) His knowledge essentially also determines choice. God's choices are eternal and essential to His nature without variance. To have God as an actually necessary being means His sovereign choice is set. This means that the level of necessity for God includes all of God's thoughts and sovereign choices eternally and immutably. God is not open in growing and gaining more knowledge and choosing in response to this knowledge. God's knowledge and choice would in fact be set within God's essential nature as determinative for the existence, essence, and choices the whole of creation makes. With God's knowledge and choice as essential to His nature, then there is no logical order in God either. This means that all the reformation options expressing the order of the decree would in fact be contradictory to God's essential nature. There would not be a logical sequence within God Who simultaneously knows and chooses without sequence (i.e. eternally). This should not surprise us, for there are no Biblical texts that talk about any logical or chronological sequence within God of an order of salvation either; all these claimed texts at best indicate that when it comes to the application of God's choice out into the chronologically changing creation that such choice has a sequence of application only for the recipient. For example, there is a clear logical and chronological sequence in applying the divine election (*ekletois*) as foreknown, preparative sanctifying of the person so that the outcome (*eis*) of this sanctification ushers in obedience and atonement (1 Pet. 1:1-2). At other instances of sequence of the application of salvation there is encouragement for the Christian who has experienced some of the salvation benefits, like justification, who can be reassured that the other benefits, like glorification, will also be his in time (e.g. Rom. 8:29-30). So the whole post-reformation discussion of the order of the decree and the order of salvation within God was an unfortunate exploration that does not apply to this necessary, immutable, and eternal God. Any linkage of logical order or chronological sequence in such works of God is an expression of application order or revelation purpose. Any attempt to communicate eternal truths into a constantly changing environment like the creation will reflect them in sequential ways partly because of the sequential nature of our environment and partly to accommodate to our human understanding. For example, the textual sequences above convey that God graciously applies and guarantees the fullness of salvation to each Christian personally, which is a revelation purpose consistent with God's immutable nature. Any apparent change in God is actually the refraction of a changeless God through the lens of the changing environment for purposes of applying some benefit to the creation, such as salvation or the communication of certain select truths to a certain group in time. The fact that the truths of God are accommodated to the means of communication does not limit the truths of God, but the context indicates the primary hermeneutical purpose and how the descriptions of God are merely supportive of this purpose.

The emphasis of predestination (*proorizō*) in the Biblical text is in the positive direction so that while I hold to a double deterministic view it would not be best to call it double predestination. Usually predestination in the Biblical text serves to accomplish positive salvific benefits (Rom. 8:29-30; 1 Cor. 2:7; Eph. 1:5, 11), however it can be an open ended sovereign determinism of whatever was to occur such as in Christians' suffering because of rebellion and sin of those non-Christians who oppress them (Acts 4:28).

God can be viewed in this model as the continuous final causal ground for all existence and events. However, I prefer to view God through Boethius' lens and identify Him as the initial grounding efficient cause for all existence and events. So God both determines and omnisciently knows (another divine initiating and determining motif) all the creation. God continues to sustain all the creation as well. God will bring the whole of the creation within His goal, for as omnipotent and incomparable He is fully able, and as sovereign determiner He is fully willing to do so. God has no challenger who can thwart His plan.

With regard to habit and depravity the non-Christian is in bondage to his nature which still allows him to choose as he will but his nature does not offer him viable righteous options. I hold to total depravity in an Augustinian way, namely, that all men from the fall of Adam on are corrupted in all parts of their nature such that there is no way to obtain favor with God. Sinful man is dead in his sinful deeds, nature, and federal imputation from Adam's sin (Rom. 5:12-17; Eph. 2:1-5). Sinful man's condition is summed up in Romans 3 by quoting a catena of phrases lifted from Old Testament descriptions of the wicked person.

> There is none righteous, not even one;
> There is none who understands,
> There is none who seeks for God,
> All have turned aside, together they have become useless;
> There is none who does good,
> There is not even one...(Rom. 3:10-12).

This kind of bondage in sin is still probably best understood to possess free will since nothing external to oneself limits one's will in any way that compels a choice other than what is consistent with one's own nature. At this point one may recognize that there is a tension between total depravity self-limiting free will and the theoretically more open previous comments about free will from the commands, blessings, and warnings in texts such as the synoptics. This is a tension within the Biblical text itself and as a theologian I do not wish to deny or ignore any aspect that the Bible legitimately brings forward. To go off to one side tends to make one Reformed or Lutheran, to go off on to the other side tends to make one Arminian or even Pelagian. The Biblical texts present a composite that maintains a tension without simplifying it to these human constructs. For purposes of our paper here that tension affirms free will in a compatible way with sovereignty.

Salvation is a divine enlivening of the dead non-Christian from sin to righteousness (Eph. 2:1, 5: Col. 2:13). Salvation life does not come unless God creates it within the one to whom He gives faith (e.g. 2 Pet. 1:1). God justifies the believer based on the redemption that is accomplished in Christ. These transformations are wonderful expressions of God's grace and mercy. This aspect of the model can be charted like a determinism where divine control creates life in us where previously only death had been.

The process of regeneration, new covenant and glorification recover and remedy the Christian in full freedom from the flesh nature. The new birth that is caused by the Spirit's work brings about a new and everlasting life and a responsiveness in faith (Jn. 3:3-16). Paul parallels this regenerated nature with the realization that our old man (*anthropos*) dies as we enter into Christ and we become a new man (*anthropos*, Rom. 6:2-9; 2 Cor. 5:17; Gal. 2:20; Eph. 4:22-24; Col. 3:9-10). As new men we have the ability to consider ourselves dead to sin so that we will freely choose righteousness. The work of the Holy Spirit is a new covenant enabling from within so that we are prompted to choose righteousness; the Spirit is the guarantor of growth enabling us to produce the distinctive fruit of the Spirit life (Rom. 8:4-17; Gal. 5:16-24). This enablement operates as a soft determinism prompting and inclining our enlivened free wills to choose to live the life of these religious affections. While we are no longer in the realm of the flesh and we are growing in righteousness as prompted by the Spirit we still struggle with the bodily flesh condition as babes in Christ and then in longstanding struggle as the inner man seeks to live out the Law righteously while that which is peripheral about me (that is, flesh) re-entangles me in sins (Rom. 7:14-25; 1 Cor. 3:1). Ultimately glorification will redeem our bodies and we can escape the futility and suffering of this life through Christ (Rom. 7:24-25; 8:18-30). In glorification our freedom will bring about unhindered righteous living.

When I presented this paper at a meeting of the Evangelical Theological Society, Roger Nicolle asked whether this free will of humanity continued beyond the grave. In answer to this, I further contrast to Aquinas; humans retain free will into the afterlife. For example, the rich man who dies with Lazarus asks of father

Abraham that Lazarus would help quench his thirst and warn his brothers (Lk. 16:19-31). Presumably these are free will requests from the rich man to try to remedy conditions which he now realized and responded to in light of his free will. Neither request was granted. However, the saints also have free will in the afterlife. For example, in Revelation 6:9-11 the martyred saints presumably from their own free will ask God how long He will wait to avenge their deaths. Furthermore, the reward given to the faithful servants in the parable of the minas includes extending the faithful servants' responsible care from the little things of this servant condition to continued responsible care over cities in Christ's kingdom (Lk. 19:17, 19). Therefore, responsible free will continues as an everlasting condition for Christ's followers within His kingdom. When this afterlife free will is folded together with the Pauline glorification, the saints continue in glory freely, only choosing good and not sin.

I position myself as a relationally sensitive Calvinist appreciating God's relational engagement with the creation. I follow Edwards' definition of free will and a reformed commitment to determinism of God as an efficient cause parallel and redundant with the human free will. There is a compatibility of nonexclusive redundant causalities from both divine and human side that tries to maintain the multiple models and tension that the Biblical text sets forth. One implication of this technique is that most Christian models of this question will find something attractive in here and something annoying in here. My hope in this is not to be an odd target but to encourage the reader to try to be faithful to all the Biblical texts in their contexts. My dream is that in your faithfulness to these texts you will worship our sovereign God more intimately and choose to live for Him more zealously.

Problems of Evil

A certain Peanuts cartoon shows Lucy bent over and saying to Linus "Look at this tiny little bug. It's appalling how little he knows... He's not like us ... He doesn't know anything about voting, or disease, or earthquakes, or love, or Monday Mornings." To which Linus responds, "Who's better off?"

Soon after World War 2, Albert Camus crafted a specter of suffering and evil in *The Plague*[1] in which the land is darkened seemingly without cause. While the night watchman took it as fate, seeing the rats scurrying as from a sinking ship, a metaphor for modern man, Dr. Rieux puts no stock in such fatalism. Jesuit Father Paneloux, espousing a just world, called the town to self-examination before the imagery of God's judgment striking down townspeople with a plague of Exodus proportions. While the magistrate was swept up into the absolute nature of the issues, Dr. Rieux could not see how innocent children could have earned a sentence of death. In his attempts to heal, the doctor found himself fighting what the priest called the will of God. For the priest the belief was complete or nothing, one either joins Christ in love of God through this suffering or he is damned in isolation of this imprisonment of quarantine to hell. The doctor mirrors Camus' view that suffering occurs in this life therefore we should try to revolt against it by trying to do good. Dr. Rieux's attempt to remedy the problem put him outside the priest's parameters of salvation and thus, fighting God. Yet when the priest died the doctor continued to live. Many lost themselves

---

[1] Albert Camus, *The Plague*. translated by Stuart Gilbert, (N.Y.: Vintage Books, 1972).

in the collective destiny of sleepwalking through the plague, but for a few there were moments of revolt as when Grand wept in fantasies, nose pressed to the toy shop window. From the human side, Camus views suffering as futile and horrible. The only noble response is to try to do good in its midst.

Unfortunately, often the opponents in such theodicy discussions talk past each other by not even defining basic concepts of good and evil in the same way. If the definitions are not the same then the responses will not be addressing the other's felt problem. So we need to begin by giving four basic definitions so that we may actually identify which of the problems of evil are being addressed. 1) For some, especially those who approach this through Platonism, good can be metaphysically defined *as being,* and evil then is *metaphysical privation in being.* For example, my new car is made of good solid metal while my older car lacks metal as it is rusting through in several places. In these instances rust is not a thing but rather the lack of good metal; likewise evil is not a thing—it is the lack of good. 2) Good emerges from the realm of morality as *God's will or virtue.* This makes evil to be *vice or violation of God's will.* Under this category truthful statements are good and especially when they underscore a character trait of truthfulness. 3) Another definition often used by existentialists is that good is existential benefit or pleasure. To balance this evil would be defined existentially as detriment or pain. 4) A final definition of good would be one of teleology whereby that which is designed or purposeful is the good. In contrast, evil would be that which is purposeless or excess, such as in excess pain.

Terrence Tilley extends Boethius by claiming that doing theodicy is itself an evil.[2]   However, this is not what Boethius writes about when in *The Consolation of Philosophy* he is contemplating his impending execution. The problem as he says is like offering sweet medicine of comfort by providing reasons for suffering without dealing with the disease or situation underlying the

---

[2] Terrence Tilley, *The Evils of Theodicy.* (Washington: Georgetown University Press, 1991), pp. 141-58.

suffering.[3] This does not seem to be a reaction against theodicy but rather a positive underscoring of the need to call down unrighteousness wherever it is found, especially when this evil is still moving forward and crushing people. It means evil cannot be merely handled as an impassioned academic treatise, but must also address suffering in passionate ways that try to heal real problems as well. There must be a call to orthopraxis. This means that any discussion about evil needs to be taken as a whole rather than isolating a response here or there to see if evil is not in fact called down throughout in different ways.

For Johannes Metz[4] there is an irreducible horror of suffering to which an argument is inappropriate. For example, the holocaust is an assassination attempt on Israel and everything holy. In such a setting as this we cannot justify such behavior. Metz follows this with an appeal that there is a necessary need to mystically protest and plead with God in prayer after the pattern of Job, the Hebrew laments, and the prophets (refusing to be comforted). Certainly by shear volume the individual laments encourage us to follow their pattern prayers in calling for divine aid in the midst of our suffering. So I write these explanations and arguments not just to try to make sense of God when there is evil experienced, but also to foster prayer, which is always appropriate, but especially in suffering.

However, several lament psalms (and certainly Job) bring the themes of God's sovereignty together with that of prayer which leaves Job with the need to simply submit to the sovereign's will. The answer given from the sovereign God to Job is essentially that I (God) am sovereign, there is no other like me and I can do this suffering to you because in my sovereignty I get to do that which I have done. This is a harsh answer but I think it captures the essence of what is being said in Job 38–41. As I developed in the chapter on sovereignty and free will,

---

[3] Anicius Boethius, *The Consolation of Philosophy.* (Cambridge: Harvard, 1983), Bk 1, prose paragraph 1.

[4] Johann Baptist Metz, *A Passion for God: The Mystical Political Dimension of Christianity* or *Pasion de dios la existencia de ordenes religiosas hoy* (Barcelona: Herder, 1992).

God's determination of sin and evil does not make God Himself evil for occasionally God explains His rationale to be of good purposes which evidence that God is good. The supreme example of this kind of explanation is the prologue to the book of Job which identifies that Job's suffering takes place as a demonstration to Satan. Satan uses the retribution principle by accusing God that He buys off those who serve Him by blessing them. This view is shown to be wrong as demonstrated by Job's life. Job serves and worships God without requiring God to reward him (Job 1:9-12; 2:2-6). There is however no evidence that Job actually knew that His suffering happened for such a lofty purpose as this. The other side of the retribution principle is expressed through the counsel of Eliphaz, Bildad, and Zophar, who articulate that God causes sinners to suffer and good to prosper. God outright declares that their view is wrong in Job 42:7. Job needs to pray for these counselors' recovery. However, in the midst of the counsel Job is incensed by what they say, softening their claims that some sufferers are sinners and some prosperous people are good. This means that in his insistence of his innocence he claims God to be unjust. However, he repents of these demands when confronted by the awesome sovereign God, departing from this view as wrong in Job 42:2-6. Elihu reminds Job that some suffering comes to turn back rebellion, claiming that Job is sinning in his claims for innocence. There may be some truth to this counsel but in Job's state of mind it further motivates him to demand his innocence. God's answer to this whole row is not really an answer at all. God instead hit Job with questions which left Job humbled with the sovereignty and omniscience of God when compared to his own smallness. God did not tell Job why he was suffering, Job must simply submit to Him. In contemplating the sovereignly caused suffering, we do not have enough knowledge to judge God and neither are we in the place to judge Him, so we must live with a certain tension of seemingly incongruous, unexplained things which (Rom. 9:14, 19-22). The active exclusion of Esau and the hardening of Pharaoh's heart are the work of the Potter over the clay and God as potter gets to do these things without our judgment. In such situations as these submitting to the sovereign God and faithfulness to Him are the only options we have. The following arguments do not remove this need to submit to the sovereign God.

To complement this sovereign side, a range of theodicies try to make some sense of evil from the free will side. Since I argued for a compatible sovereignty and free will, both sides should be developed to give the full answer.

Early in his Christian writing career, Augustine writes a response to evil especially showing the deficiency of a dualistic Manichaeanism when compared to a rather Platonic Christian view. That is, instead of viewing evil as a rival thing, evil is seen as a lack or a privation of a good thing.[5] As previously stated, rust is not an actual thing metaphysically, it is the lack of good metal. Such a view does not make sense of all definitions of evil but when the subject of evil is approached metaphysically it is a helpful way to keep God as creator and His creation process pure of taint. An Augustinian theodicy can be briefly stated as follows:

1. God created everything good.
2. Evil is not a thing; it is a privation in a good thing.
3. All evil is either sin[6] or the punishment of sin.[7]
4. Evil only harms that which is mutable in nature (i.e. creation and not God).[8]
5. The moral agent that committed the sin is responsible for its evil, therefore in such cases God is not to be faulted.[9]
6. The punishment of sinning moral agents is just and good[10] for the world at large both in limiting evil committed and inclining any moral agents who are not punished to appreciate their good state perpetually. Furthermore,

---

[5] Augustine, *City of God*, 7.17-18; *Confessions* 5.20.
[6] Augustine, *On Free Will*, 3.17.48; *City of God*, 12.7-8
[7] Augustine, *City of God*, 5.9; 19.15
[8] Augustine, *City of God*, 12.3
[9] Augustine, *On Free Will*, 3.17.48; *City of God*, 12.7-8

those who reject salvation are condemned to hell (reclaiming God's honor).[11] These damned are still party to the best world because it is better to live with one's own free choice to do evil than to be forced to do good against one's will.

This argument reflects Platonic metaphysical concerns in premise two. However, these may also be Christian and Biblical concerns as well since in the Genesis 1 creation account, the things created by God repeatedly are pronounced as good. That is, God does not create any evil thing and nothing is essentially evil. Therefore any evil that has encroached into the creation has unfortunately done so as an expression of rebellion from God's original design. So for Augustine beings remain essentially good but in rebellion they corrupt themselves and become morally evil. So in the Genesis 3 fall of humankind there emerges a corrupt twist to our moral nature. It is as if we are all Gollum, from Tolkien's *Hobbit* and *Lord of the Rings*. In the fall we become a grotesque pathetic creature twisted by our passions as we whisper after our precious ring of sin. Every time we do the sin we twist ourselves further and also press deeply into our soul the desire to sin all that much more.

Augustine's answer to such rebellion is judgment. In fact, at rare instances he even seems to float the concept of evil on another level as existential experience so that when God judges a sinner or a nation of rebels, God's judgment is a kind of evil for these rebels as they experience His judgment. This mirrors the specific statement by Isaiah 45:7 that Yahweh brings upon the Babylonians the evil of divine judgment (*ra'*). When God does this kind of judgment, He does not somehow become evil Himself because His purposes of the judgment are good. Therefore, good and evil is seen somewhat aesthetically. If one is immersed in the darker hues of rebellion then judgment will crush these individuals but from a full view of the picture as a whole these darker hues have

---

[10] Augustine, *On Free Will*, 3.24-26; *City of God, 11.16-18; Confessions 7.13*

divine purposefulness, thus ultimately being good. For so it was that Christ's death as an evil put to flight and disoriented Jesus disciples but it fits within the overarching purposes of God as a significant salvific good. Part of these broader aesthetic purposes include things such as limiting the sin committed and cultivating the free will response of the creature. Valuing the free will can be seen as inclining any moral agents who are not punished to appreciate their good state perpetually. Furthermore, those who reject salvation and are condemned to hell are still party to the best world because, as stated earlier, it is better to live with one's own free choice to do evil than to be forced to do good against one's will. Some may find such a justification of hell distasteful, but remember in this perspective it has purposefulness and thus is experienced by God as a good because it fits into His design. An additional aspect of this design is the reordering of God's honor in its proper place by judging appropriately those who have dishonored Him.

Alvin Plantinga draws this free will defense back to a more modest expression.[12] In running a modest free will defense, he admits more ambiguity, somewhat after the pattern of Job without trying to solve all sides of the theodicy problem; only solving just enough for believers to rest within our basic beliefs.

7. In order for God to create moral agents, God must have created them with the possibility of committing moral evil.
8. If finite moral agents have the possibility of doing moral evil, then probably some will commit moral evil.
9. Some moral agents commit moral evil.
10. Therefore, moral evil can be blamed on the moral agent and not God.
11. If natural evil is a result of moral evil (human sins, satanic or demonic activity) then natural evil can be blamed on the moral agent and not God.
12. Natural evil is probably the result of moral evil.

---

[11]Augustine, *On Free Will*, 3.26.

13. Therefore, natural evil is probably to be blamed on a moral agent and not God.

The move to affirm that natural evil is probably the result of moral evil is built on the baseline of the fall in which with the initial rebellion features of corruption, like weeds, come into the creation order. Perhaps also the book of Job, with the orchestrations of Satan tries to destroy Job's loyalty to God by having Job's children killed and his wealth taken. The reader sees that the sufferer, Job, does not cause his family's suffering but that quite a bit of his suffering is caused by an angelic being. Some of this suffering is natural, as with a wind. Quite a bit of this suffering is also an expression of abuse, as with the foreign powers robbing his fields of the livestock that happen to be there. The moral choices that we humans make that unfortunately end up abusing others are our doing and we are the blameworthy party for them; the fault should not be leveled at God's feet.

John Hick popularized a view, which as a minority report, he titled the Irenaean theodicy. This approach focuses on developing virtue in this life or the salvific process of "soul-making."[13] For Hick, "the good that outshines all ill is not a paradise long since lost but a kingdom which is yet to come in its full glory and permanence."[14] This model can be constructed as follows:[15]

---

[12] Alvin Plantinga, *God, Freedom, and Evil* (Grand Rapids: Eerdmans, 1977), pp. 12-49.

[13] John Hick, *Evil and the God of Love* (N. Y.: Harper and Row, 1966) chapter 13 'The Starting Point,' also developed in Hick's *Philosophy of Religion* (Englewood Cliffs: Prentice Hall, 1970).

[14] John Hick, *Philosophy of Religion,* (Englewood Cliffs: Prentice-Hall, 1970), p. 521.

[15] If this kind of argument is run on a microscopic level it can set up a process theodicy, however there are major flaws in such process argumentation. A process theodicy would see each occasion as partially self-created and partially created by previous actual occasions. In the process model, God's power over each occasion, and in directing the stream of occasions as a whole is necessarily limited to offering the best possibility and the persuasion of a creative thrust. In this model, evil is an aesthetic measure of the extent to which God's will is thwarted (discord verses harmony, triviality verses intensity). Since a process God is finite in power, He is not to be faulted for evil in the world but instead He is to be credited whenever the evolutionary development of good occurs. However this sort of process model has some major flaws. First, a process God provides no guarantee that He will overcome evil. He is merely doing the best He can and that is better than anyone else can do. Secondly, a process God does not ultimately overcome evil because God's relationship with the created order is an everlasting relationship of making creation better, but never arriving at perfection. Furthermore, ultimate evil is the perishing of the occasions

14. Moral agent's goodness that has come about through the making of free and responsible moral choices in situations of real difficulty and temptation, is intrinsically more valuable than goodness created ready made, without the free participation of the human agent.

Perhaps this premise has implied assumptions like the following. A world with higher moral virtues is a morally better world. A world where humans are permitted to sin as a precondition to a better world is better than one where they are not.[16] For example, certain virtues such as courage, fortitude, mercy, and forgiveness are attainable only in a world where sin occurs. Additionally many virtues, such as love and kindness, are heightened by the presence of evil. Furthermore, the appreciation of something is enhanced by the threat of its loss. Likewise, trust is also heightened with a complex world in which we cannot easily figure it out but we remember that the word from God is a clear beacon within these stormy seas. For these kinds of conditional virtues, it is impossible to create or coerce directly on optionally free beings because such action would abuse their freedom. It is then best to persuade conditional virtues by good, allowing for growth in virtues, which provides one with increased knowledge, experience and commitment in these virtues. These virtues and appreciations increase with the increase in overcoming of different and diverse evil. There is no place within Christianity for finally *wasted* suffering and goodness.[17]

---

and that is never overcome. Thirdly, a process God is inherently evil, as well as good because the consequent nature of god contains all the record of past occasions (as the actuality of god), then all the evil that has ever occurred characterizes the actuality of God, such that God is limited with regard to his actual goodness. Additionally since all possibilities are within the primordial nature thus God's primordial nature would contain infinite evil possibilities amid the infinite good possibilities. Finally, there is no metaphysical everlasting life in a process God, only being remembered by God in His' consequent nature.

[16] These points are developed at some length by Norman Geisler, *Philosophy of Religion,* (Grand Rapids: Zondervan, 1974), pp. 354-77.

[17] Hick attributes this thought to D. D. Raphael, *The Paradox of Tragedy,* (London: George Allen & Unwin Ltd., 1960), pp. 43-44.

15. In order for moral agents to have genuine freedom they must be created at an epistemic distance from God.

16. Therefore, God created the universe such that real difficulties and temptations exist to foster the moral agent's development.

17. Finally, with such a great amount of evil in the world designed to foster good, a supremely great ultimate good state (i.e. blessed everlasting life) is necessary to compensate for all that has happened on the way to it.

18. Such an ultimately good state will occur.

19. Therefore, God remains good as he involves potential and actual evil in his plan, all to produce the greatest good.

This soul-making argument helps to complement the creation-focused free will arguments, for here there is a focus on the way to the everlasting goal. This argument helps to make sense of the struggle of this life as meaningful in accomplishing that glorifying goal. Any Christian salvation and life strategy that does not retain this growing-in-Christian-virtues emphasis opens itself up to a vulnerable aimless ramble in this life. However, most Christian salvation strategies include a glorification of the saved after death in which the virtues that individuals lacked in this life would be made up in glory as they are transfixed by the glory of God. Does God violate an individual's free will by creating in glory the faith for wavering believers, that they lacked in this life? Is there a problem in this theodicy with being able to finally be at the blessed goal without further development of virtues or must the quest for virtues extend through the afterlife as well? Does God violate the elect angels' free will by creating in them a will or an inclination so that they will not choose to go awry? Are these elect angels hindered in their development of virtues by not being able to violate these virtues or do they learn of these things by proxy (watching us grow)? Could the world be better if God created us all so that we would not sin and would be excellent in virtue (as we will in fact be in the bliss of glorification)? Could we somehow have a condition similar to the elect angels whereby we would learn by proxy (from someone else's struggle) or perhaps in a simulated condition that would not actually mar us along the way?

These providential, free will and soul-making theodicies do not have to be mutually exclusive, for Thomas Aquinas combines them for a full orbed approach to evil. Like Augustine, evil is not a thing, nor has an essence of its own, since it is a corruption in a good thing, which good thing is created by God.[18] Every agent acts freely for good but sometimes the unintentional or deformed inadvertently brings about evil.[19] God indirectly causes evil through defect in the instrumental cause (as a genetic deformity passed from parent to child) and the very action of causation brings about a defect (God destroys some things in the process of making others).[20] So as in Augustine, evil is seen as sin of a creature or punishment for that sin.[21] Thomas cites Isaiah 45:5, 7 and Amos 3:6 in declaring that God causes evil of penalty but not of cause of sin. The present existence is not the perfect world[22] but God is in the process of making the perfect world, which will exclude all evil.[23] Until God's design is achieved fully no court should be convened to judge God. When God's design is achieved God will be vindicated from any possible charge. God is perfect in goodness essentially and thus any expression of evil ultimately fits aesthetically within God's ultimate good plan.[24] God's perfect knowledge of evil is through the good, and thus God's knowledge consists only of good.[25] All created things are good through

---

[18] Thomas Aquinas, *Summa Theologica,* Bk. I, Q. 48, A. 3; Q. 49, A. 3; *Summa contra Gentiles* 3.7 and 11.

[19] Aquinas, *Summa Theologica,* Bk. I, Q. 48, A. 1, Q. 83, A. 1; *Summa contra Gentiles,* ch.3, 7-9; *Disputed Questions Concerning Evil,* Q. 1, A. 1.

[20] Aquinas, *Summa Theologica,* Bk. I, Q. 49, A. 2.

[21] Aquinas, *Summa Theologica,* Bk. I, Q. 19, A. 9; Q. 48, A. 5; Q. 49, A. 2; Bk I-II, Q. 79, A. 1-2; *Disputed Questions Concerning Evil,* Q. 1, A. 4.

[22] Gottfried Leibniz, *Monadology: and Other Philosophical Essays,* (Translated by Paul and Anne Schrecker. Indianapolis: Bobbs-Merill, 1965), pp. 53-55.

[23] Aquinas, *Summa Theoligica,* Bk. I, Q. 2, A. 3 Reply 1 (following Augustine, *Enchirdion* 2); Bk. I, Q. 22, A. 2, Reply Obj. 2; and *Summa Contra Gentiles,* ch 2-22.

[24] Aquinas, *Summa Theologica,* Bk. I, Q. 4, A. 1-3, and Q. 6, A. 1-3.

[25] Ibid. Bk. I, Q. 14, A. 10; Q. 15, A. 13; Q. 18, A. 4.

participating in and being supported by the goodness of God.[26] With everything by nature striving for good, the end of everything is a good.[27] Ultimately everything is directed toward the good end by the providence of God.[28] God does not permit evil to occur in His works unless He is powerful and good enough to produce good from this evil. Ultimately the end of all the creatures is to know God and to be like Him to the extent that their level of being will permit.[29] Thomas cites Revelation 22:13 in claiming that God as Omega is the last end of all.

While I largely follow this Thomistic hybrid theodicy with providential, free will and soul-making components, I wish to distance myself from the overly optimistic natural law feature which Aristotle has given to Aquinas. Instead of describing man as inclining toward good it is better to affirm that while man is essentially good (metaphysically) as a creation of God, man has corrupted himself horribly. A brief reminder of a few Biblical texts shows the depth of our sin problem. For example, Genesis 6:5 reminds us that "The LORD saw that the wickedness of man was great on the earth, and that every intent of the thoughts of his heart was only evil continually." From the wisdom perspective of Ecclesiastes 9:3, "The hearts of the sons of men are full of evil, and insanity is in their hearts throughout their lives. Afterwards they go to the dead." In the looming condition of the Babylonian captivity, Jeremiah 17:9 bemoans that, "The heart is more deceitful than all else and is desperately sick; who can understand it?" In the same captivity context Isaiah confesses "All of us like sheep have gone astray, each of us has turned to his own way" (Isa. 53:6). These damning judgments are summed up in Paul's catena of quotes applying the Psalms' description of the wicked and violent man to all of us, "There is none righteous, not even one; there is none who understands, there is none who seeks for God; All have turned aside,

---

[26] Aquinas, *Summa Theologica*, Bk. I, Q. 5, A. 3-4; Q. 7, *Truth*, Q. 21, A. 4-5.

[27] Aquinas, *Summa contra Gentiles*, ch. 16.

[28] Aquinas, *Summa Theologica*, Bk. I, Q. 22, P 2, Reply Obj. 2; an example is God permitting demons to assault men Q. 114, A. 1.

together they have become useless; there is none who does good, there is not even one" (Rom. 3:10-12). Such descriptions of total depravity make it clear that the fallen human condition excludes this Thomistic natural inclination toward good.

Norman Geisler reworks this Thomistic model with the appreciation of our sinful human condition. Geisler states that his theodicy is more explicitly the best way to the best world. As with Aquinas the eschatological goal is the arena in which we should evaluate this best world. It is in this bliss that God demonstrates Himself to be supremely good and gracious in providing His salvation for us.

20. It is morally better for God to create the morally best world possible (to do less than his best is evil for God).
21. This best way to the best world is the worst world, possibly containing the most evil possible that God can turn to the greatest good (God's character limits evil so none is excessive).
22. There seems to be pointless evil.
23. Therefore, there are reasons for God's allowing evil which we do not or maybe cannot know.
24. Since the greatest good is obtained in the eschatologically perfect world, this present world is the best way to the best world.

This hybrid strategy seems to be on target in handling the metaphysical, moral, and design aspects of good and evil. It also has the distinct advantage of culling together the strengths of the various arguments, whether they are providential, free will, or soul-making. It also does justice to the depth of human sin and grandeur of God. It also emphasizes the salvific strategy which is the Biblical emphasis in resolving the problem of evil. Sins are incorporated in God's plan as ultimately greater good. For example, the sin of selling off their brother Joseph in

---

[29] Aquinas, *Summa contra Gentiles*, ch. 17-21, 25, 37, and in chapters 26-36 Thomas itemizes what this happiness is not.

Genesis 37:12-35 is orchestrated by God as a good; "You meant it for evil but God meant it for good" (Gen. 45:4-8; 50:19). However, more needs to be developed on the practical problem of pain and the existential condition of evil within which we live.

C. S. Lewis in *The Problem of Pain*[30] explores a practical slant on the problem of evil in which he emphasizes predictability to develop the lessons for soul-making.

25. If God was to have a world in which there would be genuine moral choices along with genuine punishment for disobedience the evil behavior is possible and there would be warning signs of sufficient intensity to cause us to alter behavior

26. God provided the world with appropriate levels of pain as warning signs to deter greater evil from occurring.

27. The good warning signs of pain can result in considerable evil under certain circumstances.

28. For intelligent planning to occur the world needs to be predictable so God could not have created a world where evil results would not occur (e.g. a solid hammer for driving nails does not become a sponge as it hits a person.

29. Therefore, God has created only good, but this good can be perverted into evil when we misuse it or something goes awry with the creation.

Unfortunately we live in a day in which horrendous evils ensue. Marilyn Adams defines "horrendous evils" as evil that a person participates in which calls into question that her life could be good. "Such reasonable doubt arises because it is so humanly difficult to conceive how such evils could be overcome."[31]   A

---

[30] C. S. Lewis, *The Problem of Pain* (N. Y.: Macmillan, 1957).
[31] Marilyn Adams, "Horrendous Evils and the Goodness of God" in *The Problem of Evil* (Oxford: Oxford University Press, 1990, edited by Marilyn and Robert Adams), p. 211.

prime example of such horrendous evils is what Fyodor Dostoevsky has Ivan Karamazov[32] say:

> By the way, a Bulgarian I met lately in Moscow told me about the crimes committed by the Turks and Circassians in all parts of Bulgaria through fear of a general rising of the Slavs. They burn villages, murder, rape women and children, they nail their prisoners to the fences by the ears, leave them so till morning, and in the morning they hang them all sorts of things you can't imagine. People talk sometimes of bestial cruelty, but that's a great injustice and insult to the beast; a bear can never be so cruel as a man, so artistically cruel. The tiger only tears and gnaws, that's all he can do. He would never think of nailing people by the ears, even if he were able to do it. These Turks took pleasure in torturing children, too; cutting the unborn child from the mother's womb, and tossing babies up in the air and catching them on the points of their bayonets before their mother's eyes. Doing it before the mother's eyes was what gave zest to the amusement. Here is another scene that I thought very interesting. Imagine a trembling mother with her baby in her arms, a circle of invading Turks around her. They've planned a diversion; they pet the baby, laugh to make it laugh. They succeed, the baby laughs. At that moment a Turk points a pistol four inches from the baby's face. The baby laughs with glee, holds out its little hands to the pistol, and he pulls the trigger in the baby's face and blows out its brains. Artistic, wasn't it?

Such horrendous evils are not merely kept in literature but lived out by those ethnic groups that continue to experience ethnic cleansing, which still goes on in the twenty first century. Who learns from such situations? How many lives or limbs need to be lost until no one learns any more in such situation? It often does not look like people learn much from being in such atrocities. If we in the easy chairs reading about these horrendous evils are the ones who learn from them, then why do these atrocities keep repeating? We could all learn what there is to learn by proxy by metaphors rather than broken bones and smashed lives. Are

---

[32] Fyodor Dostoevsky, *The Brothers Karamozov* (Chicago: Encyclopaedia Britannica, 1952).

virtues developed in the wake of such contexts? Or are spirits and lives crushed, with vengeance kindled so that we only need wait until the situation has turned around and the blood feud will go the other way the next time? Are these atrocities sufficiently justified by the few who forgive and learn in the midst of the pain? Remember, with Geisler's theodicy we should expect hugely revolting horrendous evils in the midst of our world and our life. How can it all be turned to good?

We don't have to go to the big and dramatic to face the same problem; it surfaces on the personal level as well. As a seminary student finishing up my Masters degree and heading into my doctorate, my wife and I decided that we would like to have kids. When kids didn't come we prayer and consulted doctors. There were three problems; we fixed every one and kids still did not come. In our evangelical context we affirmed family, took vacations with families to help them enjoy the mountains and trails we had come to enjoy, but kids didn't come. The first couple of years we learned some lessons but then we began to feel dented and contorted. We did not like part of what we were becoming, feeling like damaged goods. We felt that God had turned His face from us. We endured some other sufferings as well during this time, some of them exquisitely painful. As the suffering continued this pounding rendered us into feeling that we were "grotesques."[33] We didn't want to be this way but we were becoming this way with a flinch every time a certain kind of situation arose. In the midst of this, our faithful dog McGreggor blew out his knees so that he could no longer get up, laying part of the day in his own feces because he could not take care of himself any longer. What did McGreggor or we learn from this? We got to a point where we didn't learn anything more from these situations, we just got further dented. As our life was tumbling down to what we felt was the dark side of God I cried out with psalm 42-43, which verses became a personal guide in prayer. "As the

---

[33] This is a metaphor from Flannery O'Connor, *Wise Blood* (N.Y.: Noonday Press, 1962) which speaks of oddly misshapen people like a "blind" evangelist who gets in his own way but God can still use him.

deer pants for water, so I pant for You, O God. I thirst for God, for the living God; when shall I appear before God's face? My tears have been my food day and night, while others say 'Where is your God?'" (Ps. 42:1-3).   What is the answer to this pain? The psalmist doesn't really give an answer except a repeated refrain of commitment. "Why are you in despair O my soul? And why have you become disturbed within me? Hope in God, for I will again praise You, for the help for my presence is God's presence" (Ps. 42:5, 11; 43:5 conflated).   The suffering did not deepen my allegiance to God but rather it revealed an already deep allegiance to Him. Years later as I look back many of the dents are deeply there, a few not as deep, but some deeper. I don't like that. God has been gracious: I have a great marriage, a good job, two wonderful kids. Even so, I have always been one who longs for kingdom and I long for kingdom now.

In such horrendous or personal experiences of evil Jürgen Moltmann takes consolation that the triune God suffers with us.[34]   God as Father grieves as the Son dies and other children suffer. From this grief, the Father woos the earth toward His kingdom. In addition, the Son as God suffers personally on behalf of and with others as their redeemer leading them through suffering toward kingdom. By extension, the Spirit as God suffers with and within His children prompting them to resist suffering and to do good toward His kingdom (fostering such activism as liberation theology). Do we join Moltmann in these sentiments? Is God heartless or does He suffer? We all know that Jesus weeps and suffers to heal our wounds (Isa. 53:4; Jn. 11:35). Perhaps God's presentation of Himself as Husband and Father to His straying people shows his emotion as well (Isa. 54:8-10; 63:7-9). The Spirit prompts us to intimate prayers as we suffer with Christ (Rom. 8:14-17).

Elie Wiesel approaches the subject with the assumption that we are existentially free to make our life meaningful. As we have seen this is difficult to

---

[34] Jürgen Moltmann, *The Trinity and the Kingdom* (Minneapolis: Fortress Press, 1993), *The Crucified God* (Wilmore: Asbury Theological Seminary, 1992), *God in Creation: A New Theology of Creation and the Spirit of God* (N.Y.: Harper & Row, 1985).

do, for we can pull very few of life's strings. In each of his novels he tells an autobiographical composite of different facets of the problem of evil. In *Night*[35] he recounts of how he survived as a living dead victim of holocaust suffering and insists on being heard as a way of working out the pain for himself and calling the world to accountability so that it will never happen again. In *Dawn*,[36] evil is a real threat, with victims becoming self-reliant freedom fighters to selflessly raise up Israel, hating their enemies. In *Accident*[37] as memories of holocaust haunt, suicide is a meaningful existential choice and there is real shame to fail in a suicide attempt, missing the train to death. In *Twilight*[38] (25 years later), the older generation force the young to join the legacy of being a witness to remember the dead and proclaim their death so it has meaning; in this context suicide is treason.

I know a few things in this life. One of them is that my wife and God know my pain, care for me and will do what they can to remedy my pain. I believe that God will do the same for others as well. This God is supremely good. This God has no limits except Himself. This God will be victorious and bring in the kingdom. The hurts will be healed. And it boggles my mind how He can accomplish this that I believe of Him, because there are a staggering number of crushed and bruised people to be healed. I am one of them, and I long for the healing.

---

[35] Elie Wiesel, *Night* (N.Y.: Bantam Books, 1982).
[36] Elie Wiesel, *Dawn* (N.Y.: Bantam Books, 1961).
[37] Elie Wiesel, *Accident* (N.Y.: Bantam Books, 1990).
[38] Elie Wiesel, *Twighlight* (N.Y.: Schocken Books, 1988).

The Sovereignty of God and Prayer

This question "Why pray if God is deterministically sovereign?" can be multiplied several times as Why evangelize or Why do any religious obligation? Of course an immediate answer is because God has commanded it. For example, we are to pray without ceasing (1 Thess. 5:17). However, these kinds of questions and the specific one about prayer is more intimate and complex than merely obedience. Such an investigation raises the apologetic question, "Is prayer significant?" However when we are in need, we go even further as we join with Job in asking the practical question, "What profit should we have if we pray unto the Almighty?" (Job 21:15). A look at the question more closely helps to unpack aspects of our spiritual life under the sovereign God in practical ways: what is prayer, why is it done, and how is it to be done best? This look also helps us to see glimpses of the intricacy of the sovereign God as He folds and envelopes our free choices into His sovereign plan.

What is prayer? From contemporary English speakers, prayer may be defined as an expression of thought and feeling toward a deity. Though almost every prayer in the Bible prays to the true God (e.g. 2 Chron. 6:14; Eph. 3:14), occasionally idolaters pray also but to their false gods (Isa. 45:20). Such an expression is so common that William James considered that virtually everyone cries out to a god who could help when they find themselves caught in desperate circumstances.[1] However, the O.T. concept of prayer is broader than these desperate petitions so as to include the wide range of emotions. That is, the Psalms (with its laments, hymns, and liturgy) fills out the broad pattern of expressing thought and feeling to the Deity. However, on emphasis of the psalm material one would say that petition still is the emphasis. Sometimes reformation influenced writers primarily view prayer as worship.[2] Whereas, in the N.T. it is helpful to recognize that the words translated prayer (*deesis, enteyxis, eychomai, parakaleo, proseychomai*) actually are words of petition, asking God for something. Often these words draw this action of petition together with an acknowledgment of sovereignty. For example, *aiteō* is always an inferior asking a superior for something. The use of these words in the N.T. points to petition as the meaning of prayer. In light of these concerns the command "Pray without ceasing" is actually a command for the corporate assembly (as evidenced by the plurals) to be characterized by repeated petitioning God for their concerns (1 Thess. 5:17).

With both the broader and more petition focused definitions of prayer, one reason to pray is that of building a relationship with God. Initially, humans were created in a context in which they conversed with God and walked in each other's presence (Gen. 2:15-17; 3:8-13). Though marred by sin humans began to recover a prayer relationship in Seth's day (Gen. 4:26). Enoch and Noah in relationship "walked with God" (Gen. 5:24; 6:9). Abraham, Isaac, and Jacob "walked before God" in a believing relationship (Gen. 17:1; 24:40; 48:15). In this Abraham was called the friend of God, focusing on his open communication and responsiveness to God (2 Chron. 20:7; Isa. 41:8; James 2:23). Moses spoke in dialogue with God (e.g. Ex. 3). David, the man after God's heart, maintained an active communication with God in hymn and lament, praising and petitioning God. Jesus Christ is the supreme example of the possible interpenetrating relationship

---

[1] William James, *The Principles of Psychology* (Chicago: Encyclopaedia Britannica, 1977), pp. 203-4

with God in prayer (e.g. Jn. 17). All these examples demonstrate that a relationship filled with vibrant communication with God is essential and desirable for the one who loves God. Such a love relationship with God is preeminent in our obligations in this life (Mt. 22:37). One of the most prominent imageries of God in relationship is that of a loving Father. As we address Him as Father in prayer we raise the issues of His sovereignty ("Thy Kingdom come, Thy will be done on earth as it is in heaven") and petition, since the imperatives throughout the Lord's prayer indicate it is a series of requests (Mt. 6:9-13; Lk.11:2-4). The essence of the prayer is that the Sovereign's kingdom may come in all its many ramifications: God's name be recognized as holy, God's kingdom rule on earth, daily physical provision, spiritual cleansing, and guidance with protection. God's sovereignty and prayer are intertwined. This same compassionate Father responds by answering prayer generously and swiftly (Lk.11:5-13). The Holy Spirit shows His leading in the believer's life by prompting us to intimately cry out "Daddy, Father!" to God in prayer (Rom. 8:15-16).

Prayer changes the one who prays. For example, anyone who is anxious or concerned about anything is commanded by Paul to pray (Phil. 4:6-7). God supplies a promise that His peace, which surpasses our comprehension, will guard your minds and hearts in Christ Jesus. Presumably the anxiety that spurred the prayer in the first place will be removed as the prayer involves the person with the God of peace. There may be many other changes as well as we humbly admit our dependency upon God and increase our faith as our prayers are answered in the affirmative. Certainly the wonderful religious affections and fruit of the Spirit which are developed in the midst of an intimate relationship cultivated with God involve prayer in the process. However, the change of the praying person's emotions is not the primary reason to be praying. The petitions identify specific requests sometimes beyond the person who prays. So it is partly why Paul shows us the specific prayers for his disciples character in Christ as he begins most of his

---

[2] E.g. John Hannah, "Prayer and the Sovereignty of God," *Bibliotheca Sacra* 136 (1979)

letters. Paul lets his readers know what he prays for in their character and thanks God when he sees these character traits develop.

With an eternal sovereign God who determines everything, the human prayer and the answer are both expressions of His deterministic choice. C. S. Lewis elaborates this.

> If our prayers are granted at all they are granted from the foundation of the world. God and His acts are not in time. Intercourse between God and man occurs at particular moments for the man, but not for God. If there is–as the very concept of prayer presupposes–an adaptation between the free actions of men in prayer and the course of events, this adaptation is from the beginning inherent in the great single act.[3]

Wayne Spear defends that God ordains *means* as well as *ends* and thereby gives prayer its meaning.

> Paul finds no contradiction between prayer and God's eternal decree. In his most extended discussion of predestination, where he shows that the salvation or rejection of Israel rests upon God's purpose of election (Rom. 9-11), he can say, 'Brethren, my heart's desire and prayer to God for them is that they may be saved' (Rom. 10:1). He is confident that God will complete the work of salvation which he has begun in the Philippians (Phil. 1:6; cf. Rom. 8:29-30); and what he is sure God will do, he prays for (Phil. 1:9-11).[4]

With God's determinative sovereignty including our praying and the answer to these prayers we should willingly pray as participation within the plan of God.

The implementation of this decree is providence. *The Westminster Shorter Catechism* defines this succinctly as "God's works of providence are his most holy, wise, and powerful, preserving and governing all his creatures and all

---

345.
     [3] C. S. Lewis, *Letters to Malcolm: Chiefly on Prayer* (N.Y.: Harcourt, Brace & World, 1963), p. 48.
     [4] Wayne Spear, *The Theology of Prayer* (Grand Rapids: Baker, 1979), p. 69.

their actions."[5] God's providence is comprehensive and unconditional. As Paul says, "So then it does not depend on the man who wills or the man who runs, but on God who has mercy. . . So then He has mercy on whom He desires, and He hardens whom He desires" (Rom. 9:16, 18). God says, "I am God, and there is no other; I am God, and there is no one like Me, declaring the end from the beginning and from ancient times which have not been done, saying, 'My purpose will be established, and I will accomplish all My good pleasure'" (Isa. 46:9b-10). This providential control covers all areas (e.g. Eph. 1:11) even down to giving specific answers to prayer (eg. 1 Sam. 1:19; 2 Chron. 33:13; Ps. 65:2; Isa. 20:5-6; Mt.7:7; Lk. 18:7-8). The proper response to this sovereign God is worship, "Now to the King everlasting, immortal, invisible, the only God, be honor and glory forever and ever. Amen...He who is blessed and only sovereign, the King of kings and Lord of lords; who no man has seen or can see. To Him be honor and everlasting dominion! Amen." (1 Tim. 1:17; 6:15-16).

At times God is shown authoring prayer. For example, when Abraham journeyed into the Negev he and Sarah deceived King Abimelech into thinking that Sarah was not Abraham's wife. As a result Abimelech took her to be his wife. God put him under a curse of death with only one way out: restore Sarah to Abraham and have Abraham pray for him. "Then God said to him in a dream... he will pray for you, and you will liv" (Gen. 20:6-7). It was God's idea for Abraham to intercede before God, not Abraham's idea. This is not an isolated instance of God authoring the prayers of those who are His. Along these same lines, God restored Job's fortunes when he prayed for his friends, but the prayer of Job originated with God (Job 42:8, 10). Some of the council's of the church have even made pronouncements on the fact that God initiates at least some prayers, especially the prayer of initial faith by which believers begin their initial salvation. For example, the Council of Orange, A.D. 529, settled this issue in the third canon saying, "Whoever says that the grace of God can be bestowed in reply

---

[5] *The Westminster Shorter Catechism*, question 11.

to human petition, but not that the grace brings it about so that it is asked for by us, contradicts Isaiah the prophet and the Apostle (Isa. 65:1; Rom. 10:20)."[6] However, the prayers which God initiates are not only those of rescue and salvation. For the Christian there is a developing spirituality dependent upon the Holy Spirit transforming them. Paul develops this in the leading of the Spirit, in which the Spirit prompts the believer to cry out in intimate prayer "Abba, Father" (Rom. 8:14-15). In commenting on the poem, *Dream*, C. S. Lewis says, "If the Holy Spirit speaks in man, then in prayer God speaks to God... 'God did (or said) it' and 'I did (or said) it' can both be true."[7]

Some authors claim that prayer powerfully changes things.[8] For example, Luther writes in language characteristic of those who are sure God has made specific response to their petitions.

> No one believes how strong and mighty prayer is and how much it can do except he whom experience has taught, and who has tried it. It has raised up in our time three persons who lay in danger of death, myself, my wife Katha, and Phillip Melanchthon in 1540 at Weimar.[9]

In such a view prayer, Kierkegaard writes, "The archimedian point outside the world is the little chamber where a true supplicant prays in all sincerity–where he lifts the world off its hinges."[10] Such a posture often expresses itself as though prayer was the cause for accomplishing the request. Jesus often enough told parables that fit this kind of model. For example, there was a friend who was without bread when another friend returned from a long journey (Lk. 11:5-13). The host wishing to be hospitable to the traveler went to another friend late at

---

[6] *The Council of Orange*, third canon, as expressed in Joseph Cullen Ayer, *A Source Book for Ancient Church History* (N.Y.: Charles Scribner's Sons, 1949), p. 473.

[7] Lewis, p. 68. For further development see the chapter in this book on "Sovereignty and Free Will."

[8] Examples include E.M. Bounds, *Power Through Prayer* (Grand Rapids: Zondervan, 1962) and Charles Blanchard, *Getting Things from God* (Wheaton: Sword of the Lord Publishers, 1915).

[9] Quoted by George Buttrick, *Prayer* (N.Y.: Abingdon-Cokesbury, 1942), p. 82.

night and woke him to obtain bread. Though his friend might not give the bread for friendship's sake to get back to sleep he might still give the bread. Summarized as "Ask and it shall be given; seek and you will find; knock, and it shall be opened to you. For everyone who asks, receives; and he who seeks, finds and to him who knocks, it shall be opened." (Lk. 11 9-10). Other parables present the same point, like the persistent widow (Lk. 18:1-8). However, these texts do not leave us with such a resistant uncaring individual to whom we pray. God is better than a loving father who would only give good things. "If you being evil know how to give good gifts to your children, how much more shall your heavenly Father give gifts like the Holy Spirit to those who ask Him?" (Mt. 7:7-11; Lk. 11:11-13). Relationship with such a loving Father tends to soften the need to see the prayer as the cause; a prayer becomes taken into account by the loving Father, Who has fostered our inclination to pray in the first place. C. S. Lewis develops this idea of "taken into account."

> I agree that my deliberately vague expression about our prayers being 'taken into account' is a retreat from Pascal's magnificent dictum ('God has instituted prayer so as to confer upon His creature the dignity of being causes'). But Pascal really does suggest a far too explicit agent-and-patient relation, with God as the patient. And I have another ground for preferring my own more modest formula. To think of our prayers as just 'causes' would suggest that the whole importance of petitionary prayer lay in the achievement of the thing asked for. But really, for our spiritual life as a whole, the 'being taken into account,' or 'considered' matters more than the being granted. Religious people don't talk about the 'results' of prayer; they talk of its being 'answered' or 'heard.' Someone said, 'A suitor wants his suit to be heard as well as granted.' In suits to God, if they are really religious acts at all and not merely attempts at magic, this is even more so. We can bear to be refused but not be ignored.[11]

---

[10] Ibid.
[11] C. S. Lewis, pp. 52-3.

In petition we speak to God as a loving Father Who is already aware of these issues, "for your Father knows what you need, before you ask Him" (Mt. 6:8).

Some human petitions are definitely spoken against in the sovereignty of God. Moses petitioned God to allow him to enter the Promised Land but Yahweh cut off his prayer saying, "Enough! Speak to Me no more of this matter" (Deut. 3:26). Perhaps the most dramatic was that of Jeremiah who petitioned God in trying to hold off the captivity. In answer to his prayers, God said forcefully, "As for you, do not pray for this people, and do not lift up cry or prayer for them, and do not intercede with Me; for I do not hear you" (Jer. 7:16; 11:11-12, 14; 14:11-12; 15:1). Even if God's actions are determined, petition against them is natural but not effective. For example, God told Jeremiah to stop petitioning Him on behalf of Israel, since their sinning rendered divine judgment inevitable (Jer. 7:16; 11:14; 14:11). Nevertheless, Jeremiah continued to intercede on behalf of the nation (Jer. 14:7-9, 13-22).

Though God's acts are sovereignly fixed, prayer may have an effect as to when these events will occur. At times God has revealed what He will do but did not reveal when He would do them (Ex. 5:22-23; cf. 1 Pet. 1:9-21). In such situations human prayers effect God's providential timing. Intercession slowed the coming of divine judgment (Ex. 32:34; Num. 14:27; Deut. 9:18-20, 25-29) and hastened the arrival of His promises (Isa. 62:6-7; Ex. 36:37).

Some of God's acts are providentially conditioned on petition for their execution. Petitioning God is required if one is to receive certain blessings from God (Luke 11:5-13; James 4:2). Petition is a means established by God for the accomplishment of His foreordained purposes (Mt. 9:38; 24:20; 2 Cor. 1:11). Some divine events occur as a direct result of human petitions (Josh. 10:12-14; 2 Sam. 15:31).

A few events even seem to be changed by prayer from what God has revealed. A good example of this is when Hezekiah was mortally ill, God sent Isaiah to him with the message, "set your house in order, for you shall die and not live" (2 Ki. 20:1). His response was one of true repentance in which He cried out sincerely to God in prayer. God responded with giving him fifteen more years to live (2 Ki. 20:1-6; 2 Chron. 32:24; Isa. 38:1-5). In essence this is just the slowing of the approach of death as a result of a man's petition. It is complicated, however, by the forceful language used which does not appear to leave room for a condition. One is left with one of two choices. Either God deceived Hezekiah knowing full well that he would receive fifteen more years but desired him to repent and pray, or else prophetic statements revealed by God directly to the person in question may be conditional in spite of forceful, seemingly unconditional language. God cannot deceive, for He is the source of truth so much that He cannot lie (Titus 1:2). From the context of the story it is probably true that God desired Hezekiah to change his attitude and exhibit the change through petitioning Him. It could not be that He practiced deception, an act which He condemns as sin. One is left with only the possibility that some prophetic statements revealed by God are conditional though they do not have a condition attached. Jonah's proclamation to Nineveh is another prophecy without a revealed condition, which prophetic judgment was not realized due to the Ninevites repentance and petitions. This Jonah prophecy is significant because a time limit was even attached. So, some prophecies are conditional and thus can actually be changed from occurring. However, believers do not know which statements are conditional and which are not conditional. Probably conditional prophecies are addressed to the individuals to whom they concern so that they can make the desired response and thus avert judgment or receive blessing. One need not wait until history fulfills prophecy to determine the conditional nature of some prophecies. Petitioning God works because God actively and willingly works in our world.

Summarizing part of this answer, some things cannot be changed from what God has revealed. Some things, while they cannot be changed, can be seemingly hastened or slowed in their arrival times. The act of petitioning God for answers is included within the decree as one of His means. Within this range of options, some things can even be changed from what God reveals them to be as He decides.

As humans we do not know what God knows. Believers are required to live within the perspective of the truth that is revealed. When we pray in line with the revealed will of God we can have confidence that He hears us and that we will have the answers which we have asked from Him (1 Jn. 5:14-15). So in this context, petitioning for everlasting life and the assurance of this salvation are requests, which we will confidently receive. Praying in line with God's will is well illustrated by Daniel who records that while he was reading the book of Jeremiah, he noticed that the captivity was to last seventy years. He made some quick calculations and rightly concluded that the time was almost over, so he petitioned God concerning the matter. When explicit commands and consequences are delineated in the Bible praying in line with these is guaranteed. For example, Elijah is righteous in praying for draught in line with God's covenant curse when Israel was disobedient to the Mosaic covenant, and praying for rain in line with God's covenant blessing when Israel became obedient to the Mosaic covenant in killing the prophets of Baal (Deut. 11:13-17; 1 Ki. 17:1; 18:1-46; James 5:16-18). Petitioning God in line with His revealed will should be done by all believers. This would tend to encourage us to: give God our anxieties, pray for Christian virtues, and petition that Christ and kingdom would come.

The Biblical text also provides a range of prayers that can serve as patterns for our prayers. In these we have no guarantee of getting our requests answered affirmatively but the example does provide guidance in how to pray. One such prayer might be if one prayed for the salvation of some Jewish friends based on Paul's example (Rom. 9:1-5; 10:1). Answers to this type of prayer are not guaranteed but it is likely that the answer might be favorable, and either way a person is in good company patterning their prayers off the prayers recorded in the Bible. It is of this type of prayer that David says, "Delight yourself in the Lord and He will give you the desires of your heart" (Ps. 37:4). As a believer draws closer to God, he will become more like Him in character. As a person develops this relationship with God over a period of time, his desires are changed into God's desires. From this desire for God's will and ways, he petitions God closer and closer to His will progressively into maturity. Thus, these answers may often be favorable. Anyway around it, it is always appropriate to go to the Sovereign and pray.

PROVIDENCE VIEWS[1]

	Process	Openness	Redemptive Intervention	Molinist	Thomist	Relational Calvinist	Calvinist	Fatalist
Description	God persuades to good possibilities while occasions make the choices.	God is open to the future of His creatures libertarian free will.	God knows all so as to plan responses to His creatures libertarian free will.	God knows all possible worlds, so He can choose the best as the actual one.	Nonexclusive redundancy of God's first cause and man's efficient free-will.	God is comprehensively deterministic with humans having free will, and God relates to creation in time.	God is comprehensively deterministic with human having free will.	God determines all.
God's experience of time	Temporal	Temporal	Could be either	Could be either	Timeless	Could be timeless, but He is temporally related to creation	Timeless	Timeless
God knows the actual future totally	No	No	Yes	Yes	Yes	Yes	Yes	Yes
God knows counterfactuals	No	No	No	Yes	No	Could be either	No	There are none
God takes a risk in creation	Yes	Yes	Yes	Yes	No	No	No	No
God specifically permits all evils	No	No	No, only generally	Yes, in choosing this world	Yes	Yes	Yes	No, but actively brings them about
Human freedom is:	Libertarian	Libertarian	Libertarian	Libertarian	Compatibilistic Libertarianism	Volitional	Volitional	Illusory
Human effort and prayer affects the outcome	Yes	Yes	Yes	Yes	Yes	Yes	Yes	No
Prayer changes God's mind	Yes	Yes	Influenced the plan but does not change it now	Influenced which plan God choose but does not change it now	No	No	No	No
Adherents	Whitehead, Tielhard de Chardin	Clark Pinnock, John Sanders, William Hasker	Bruce Reichenbach, Jack Cottrell	Louis de Molina, Bill Craig, Tom Flint	Thomas Aquinas, Norman Geisler	Terrance Tiessen, Doug Kennard	John Calvin, Paul Helm, J.I. Packer	Islaamic Kadari sect

---

[1] This chart is a modification of the one in Terrance Tiessen. *Providence & Prayer: How Does God Work in the World?* (Downers Grove: InterVarsity, 2000) pp. 363-4.

Thy Kingdom Come

The Jewish concept of kingdom includes Yahweh's covenant reign over Israel but has ultimate expression in the eschatological defeat of Israel's enemies and the setting up of a glorious future for Israel. This sentiment can be seen repeatedly throughout the prophets, inter-testamental books, and the New Testament. As it moves into the New Testament, Jesus Christ is seen as the King Who brings this kingdom into reality. One such statement is Zacharias' prophesy at the birth of his son John the Baptist (Lk.1:68-75).

> Blessed be the Lord God of Israel,
> For He has visited us and accomplished redemption for His people,
> And has raised up a horn of salvation for us
> In the house of David His servant-
> As He spoke by the mouth of His holy prophets from of old–
> Salvation from our enemies,
> And from all those who hate us;
> To show mercy toward our fathers, And to remember His holly covenant,
> The oath which He swore to Abraham our father,
> To grant us that we being delivered from the hand of our enemies,
> Might serve Him without fear,
> In holiness and righteousness before him all our days.

Zacharias anticipates John's role as preparing the way for the Christ, Who brings in the kingdom.

As Jesus comes He is not quite what the people expect such a king to be, but He affirms that the disciples have it right in recognizing Him as the King "the

Christ, the son of the living God" (Mt. 16: 16). When Jesus unpacks this eschatological kingdom associated with His second coming, He does so promising everlasting reward and continuing responsibility for His righteous faithful servants (Mt. 25:14-46; Lk. 19:11-27). This conception fits with the apocalyptic hopes of the Jewish people. The timing of the establishment of this eschatological kingdom is set by God the Father (Acts 1:7). However, in the midst of anticipating an eschatological kingdom, Jesus also identifies that certain virtues in relation to Christ identify the poor in spirit and those who are persecuted for the sake of righteousness as already within kingdom (Mt. 5:3, 10). This kingdom is like mustard seed and leaven; the kingdom starts small (as in Jesus' band of disciples) and then grows large and permeate the whole (Mt. 13:31-33). This world already lives in the kingdom of Christ awaiting the eschatological expression of the kingdom of the Father to come (Mt. 13:38, 41, 43).

Jesus demonstrated a deep commitment to prayer in His life and prayed repeatedly. These New Testament words for prayer are words describing petition. His disciples noticed His practice and asked Him to teach them to pray as John the Baptist had taught his disciples to pray. The features of the prayer are not altogether novel since Jews had prayed to "our Father" before this and as one compares the following quaddish prayer one can see similarities, "Exalted and hallowed be Thy good name in all the world which He created according to His will. May He let His kingdom rule in your lifetime and in your days and in the lifetime of the whole house of Israel, speedily and soon." Jesus' prayer is however deeply personal and compassionate, applying kingdom to life. Jesus gives his disciples a pattern for them to pray (Mt. 6:9 makes it clearer that it is a model; Lk. 11:2-4). Each line in the prayer expresses an application of a kingdom quality into life. "Father, let your name be regarded as holy." The unique separateness which Isaiah had expressed as holiness had been that God was the everlasting king (Isa. 6:1, 3). "Father" could also be a kingly title, but more personal. In the eschatological era the living creatures near the Father's throne continue to celebrate the Father as the everlasting God Who has the almighty power to bring about His reign (Rev.4:8). This is certainly a request that God's name be highly honored. "Thy kingdom come" is a request that resonates with Jewish expectation and petition of longing for the eschatological kingdom. The kingdom is however encroaching already in practical ways, so a practical request follows for the next days' sustaining food or bread. This connects with the average peasant's life, where income was earned day to day, and was paid at the end of the day for the next days' food needs. "Forgive us our sins in the manner that we also have forgiven everyone indebted to us." There own pattern of forgiveness identifies the extent to which they are praying for their own forgiveness as indicated by the *hōs*, which is translated "as" or "for." I have elsewhere argued that the synoptic linkage of divine forgiveness after the pattern of our virtue of forgiveness is seen as salvific in identifying who gains kingdom and misses hell fire.[1] This request is one for continued benefit in relationship with the Father and gracious inclusion in this kingdom program by the Father. It is however a request that we need to have a track record compliance. We must be forgiving people. But life is not simply composed of our choices as though God was a vending machine; God is sovereign. The final request comes, "lead us not into temptation" because God is the sovereign one who leads and has lead Jesus out into temptation (Lk. 4:1), and Jesus is asking his disciples to pray this that they would not have similar trials under God's oversight. Each petition in this prayer has to do with applying aspects of the Father's kingdom to our lives.

The Lord's pattern prayer is immediately followed by parables for persistence and confidence in getting our petition answered in the affirmative. Suppose a friend has arrived late at night, perhaps traveling because of the heat of the sun in the desert. Hospitality requires feeding people, but as a   peasant you

---

[1] Doug Kennard, ed. *The Relationship Between Epistemology, Hermeneutics, Biblical Theology and Contextualization* (Lewiston: Mellen Press, 1999) pp.128-133.

may have no more food for that day, so you wake up a neighbor requesting food from him. Though the neighbor makes excuses about his family already laying out on their mats, but because you are persistent he will get up and give you as much as you need. This neighbor's reluctance is overcome by persistence. However, God, the Father is not reluctant. The asker will receive and the seeker will find (Lk. 11:10). Perhaps such encouragement to be persistent in prayer for application of the kingdom is informed by such requests actually having an effect of bringing in the kingdom, with its benefits. Jesus then follows this with a fatherly perspective that when a son makes a request for food, fathers would not give their son something hazardous to his health, like a snake or a scorpion. "If you being evil, know how to give good gifts to your children, how much more shall your heavenly Father give the Holy Spirit to those who ask Him?" (Lk. 11:13). The giving of the Holy Spirit was identified as the enablement for the kingdom era (e.g. Joel 2:27-29). So unlike the neighbor, God is eager to give that which will bring in the kingdom and apply these kingdom benefits. Perhaps our persistent prayers make a difference. Remember that the Spirit and the bride request Lord Jesus to come (Rev. 22:17). Jesus responds, "Yes, I am coming quickly" (Rev. 22:20). The apostle John joins in this sentiment that Jesus is urging us to pray, "Come Lord Jesus." Perhaps these prayers for the coming and establishment of the kingdom make a difference. Anyway around it, on Jesus' authority, and John's authority, and God's authority we should be praying for the kingdom to come. O Lord Jesus come to establish your kingdom!

The imminence of God's coming is balanced in Peter between God's timing and man's participation. Peter emphasized that Christians beloved by God need to remember that God's time is different than the way man counts time; "with the Lord one day is as a thousand years, and a thousand years as one day" (2 Pet. 3:8). This different divine timing is not a chiliastic argument for a six thousand year development of the creation with a thousand year kingdom rest.[2] In

---

[2] Contra *Epistle of Barnabas* 5:4; Irenaeus, *Adv. Heb.* 5:23.2; 5:28.3.

fact, Peter's statements argue the opposite of a known time frame; he points out that one cannot calculate when these events will take place. Neither does the verse mean that God is contemporaneous with time[3] because Peter still describes God as experiencing time as days and years. Furthermore, God's counting of days and years as being different than a human assessment does not make time meaningless. God's time as with His attributes are measured on a much greater scale than a human normally considers. The fact that God's timing has not been reached provides no grounds for viewing it as slow, which would raise a concern of God's indifference or impotence (2 Pet. 3:9). Presumably some had regarded it as slow but Peter exhorts believers to regard it as an expression of God's compassionate patience in bringing in salvation for them and others who would repent (2 Pet. 3:9, 15). However, to those who mark God as impotent or indifferent, judgment will come quickly when they are not ready (2 Pet. 3:4, 9-10). God's timing seems to hinge on His accomplishing a salvific goal rather than an arbitrary date.

Peter exhorts us to look for and hasten the coming of the Day of the Lord (2 Pet. 3:12). The first word (*prosdokaō*) describes an expectant waiting and observing, with hope and perhaps fear about what will take place. The second word (*speudō*) describes zealous industry to hasten the coming. This concept is not hastening toward the coming, for that would require a preposition like "toward" in the text, however there isn't one there. Therefore, from the free will side it is our zealous industry that actually moves up the calendar day for the day of God to come. The kind of behavior we are to do to bring God's day sooner is zealous holiness and godliness (2 Pet. 3:11-12). This coming of the Day of God has a judgment primarily on the ungodly men and not the heavenly bodies (2 Pet. 3:7). Apparently, the destruction of the existing heavens and earth is the extreme cost it takes to judge ungodly men. The person who considers this message should be zealously holy and godly, identified with the way of salvation and

---

[3] Contra *Jubilees* 4:30; *Apocalypse of Abraham* 28; *Enoch* 91:17; and 2 *Enoch* 33.

secluded from the way of judgment (1 Pet. 1:13-16; 2 Pet. 1:5-6, 11; 3:11). The believer should live his life in such a way as to be recognized by the God who judges, as identifying himself with Christ's spotless and blameless character (1 Pet. 1:19; 2 Pet. 3:14) and far from the false teachers' character of blots and blemishes (2 Pet. 2:13). Furthermore, any length of time it takes for the cataclysm to come should be considered as the Lord's patient salvation work and not an opportunity to sin.

Christ reigns currently in his everlasting kingdom but there is a future expression of this reign in the restoration of all things. As with the exhortation to look for the coming of the Lord, Peter describes himself and his readers as in the condition of looking for (*prosdokaō*) the new heavens and earth (2 Pet. 3:12-14). They are expectantly waiting and observing with hope and perhaps fear about God's bringing into existence this remarkably new order which serves as the salvific goal, completely characterized by righteousness. The newness of these heavens and earth evidence that the new order is not merely a remaking or refurbishing of the present order, but a whole new order.

The restoration of all things is another description of either the same age or an earlier stage approximating it. *Apokatastasis* refers to a restoration of everything either to a previous state or to perfection. Such a restoration of everything in Judaism took a teleological framework instead of the Egyptian and Babylonian cycles of endless recurrence. The concept of restoration includes restoring Israel back into the land after the exile (Jer. 16:15; 23:8; 24:6). The restoration eschatologically raises Israel to its full former glory (Ezek. 16:55). In this restoration Elijah the prophet restores all things (Mal. 4:6; Matt. 17:11; Mk. 9:12). The objective restoration of all things begins when Jesus Christ returns from heaven to earth (Acts 3:20-21). The prophets spoke about the coming of Christ initiating the restoration; it is characterized as the time when the Abrahamic blessings are realized by the repentant and Christ functions as the Mosaic mediatorial prophet on earth (Acts 3:21-26). The fact that the non-repentant are excluded from these blessings of restoration indicates that this restoration is not a universal salvation. This indicates that the restoration is to a state of perfection, excluding the unrepentant that expresses a continuum with the best of the past but excelling beyond it.

This objective restoration is identified with the subjective times of refreshing (*anapsyxis*, Acts 3:19-29). With the aorist verb and the relationship with the noun "time" (*kairos*), times of refreshing cannot be mere personal or corporate breaks in end-time afflictions; it needs to be seen as the definitive age of refreshment. The concept of *anapsyxis* includes breathing space, relief, relaxation, refreshment, and of course the Messianic age that brings rest. The definitive age of restoration and refreshment objectively begin together when Christ comes back to earth. However, Peter develops a subjective effect of when that might be. The Jews' repentance, which provides them with forgiveness serves as a condition enabling the divinely purposed Messianic age of rest to come (as an age, and not merely an individual experience). This means that while the age begins with Christ's coming, the repentance of these Jews (and maybe other non-Christians) has an effect on when Christ will come to initiate this age. That is, perhaps responsiveness in repentance and maybe evangelism could bring the Messianic age of rest sooner than might otherwise be the case.

So, we have seen that the sovereign Lord's eschatological kingdom might be brought sooner than otherwise might be by the following: prayer, holy and godly living, repentance and evangelism. Yet we do not bring in the kingdom; Christ brings in the kingdom. Of this Christ in the divine throne room the myriads say, "Worthy is the Lamb that was slain to receive power and riches and wisdom and might and honor and glory and blessing" (Rev. 5:12). All creatures responded saying, "To Him who sits on the throne, and to the Lamb, be blessing and honor and glory and dominion forever and ever" (Rev. 5:13). With God and Christ (at His second coming) bringing in the eschatological kingdom, we must wait for Him to accomplish this level of His reign, and do what we can to help His reign be soon. So I pray, O Lord Jesus come! Thy kingdom come!

Index

Index

TORONTO STUDIES IN THEOLOGY